EUGENE H. BERWANGER

The Rise of the Centennial State

COLORADO TERRITORY, 1861–76

UNIVERSITY OF ILLINOIS PRESS
URBANA AND CHICAGO

c 5 4 3 2 1
♾ This book is printed on acid-free paper.

Library of Congress Cataloging-in-Publication Data

Berwanger, Eugene H.
The rise of the Centennial State : Colorado Territory, 1861–76 /
Eugene H. Berwanger.
p. cm.
Includes bibliographical references and index.
ISBN-13: 978-0-252-03122-9 (cloth : alk. paper)
ISBN-10: 0-252-03122-9 (cloth : alk. paper)
1. Colorado—History—To 1876. 2. Frontier and pioneer life—
Colorado. I. Title.
F780.B54 2006
978.8'02—dc22 2006029387

To the Memory of

My Brothers and Sisters

Contents

Preface

In the 1950s Earl Pomeroy and Clarence E. Carter each in turn challenged fellow historians to examine in greater detail the territorial history of the United States, especially that of the West.[1] Interest picked up on the task, with monographs on the western territories appearing over the next several decades.[2] Still, despite the number of studies completed, no single-volume history encompassing the entire territorial period for Colorado has ever been published. To be sure, Howard Roberts Lamar devoted four of his nineteen chapters in *The Far Southwest* to Colorado's territorial years. And Duane A. Smith, in his important work on the topic, still chose to conclude *The Birth of Colorado: A Civil War Perspective* with the year 1865.[3] As a result, the culminating decade of Colorado Territory's history, 1866–76, continues to invite investigation.

If the Civil War years signaled the coming into existence of Colorado, as Smith suggests, the ensuing years witnessed growth even more important for the territory. With the end of the Civil War, Colorado would experience a resurgence in its economy. For one, new techniques brought greater profits from the mining of gold and silver. And new modes of transportation, notably the Union Pacific and Kansas Pacific railroads, would open Colorado to eastern markets. With railroads came faster and more comfortable travel and settlers would arrive in ever increasing number, encouraging dramatic growth in the population once the Native American threat had lessened on the Colorado plains. In this way would farms, ranches, and towns take hold, with livestock and dryland farming finding their place alongside mining in importance to the territory's economy and culture. In all, new settlements grew up on the High Plains where only wind, dust, and tumbleweed had thrived.

This book traces the history of Colorado from its inception as a territory in 1861 to the eve of statehood in 1876. In doing so, it describes a temporary period of population decline during the Civil War, conflict with Native Americans, and technical limitations in the mining industry. The book also explores a postwar era of growth attributable to technological improvements, a more diversified economy with the expansion of agriculture and the introduction of railroads. Finally, it concludes with a discussion of the politics of personality and corruption at the highest levels of territorial government. While the book focuses on the period following the Civil War, it in no way purports to diminish the significance of the earlier mining frontier or its role in stirring Colorado's initial growth. Without the discovery of gold in 1858, the territory would not have developed so rapidly. The mining frontier brought a rush of fortune seekers to Colorado's mountain streams even if many of them moved on just as quickly. Those who stayed were determined to see the territory grow, and together with the ensuing arrivals they worked to achieve statehood for Colorado.

Samuel Bowles, editor of the *Springfield Republican* in Massachusetts, was among the first to recognize the importance of the postwar period for Colorado. He visited the territory in 1865 and again in 1869. On his second visit he took note of advances that were occurring and their effect on the territory's development. In his view, the post–Civil War years would prove to be the "kernel" years for Colorado. Whereas in 1865 Bowles, like most visitors, noted decline and predicted a bleak future for the territory, by 1869 he had changed his view, acknowledging the growth taking place and gauging its importance for the territory's future.

Colorado Territory came into its own during the Reconstruction period, culminating in 1877. Over all, this was an era noted for Congress's efforts to endow the freedmen of the South with basic political and civil rights. Still, it has its negative side. Antagonism surged between Congress and Andrew Johnson, Lincoln's successor, very nearly bringing national politics to a standstill. Outright corruption in government was another factor, causing an increasing lack of confidence among the citizenry.

In addition to attempts at political uplift there were, during Reconstruction, other efforts at reform, most notably at the state and local levels. Woman suffrage, prohibition, care for the disabled, eliminating political corruption, and ending prostitution each in turn was a topic for discussion. So, too, would these issues be raised in Colorado, though with impact less far-reaching. Still, reform efforts in the territory confirmed that Colorado was neither politically isolated nor unmindful of events going on elsewhere in the nation.

In all, Colorado Territory appears to have gained from the turmoil of Reconstruction. By the mid-1870s the Republican Party, which had controlled national politics since 1861, witnessed a decline in its fortunes. Fearful of losing the presidential election of 1876, party leaders urged the admission of Colorado, with its three electoral votes, in order to offset the Democratic resurgence. While statehood fulfilled the long-sought goal of many Coloradans, in the end it would have a pivotal role in the most contested presidential election in the nineteenth century.

To the many people who came to my assistance on this project I owe a debt of gratitude. I am particularly grateful to the staffs in the Western History Department at the Denver Public Library, the Colorado State Archives, the Colorado State Historical Society Library, the American Heritage Center, the Pueblo Public Library, the Penrose Public Library in Colorado Springs, and the Fort Collins Public Library. So, too, do I appreciate the help of library personnel at the University of Colorado, the University of Northern Colorado, Colorado State University, and the University of Wyoming.

Within these institutions several individuals deserve special mention. David Hayes, director of the Western Americana Collection at the University of Colorado, guided me to a number of sources that I might otherwise have overlooked. Fred Schmidt, federal documents librarian at Colorado State University, regularly set aside volumes of the *Congressional Globe* and the *Congressional Record* so that I might research them at leisure. In advance of my arrival in Laramie, Carl V. Hallberg and Richard G. Ewig of the American Heritage Center answered my many questions and expedited my research there. And in Denver, Terry Ketelsen, director of the Colorado State Archives, allowed me access to files not generally available to the public. Chris Geddes, national and state register historian at the Colorado State Historical Society, checked and clarified minor matters and saved me many trips to Denver. Ellen Zazzarino and Erin McDanal, senior archivists at the Denver Public Library and the State Archives, aided me in obtaining negatives of the photographs that are reproduced in the book. At the University of Illinois Press, Laurie Matheson, western history acquisitions editor, encouraged me while I edited the manuscript for publication. Finally, I would be remiss if I failed to mention the many local Colorado historians whose own writings helped to clarify and enliven my research.

Four other individuals are deserving of special note. Fred Anderson, professor of history at the University of Colorado, made available an unpublished paper he had written on prohibition in Fort Collins, thus enabling me to clarify conflicting information from other sources. Albert Castel, scholar on Kansas Territory and the Civil War in the West; John Albright, former historian for the National Park Service; and the late Liston E. Leyendecker, Colorado mining historian, read early drafts of chapters and offered suggestions for improvement and interpretation. Even so, I accept responsibility for any errors that appear in the published book.

THE RISE OF THE CENTENNIAL STATE

Prologue

The American territorial system, initiated by the Northwest Ordinance of 1787, underwent significant changes in interpretation by the latter half of the nineteenth century. The original document provided for limited public participation in government. Under its provisions the federal government guaranteed private property and the right of habeas corpus, jury trial, and freedom of religion to all settlers. Only the landowning classes, however, were permitted to vote and hold office. As a result, the territorial assembly, the sole authorized legislative body, represented a narrowly defined voting public.[1] At the same time, the federal government addressed the needs of the people by relegating the Native Americans to less settled areas, adopting more liberal land policies, and reducing potential foreign threats by purchasing the Louisiana Territory outright and by pressuring Spain to cede Florida. And in the appointment of territorial governors it selected persons of national or local renown who were generally well-regarded by the local population. Among them were such prominent names as Arthur St. Clair (Northwest Territory), William Henry Harrison (Indiana Territory), Andrew Jackson (Florida Territory), and William Blount (Southwest Territory).

With the advent of the 1820s and 1830s calls for democracy and greater participation in the political process increased throughout the nation. The states responded by removing land ownership qualifications for voting and office holding and by providing for the popular election of the president. So, too, did Congress extend democracy in the territories. After 1825, in fact, no territory underwent the first stage of the ordinance stipulating rule by an appointed governor and three judges alone. Congress now authorized legislatures with each territory's establishment. Neither would voting rights be so restrictive. Both the territorial council, appointed under the provisions of the ordinance, as well as the assembly were to be elected by the citizens at large and voting requirements became so liberal as to make white manhood suffrage a distinct possibility. By the 1850s Stephen A. Douglas's doctrine of popular sovereignty caught on in the territories and people began to demand greater freedom to control their own affairs. While historians have long stressed popular sovereignty as a concept relative to the slavery question, it had far broader meaning for people living in the territories. As Robert Johannsen has shown, "The Democratic party doctrine of popular sovereignty was interpreted on the frontier to mean full and complete territorial self-government and it appealed to all elements despite party background."[2]

The official attitude toward territories underwent definitive change once the Republicans gained control of the federal government. From 1861 until 1889, Republicans increasingly regarded the territories for the impact they might have on the party's national objectives. To that end, they insisted that federal control be paramount in all territories. They began scrutinizing territorial reports more carefully, monitoring expenditures in closer detail and, after 1869, limiting territorial legislative sessions to every two years. At the same time, Republicans came to view the territories as a source of patronage and used territorial offices to pay off political debts or to provide jobs for defeated colleagues. As a result, wrote Louis L. Gould, the West became "a convenient dumping ground for obstreperous hacks and a suitable reward for deserving second-raters." Indeed, many federal appointees were more interested in improving their personal fortunes than in governing and spent most of their time speculating in land, mines, or railroad stock.[3] In addition there was the statehood question. While Republicans were quick to create territories, establishing seven new ones during their first eight years in office,[4] still they exhibited a reluctance to confer statehood. If over the seven decades spanning 1792 to 1861, Congress saw fit to admit twenty states, over the next twenty-seven years culminating in 1889, only three territories—Nevada, Nebraska, and Colorado—were granted statehood.[5]

Colorado Territory's inability to achieve statehood quickly rankled with an element of the population. Many citizens took a narrow view of federal appointees, especially those from outside the territory. Imbued with the doctrine of popular sovereignty and believing themselves capable of self-government, Colorado settlers craved greater independence from outside control. Almost from the discovery of gold along Cherry Creek, in fact, a faction of the population expressed their desire for self-determination, which among Denver politicians only became stronger as the territorial years progressed.

From 1854 and 1861 the eastern plains of modern-day, central Colorado were part of Kansas Territory. The territorial legislature established Arapahoe County in 1855 but failed to organize it. This western-most county, extending to the Continental Divide, was just too far away to be of much interest to lawmakers whose greater concern was the ongoing struggle between pro- and antislavery factions in eastern Kansas. Only after the news of gold in Cherry Creek did Kansas officials finally take action, directing that a board of commissioners be established there. But it was too late. Local citizens had already taken matters in hand, electing their own county officials. They also sent Hiram J. Graham as delegate to Congress, but he failed to win recognition. Still, the mining regions did have champions in Congress. In 1859 Representative Schuyler Colfax of Illinois introduced a bill organizing them as the Territory of Colona, but Congress failed to take action.

Finally, in frustration over the lack of organized government in the face of increasing population, Denver area citizens made a move. In May 1859, they elected a convention and wrote a constitution for the "State of Jefferson." The electorate, however, rejected the document, fearing the increased taxes that statehood was sure to bring. Outside of Denver there was also concern about the city's political power in the new state. In fact, this uneasiness about Denver's prominence in politics would linger throughout the entire territorial period. Failing to secure approval of the new constitution, its protagonists pulled back and, in October 1859, proclaimed the "Territory of Jefferson." Within a few months it elected both a slate of territorial officials and a representative to Congress. Similarly, the legislature passed civil and criminal codes, established a court system, and went on to create a number of counties.

In the end Congress never recognized the Jefferson territorial government. Neither would the initiative overcome local disfavor, and within months it ran into opposition. Those not involved in establishing Jefferson Territory rejected its authority by refusing to pay the taxes imposed. Some mining districts were still unclear about where the authority lay and sent representatives to the Kansas territorial legislature, hoping it would assume jurisdiction after all. Others continued to act independently. From 1858 to 1861, the mining districts had no effective government other than the miners' own laws and impromptu municipal organizations.[6]

There are several explanations for this situation. By 1860 Kansas was on the eve of statehood and its new western boundary did not include the mining districts. And in Washington, D.C., lawmakers had been quarreling over the question of slavery in the territories for nearly a decade, and many were loath to create a new territory and again bring up and intensify the slavery issue. Not until the secession of the southern states, in fact, did Congress seriously consider creating a territorial government for the mining districts. It would not be first time Colorado Territory benefited from the nation's political distress.

1 *The New Territory*

Colorado Territory was created on the eve of the Civil War. Following the admission of Kansas in January 1861, Congress realized the need to establish a government for the people who had poured into the western region of Kansas Territory during the gold rush of 1858–59 and who now lived along the eastern slope of the Rocky Mountains and in mining camps at the base of the Continental Divide. To give the new territory a more viable economic base and to make its size more equal to those around it, Congress enlarged Colorado by attaching parts of the neighboring territories. From Nebraska Territory came the land between the 40th and 42nd parallels and east of the Continental Divide, a region that contained much of the South Platte River Valley. The economic interests of the people living there, mainly in Boulder, in Julesburg, and on isolated farms, were more closely tied to the mining districts and to Denver, and they had no desire to remain in Nebraska. To the south Congress attached the area north of the 37th parallel, taking from New Mexico Territory the land along the Arkansas River and the agriculturally rich San Luis Valley. The Hispano population resented being separated from its New Mexican roots and remained a group apart during the territorial period and beyond. Mormons showed little concern about the portion taken from Utah Territory, the land west of the Continental Divide. Not only was it distant from their settlements around Salt Lake City, but almost nothing was known about it.[1]

The bill to establish Colorado was introduced in early February 1861, and signed by President James Buchanan before the end of the month. Quick passage was stimulated by the desire to bond the territory, with its wealth in precious metals, more closely to the Union and was made easier by the withdrawal of southern states. Had southern representatives still been in Congress they would surely have raised the question of whether or not slavery would be permitted. Republicans, who now controlled Congress, decided against mentioning slavery; thus, the Colorado Organic Act was silent on the issue. Possibly, most congressmen believed that slavery could not take hold in the rugged western mountains. More likely, Republicans hoped that softening their strong stand against the expansion of slavery into the territories might keep the border slave states from seceding.[2]

More controversial was a name for the new territory. Congress rejected "Jefferson" because many members opposed naming states after individuals. A substantial number of lawmakers favored "Idaho" but were won over to "Colorado" after the territory's delegate pointed out that the Colorado River rose in its mountains and hence there was particular fitness to the name.[3]

It was left for Abraham Lincoln to select the new territorial officials and he chose William Gilpin as the first governor. A member of Philadelphia society, Gilpin had been educated in England and attended West Point. He had acquired a familiarity with the West in 1841 when he accompanied John C. Frémont's expedition to Oregon. Later Gilpin served in the campaign against Santa Fé in the Mexican War and during the 1850s wrote extensively on the West and its economic potential.[4]

Upon his arrival in May 1861, Gilpin worked expeditiously to organize a territorial government. Within four months he ordered a census, called for the election of a territorial legislature, created three judicial districts, and toured the mining regions. When the legislature met, he persuaded the lawmakers to pass civil and criminal codes and fix a levy for territorial taxation. While his efforts brought order to the territory, Gilpin complained that he had to manage "the *legislature,* the *Indians,* the *military,* the *courts,* and this *wonderful population*—30,000 (all *Males*)— . . . without a single skilled assistant."[5]

Besides governing the territory, Gilpin was determined that Colorado would remain loyal to the Union. His summer tour of the mining districts convinced him that the Confederate threat was large and growing, and he became especially concerned about a Confederate invasion from Texas to seize the gold mines. A Republican with strong antislavery leanings, he came to believe that individuals who did not express strong feeling against slavery must be Confederate sympathizers. Within a short time he felt himself "surrounded by assassins, . . . and it seemed to be part of their plan to get rid of men they did not like." Contemporary events indicate that Gilpin exaggerated the extent of southern sympathy. During the spring and summer of 1861 Union rallies were held in Golden, Central City, and Denver, and the demonstrators insisted that prominent citizens declare their sympathies. Susan R. Ashley noted, upon her arrival in Denver in 1861, that southern sentiment existed in the city but was by no means predominant.[6]

In order to protect the territory from possible invasion, Gilpin organized the First Regiment of Colorado Volunteers. Certain that federal officials would favor his action, he did not bother to seek their approval. To outfit and pay the troops Gilpin issued drafts on the federal treasury, which the government refused to honor when they were first presented for payment. Nor were officials in Washington impressed by his argument that Colorado was in danger. With southern troops amassing almost within sight of the national capital, threats of a Confederate invasion two thousand miles distant were not a vital concern. The federal government finally agreed to pay the unauthorized drafts, totaling $300,000, after Colorado troops stopped Confederate forces at Glorieta Pass. Yet, Gilpin's actions cost him the governorship. When he rushed east to Washington, D.C., in December 1861, to defend his policies, Gilpin found himself without friends. Even Francis P. Blair, who had suggested his appointment, recommended Gilpin's removal and replacement with "some man of good common sense." Lincoln dismissed the well-meaning governor after one year in office despite his success in establishing the territorial government and in halting a Confederate incursion into the Mountain West.[7]

John Evans replaced Gilpin in the governorship. A native of Waynesville, Ohio, Evans earned an M.D. at Clarmont Academy in Cincinnati. After practicing medicine in Indiana, he joined the faculty of Rush Medical College in Chicago. Investments in railroad companies and real estate made him wealthy enough to further his interests in education and politics. He assisted in establishing Northwestern University in Evanston, Illinois, a town named in his honor. An ardent antislavery advocate, he played an instrumental role in establishing the Illinois Republican Party and supported Lincoln's presidential nomination in 1860. Although Evans was forced to resign the governorship in 1865 for staunchly defending the action of Colorado troops during the Sand Creek Massacre, he remained in Denver and played a pivotal role in railroad building and furthering education in the territory.

Along with the new governor came Samuel Elbert, who had struck up a close friendship with Evans at the Republican National Convention in 1860. Within a short time the relationship strengthened when Elbert married Evans's daughter Josephine. A graduate of Ohio Wesleyan University, Elbert moved in 1854 to Nebraska Territory, where he practiced law and served in the territorial legislature. Evans used his influence with Lincoln to secure the territorial secretaryship for his new son-in-law. Elbert's political career in the years following would have its ups and downs, but along with Evans, the duo had substantial influence on Colorado's growth and politics during the territorial period, and even beyond.[8]

Unlike most American territories, Colorado did not move steadily forward. In fact, by 1862 the territory was declining. William Byers, editor of the *Rocky Mountain News* and one of Colorado's most ardent boosters, had to admit that there was an "air of desertion" surrounding the villages in Clear Creek Canyon. According to a resident of Empire, towns that predicted "pretentious greatness" a year or two earlier had almost disappeared in the meantime.[9] While there were many reasons for this decline, chief among them was the failure of Colorado to become another El Dorado.

Most men who had rushed to Colorado in 1859 and 1860 were seekers after placer or "free" gold. This was especially true of those who came from California, where placer gold was more abundant than in Colorado. Placer gold exists in the form of nuggets or flakes in stream beds or along creeks. Once located, it is washed in a pan, thereby separating the gold from the sand and gravel. But the narrow, steep canyons that characterized the greater part of Colorado's mining region contained a limited field for placer mining. Frank Fossett, who detailed the territory's mineral and agricultural resources, wrote that placer gold production reached its peak in 1862, when $3,400,000 worth was panned. Thereafter it began to drop off drastically and by 1866 placer mining had almost disappeared. Hence when gold was discovered in Montana and Idaho in 1862, Colorado miners took off for more lucrative fields, while those who remained resorted to lode mining.[10]

Lode gold exists in veins or streaks in combination with rock or quartz. If the vein lies near the surface, the gold usually has been oxidized and is easily extracted. But when veins run deep into the earth or mountainside, the gold ore resists oxidization. In Colorado this rock, called "refractory" ore, had to be brought to the surface and crushed before the gold fell free. Early on miners crushed it in Spanish arrastres, two large stones rotated by oxen or other animals. Later stamp mills were used. They consisted of heavy weights raised by water or horse power and dropped on the ore. Whichever process miners employed, the ore was then mixed with mercury to form an amalgam. The process was both laborious and disappointing because many of the gold particles were often too embedded in the rock to amalgamate with the mercury. As a result the loss of precious metal was substantial. In 1866 a *New York Times* correspondent estimated that "not more than 30 per cent of the gold has ever been secured." Ovando Hollister, editor of the *Daily Mining Journal* in Black Hawk, thought the figure was closer to one-half. No matter the estimates, lode mining was so inefficient that in 1868 Colorado produced only $2,010,000 worth of gold whereas California produced $17,500,000 during the same year.

Besides the small return, the expense and danger involved discouraged lode mining. Cave-ins were common and accumulated water had to be pumped out of the mines. The deeper the mine, the more necessary it became to provide fresh air to prevent sickness caused by the foul air that accumulated below ground.[11]

If some miners left Colorado because of their disappointment in not striking it rich, others left the territory to take part in the Civil War. Even though Colorado miners were far from the eastern battlefields, they remained emotionally attached to either the Union or Confederate cause. As a result, many returned home and enlisted in the military. It is estimated that nearly five thousand Coloradans served in the Union army while another fifteen thousand enlisted in territorial militia units during the war.[12]

Lewis L. Weld, the first territorial secretary and nephew of the noted abolitionist Theodore Dwight Weld, was the highest-ranking political figure from Colorado to serve the Union. Following the battle of Bull Run, he returned east to join the Army of the Potomac and was eventually promoted to major in command of a unit of black troops. He died from exposure during the siege of Petersburg, Virginia, in 1864. Unionists not inclined to trek back east served their country by joining Colorado militia units. In March 1862, the First Regiment, Colorado Infantry Volunteers, commanded by Major John Chivington, encircled Confederate troops at Glorieta Pass, destroying their supply train and forcing their retreat to Texas. Two years later, in the summer of 1864, the Second Colorado Cavalry, under Colonel James H. Ford, was ordered east to subdue Missouri bushwhackers. The Missourians were "impressed by the fine horses and 'sand' [the Coloradans] showed in their fighting." Later in October, the same unit helped defeat Confederates at Westport, Missouri, causing them to scatter into Texas and Arkansas. Indeed, Colorado contributed more to the Union war effort than any other Far Western territory.[13]

Southerners also left the territory in substantial numbers. While 8,231 Coloradans listed their birthplace as a southern state in 1860, that number had declined to 3,810 ten years later. Many returned to the South to serve in the Confederate army but because of poor record keeping the number remains unknown. But not all southerners went back home. There are indications that a substantial number relocated to the northern Rockies. At least, David Ballard, Republican governor of Idaho Territory, reported that southerners made up the majority of the population and were the dominant element in his territory until they began to return to the South in 1869.[14]

The most notable southerner to serve the Confederacy was William Green Russell, who made one of the first gold discoveries along Cherry Creek. An avowed secessionist, Russell was regarded with suspicion and closely watched by Colorado authorities once hostilities between North and South began. When he attempted to return to the South by way of New Mexico, the commander at Fort Union incarcerated him for several months. He finally succeeded in leaving Colorado by traveling through Nebraska. Once back home he served as a captain in the Georgia Cavalry, along with contributing $20,000 in gold to the Confederate cause.[15]

As paradoxical as it may seem, the hardship of crossing the plains did not discourage travel eastward. Most men in Colorado were young and unattached—28,115 of the 32,691 males in the territory were between the ages of twenty and forty. Accustomed to traveling light, they sold or gave away unneeded possessions; then, usually banding in groups for protection, they made the trip eastward as quickly as possible. Unlike those who had traveled to Oregon and California in earlier decades, the argonauts of 1859 did not have to contend with the passes of the Sierra Nevada or the arid desert of the Great Basin on their trip home. As one historian has observed, "Perhaps this helps to explain why more people left Colorado than stayed."[16]

How great was Colorado's population decline? Given census inaccuracies plus exaggerations by Colorado's critics and supporters, it may never be possible to reach a precise number. Frank Fossett claimed that 100,000 people lived in the territory during the 1860s, but the number seems excessive. Perhaps a more accurate estimate can be reached by comparing federal and territorial census figures. The 1860 census listed Colorado's population as 34,277, but that included only the portion taken from Kansas. Historians have adjusted that number by adding the population of the areas taken from Nebraska and New Mexico, 4,223 and 5,000 people respectively. Thus, the number in 1860 was closer to 43,500. A legislative census in 1866 claimed the territory's population was 27,901. These figures indicated that some 15,000 to 16,000 left Colorado between 1860 and 1866.[17]

Many Coloradans who failed at mining or had no interest in military service turned their attention to agricultural pursuits. Nor was this a totally new venture. The Hispano population in southern Colorado had operated farms even before the gold rush. Besides raising food crops for their own use, they grew extensive quantities of grain for their livestock and to sell to travelers. Indeed, the early gold rush proved a boom for Mexican Americans as they became chief suppliers for the mining regions. Even a federal government report in 1862 called special attention to the grain-growing farms along the Huerfano and Arkansas rivers.

The first large-scale, commercial farming in northern Colorado may have been undertaken in 1859 near Boulder by the Wellman brothers. By the next year the census reported two hundred farms in the Denver vicinity and along the South Platte River but did not specify whether their owners engaged in subsistence or commercial agriculture. Farming in Colorado required some adjustment on the farmers' part. While the Piedmont soil along the creek and river bottoms was similar to that of some eastern regions, the sparse rainfall on the High Plains was inadequate. Early Colorado farmers would have agreed with Newton S. Pettis when he wrote, "Irrigation is absolutely necessary to the growing of any crop of grain." To overcome the difficulty farmers adopted the Mexican American irrigation system: short, shallow ditches running off creeks or streams. Because they were dug by one or two individuals their length was limited and they seldom extended farther than one-half mile on either side of a watercourse. But still these ditches were prototypes for the community-built irrigation canals of the later territorial period.[18]

The second difficulty Colorado farmers faced was grasshoppers. The first major plague of many that would come during the territorial years occurred in 1865. Indeed, the *Rocky Mountain News* reported that except for the grasshopper, the territory would have produced enough grain and vegetables to feed its entire population and livestock. By May, according to the *News*, the pests had eaten three-fourths of the wheat, barley, and oat crops in the Boulder Valley, and farmers were replanting their fields in corn, hoping the infestation would be over by the time it ripened. By July the Wellman brothers lost thirty-five of the eighty acres they had planted in wheat and expected greater losses. At the end of the 1865 growing season, one correspondent could only write: "But for the grasshoppers! Why they come in morning, and before night the place looks as if it had been burnt over—not a vestige of green is left. But they don't come every year, and I don't think that they will come next."[19]

Despite the problems, farming was more profitable than mining for many. The *Rocky Mountain News* reported that John Lilly, farming eight miles from Denver, made a substantial profit from the wheat, barley, and oats he had raised on forty-one acres. Another farmer predicted that he would earn $10,000 in 1866 from vegetables he had planted for sale in the mining districts. The previous year he had netted $2,500 from his one-half-acre tomato crop alone.[20]

The successes of farming aside, Colorado continued to lose population during the war. Moreover, the number of immigrants did not equal those who had left, and the new arrivals were regarded with suspicion. Men of military age were often believed to be draft dodgers and Coloradans had little good to say about them. Captain Eugene Ware, stationed at Fort Sedgwick near Julesburg, described the men passing through the area as "bounty jumpers, secesh, deserters [and] people fleeing from the draft." Samuel Bowles, editor of the *Springfield* Massachusetts *Republican,* referred to Colorado's wartime immigrants as "neutrals and cowards, willing to run any risks but those of fighting for their section or their nation."[21]

There were valid reasons to stay away, however. The war had expanded the labor market and jobs were plentiful in the East. Further, Native American depredations on the plains increased as seasoned troops were sent to eastern battlefields and replaced by locals or untrained militia units. But for the great majority of easterners, Colorado was too isolated, too far away. Travel there was difficult and even communication was not reliable. "All our ills now may not unjustly be traced to the lack of communication with the Atlantic cities," complained a *New York Times* correspondent. The most rapid means of communication was the transcontinental telegraph, but it did not arrive in Denver until 1863. Although the line had been completed to Julesburg in 1861, it took two years for citizens of Denver to persuade the Overland Telegraph Company to build a branch line to the city. And Denver citizens had to pay the entire cost of construction. Still, the telegraph remained unreliable. High winds often blew down the lines or Native Americans cut them. In 1865 the local agent for the Overland Company lamented that Native Americans had burned eight miles of telegraph poles and it took him almost a month to locate and replace them.[22]

Nor had travel advanced beyond the days when Americans plied their way along the Oregon Trail to the West Coast. During the Civil War the only protected route to Colorado lay along the Platte River, and Denver was over six hundred miles west of populated settlements in eastern Nebraska. The region in between remained uninhabited except for military posts, Native Americans, and isolated settlers. Earlier there had also been a route through Kansas but when the government pulled troops away it became too dangerous to travel because of Confederate guerrillas in Kansas and Native Americans in the Republican and Smoky Hill river valleys. "Do not come by the Butterfield route as the 'Friendlies' has [*sic*] made an outbreak on that route," Alexander Steele warned his business partner, John Harper. Steele suggested that Harper take the Platte River route because it was guarded but still he should "Come Armed."[23]

For those traveling by wagon train, the trip from Omaha to Denver took four to six weeks, depending on the time taken out for rest, repair of equipment, or delays due to Native American raids. The stagecoach trip was faster but it was both expensive and uncomfortable. Traveling in pairs for protection, stages operated twenty-four hours a day, and took six days if there were no breakdowns or Native American troubles along the route. James Rusling described the trip as tedious and dull: "The plains after a while become somewhat of a bore, they are so vast and outstretched, and you long for a change, something to break the monotony." The Reverend William Crawford was more concerned about the expense. He paid $100 for a one-way ticket and 50 cents a pound for baggage over the twenty-five-pound limit. In addition, he had to purchase meals at relay stations that cost between $1.25 and $1.50 each. Crawford insisted the trip could not be made for less than $150 and implied that the price could be reduced if passengers carried their own provisions. Both George Kassler, who became a leading banker in Denver, and Nathaniel P. Hill, a future U.S. senator from Colorado, would have agreed with the suggestion because of the quality of the food. "I cannot recommend the eating stations along the road," Kassler wrote to his wife. Similarly, Hill thought the meals "too poor to describe."[24]

The only breaks in the trip came at stations where coaches changed drivers and horses or made necessary repairs. They usually contained the most rudimentary facilities but still gave the passengers a chance to refresh themselves. Most stations consisted of one room with or without eating facilities. The exception was at Julesburg, where there was also a general store. Louis L. Simonin, a Frenchman traveling to Colorado to inspect the mines, wrote an amusing description of stage stations: "At the relay station you will find a hand basin and a pitcher of water, with soap and a towel that turns endlessly on a roller. You will find mirrors, combs, and brushes, and even tooth brushes, all fastened to a long string, so that everyone may help himself and no one will carry them off. You might laugh in Paris at these democratic customs; here they are accepted by all and are even welcome, except for the tooth brush, which is regarded with a suspicious eye."[25]

The exodus from Colorado and the failure to attract substantial immigrants affected almost every town in the territory. While Denver remained the largest city, it lost 1,226 people during the Civil War years. Located at the western edge of the Platte River route, the city was a major distribution center for mining districts to the west, with the result that its economy was chiefly based on mining. Less than 3 percent of its dollars were invested in milling, manufacturing, or transportation. Thus, as mining declined so did the city. And it suffered in other ways. On April 19, 1863, a fire in the business area destroyed seventy buildings, causing $197,200 in damage. Then on May 20, 1864, a devastating flash-flood roared down Cherry Creek, which ran through the center of the city, inundating large sections and killing eleven people. Because of the city's remoteness, many individuals, especially Europeans, were unsure of its exact geographical location. Maurice Morris, an Englishman visiting Denver in 1864, received a letter from his banking firm in London addressed to Denver, Nova Scotia.[26]

The loss of population and natural disasters had telling effect. The Rev. Crawford declared that the entire town looked as if "fire had passed over it." While preaching in the Presbyterian church in July 1863, he was overcome by the urge to have the congregation sing a hymn entitled, "Lord, what a wretched land is this!" But Crawford's mood became more positive several years later when he reported that Denver was being rebuilt with "substantial and elegant brick blocks," and most people looked toward a brighter future. For some, however, that future seemed slow in coming. Clarence J. Clark wrote, "There is nothing of interest going on in Denver." Even the *Rocky Mountain News,* the town's most ardent booster, admitted that, "Business is almost at a standstill." Merchants refused to lower prices and citizens retaliated by not buying. General William T. Sherman first visited Denver in 1866 and then again in 1868. On his second visit he thought the town "is even duller by reason that the Rail Road carries travel past, and nobody comes here unless on business pertaining to Colorado."[27]

Denver made varying impressions on visitors. On the one hand, William Dixon described the city as having ten or twelve streets, two hotels, a bank, a theater, six chapels, fifty gambling houses, and one hundred grog-shops. "Every fifth house," he wrote, "appears to be a bar, every tenth house a brothel or gaming house, often both." American poet and essayist Bayard Taylor, on the other hand, concluded that while business seemed dull and people dispirited, "Denver seems to me to have a very brisk and lively air. A number of substantial buildings are going up, there is constant movement in the streets, . . . and the people one meets are brimful of cheerful energy."[28]

Other towns suffered similar or greater losses. James Rusling estimated that only five hundred people lived in Golden in 1866. If he was correct, the city lost half of its population since 1860, when the census reported 1,014 residents. Colorado City (later incorporated into Colorado Springs) and Cañon City virtually disappeared during the war. Both were founded in 1859 and both were service centers for miners in South Park. Early settlers in Colorado City had great hopes for their town. Its representative in the first territorial legislature, stressing the village's central location in the territory, persuaded the lawmakers to designate Colorado City as the territorial capital. When the legislators convened there and discovered that the city lacked both a meeting place and facilities to house them, they immediately adjourned to Denver. Southerners established Cañon City and by all reports it was a thriving trading center with 727 residents in 1861. By the end of the war the situation had completely changed. James Rusling, visiting both towns, recalled that Cañon City had "good buildings, the equal, indeed, of any in Colorado," but they were all empty. He encountered only two people in the entire town. "Colorado City," Rusling concluded, "was in a bad way." Town lots were for sale, "dirt cheap." There was scarcely any population, and the hotel and tavern were forlorn and dirty, with the people in them idle and listless.[29]

Pueblo had been founded in 1846, earlier than either Colorado City or Cañon City, and until the gold rush was a thriving trading post and rendezvous for hunters and trappers. Yet, at the end of the war it contained less than fifty people. Economic decay set in because travelers avoided the city due to Native American outbreaks and the closing of trade routes through Kansas. Still, the city was able to maintain both weekly mail and stagecoach service to Denver. When James Meline came across Pueblo during his travels, he noted that most of the people were Americans and the town consisted of a dozen houses, three stores, and a tavern.[30]

Trinidad seemed a world apart to most white Coloradans; indeed, many were unsure it was even located in the territory. Laying just twenty miles from the New Mexican border, everything about the town appeared more Mexican than American. The pueblo style dominated the architecture and most residents spoke Spanish. C. H. Waltz, a Protestant clergyman, decried the strong influence of the Roman Catholic Church in the town. The parish priest dominated both politics and society and two nuns controlled the local school. Little money was spent on actual education because "most of the school money . . . is used in erecting edifices for the Jesuits." While the town did not undergo a great population loss, it still remained a crude place on the Santa Fé Trail heavily dependent on trade and travelers.[31]

Boulder, La Porte, along with Julesburg, apparently retained their residents during the war. La Porte was little more than a cluster of houses around Camp (later Fort) Collins established to protect travelers on the Overland Trail from Native Americans. Although mining took place in Boulder County, people living in the Boulder Valley depended on farming for a livelihood, and agriculture was a fairly profitable business. The *Rocky Mountain News* estimated Boulder's population to be two hundred people at war's end and reported substantial construction in the town even though it lagged throughout the rest of the territory. Julesburg was little more than a glorified stage station. Its importance was as a transfer point for people traveling to the West Coast and those going south to Denver. The town contained a telegraph office, a general store, a livery barn, a blacksmith shop, a warehouse, a billiard-saloon, and six houses. Its residents numbered about fifty people and most travelers described it as too rustic to attract a more permanent population.[32]

Besides a weakening economy and a declining population, Colorado's image was tarnished by misconceptions about its mineral wealth. Eastern speculators in gold were especially bitter about the losses they had incurred during the gold boom of 1863–64. Rich with wartime profits, they began to speculate in Colorado gold mines when prices of the precious metal soared in 1863. "Never in the history of the country," wrote the *Daily Mining Journal,* "did the excitement in mining speculation run so high as at present. Men are every day receiving wind falls in the shape of receipts from the sale of claims to Eastern capitalists." But too often Colorado miners spent the new money frivolously before enough ore had been extracted to justify the investment. In addition, many claims turned out to be fraudulent. When the price of gold declined in late 1864 and suspicions about the wealth of Colorado mines began to surface, investors dumped their gold stock on the market. Those who failed to move fast enough lost money and blamed Coloradans for their losses. As historian Duane Smith wrote, "Colorado had not fared well with easterners and its reputation was now besmirched."[33]

After 1864 miners found eastern backing difficult to obtain and few could afford to import the equipment necessary to do the job. The uncertainty of the war's outcome, moreover, discouraged the investment of foreign capital. Thus, Bayard Taylor reported: "The deserted mills, the idle wheels, and the empty shafts and drills for miles along this and the adjoining ravines—the general decrease in the population everywhere in the mountains—indicated a period of doubt and transition. . . . My friends in Central City will not take offence when I say I left—not them but the place—with a cheerful sense of relief." John Tice, a visitor, noted that "crumbling walls and tottering chimneys of 'played out' reduction works, ponderous broken, and rusted machinery and curious shaped furnaces, whose fires have been extinguished for years, meet the eye everywhere and chill the hearts of capitalists anxious to invest in the rich mining of these mountains."[34]

Colorado also had a reputation as a land of high prices and scarce goods. Miners' letters back home as well as contemporary statements strengthened the impression. True, wartime inflation and freighting charges (usually 10 cents to 20 cents a pound per mile) increased prices for goods shipped from the states. Scarcity, too, especially when wagon trains were halted because of Native American problems, only exacerbated the situation. "We cannot live here on a small salary, and the people cannot pay us a large one," the Rev. Crawford informed the American Missionary Society. Bayard Taylor called Central City "the most outrageously expensive place in Colorado. You pay more and get less for the money than in any other part of the world." Women often complained about prices in their letters home. Ellen Pennock paid 90 cents for a yard of bleach muslin and 65 cents for calico. Amelia Buss chaffed at having to pay $125 for a cord of wood and that "for one cord of pine wood." Eggs in Denver sold for $2.00 a dozen, flour for $25 a sack, and butter for $2.00 a pound. Buffalo meat was the least expensive item in town, at 3 cents a pound, but most people refused to eat it. Table board cost $15 a week, while in Chicago it was advertised at $3.50.[35]

Wages somewhat offset higher prices but not enough to please most people. One Denver resident felt that despite higher wages, the cost of living had soured a close relationship with his former Ohio neighbors. At his urging they moved to Denver but found, even with higher wages, their lifestyle had deteriorated. And they blamed him for the predicament. "Wages are high because living is so dear," wrote a *New York Times* correspondent, "and the price of food and all other articles depend upon having free communication with the East. Teaming 600 miles is, of course, expensive, but the Indians are the chief trouble, and this is what exasperates the people here so much about the red-skins."[36]

The most lasting impression of Colorado and its people came as a result of the Sand Creek Massacre. Like most Americans who moved westward, Coloradans, almost from the beginning, demanded the removal of the Native American population. The major tribes in eastern Colorado were the Arapaho and Southern Cheyenne. By the Treaty of Fort Wise in 1861 some bands did agree to move to a reservation in southeastern Colorado. Within a short time, however, crop failure, the lack of game, plus the federal government's failure to deliver promised blankets and foodstuffs caused discontent. By the spring of 1864 Native Americans were raiding farms and stealing food, cattle, and horses. Chivington, now a colonel, responded with raids on Cheyenne camps, killing some fifty braves. The situation became more intense after the Native Americans retaliated by attacking settlers. In June 1864, a band of Arapaho marauders killed and scalped the Nathan Hungate family, consisting of the parents and two children, who lived on a ranch southeast of Denver. Within days the "bloated festering bodies," wrote Byers, were "drawn naked through the streets in an ox wagon" and put on display in the city. In August Native Americans captured Lucinda Ewbanks (sometimes spelled Eubanks) and subjected her to sexual abuse and harsh treatment before releasing her.[37]

By the fall of 1864, Denver citizens were near panic, and calls for extermination of the Native Americans became common. Charles Dilke, an Englishman who had an unpleasant encounter with Native Americans on the Plains, agreed. Even "Mrs. [Harriet] Beecher Stowe," he wrote, "would go in for the western 'disarm at any price, and exterminate if necessary' policy if [she] lived long in Denver." Explaining the general attitude in the city, Alexander Hunt, later governor of the territory, commented: "That feeling [extermination] prevails in all the new countries when the Indians have committed any depredations. And more especially will people fly off the handle in that way when you exhibit the corpse of someone who had been murdered by the Indians. When they come to their sober senses they reflect that Indians have feelings as well as we have, and are entitled to certain rights; which, by the way, they never get."[38]

Relations between Anglos and Native Americans continued at an impasse. Governor Evans, in 1864, issued a call for the Third Colorado Volunteer Cavalry Regiment to serve for one hundred days and limited its duty to fighting the Native Americans. Then, in early November he left for Washington to request more troops. During the governor's absence Chivington decided to deliver a telling blow. On the 29th he attacked a peaceful Cheyenne encampment on Sand Creek, and according to his own estimate, killed five hundred Native Americans, although historians calculate the actual number closer to two hundred. Much of the soldiers' fury was motivated by their belief in the innate inferiority of Native Americans and the desire to see them eliminated from the Plains. Even Governor Evans asserted that "the benefit to Colorado of that massacre, as they call it, was very great for it ridded the plains of the indians [*sic*]."[39]

While many people in the East and officials in Washington, D.C., did not have a higher opinion of Native Americans, they were genuinely shocked by the slaughter of innocent women and children, and their reaction was immediate and caustic. It was one of the most atrocious events in white-Indian warfare, screamed the *New York Times*. The federal commissioner of Indian affairs denounced it as a massacre, and Benjamin Wade, U.S. senator from Ohio, declared Sand Creek to be "the scene of murder and barbarity . . . of the most revolting character." An investigation conducted by the House of Representatives condemned Chivington for having "deliberately planned and executed a foul and dastardly massacre which would have disgraced the veriest savage among those who were the victims of his cruelty." It also criticized Evans for defending Chivington and portraying the Native Americans at Sand Creek as hostile when he was fully aware they were not. As a result, the president demanded the governor's resignation, and the army ordered a court of inquiry into the incident.[40]

Mining towns took a critical view of Sand Creek. The Montana Literary Society in Central City, "*Resolved*, that indiscriminate massacre of all Indians, without reference to age or sex, is contrary to humanity, religion and common sense."[41] In Denver, however, most people praised the massacre as an outstanding victory. The *Rocky Mountain News* called it a "brilliant feat of arms in Indian warfare" and wanted to know how long citizens of Colorado "will have to be maligned for Sand Creek. Indians are thinning our sparse settlements along the Platte and when we strike back they call it a 'massacre.'" When U.S. Senator James Doolittle arrived in Denver seven months after the event to conduct a congressional inquiry, he held an open meeting hoping to gauge public opinion. Instead of finding the audience remorseful, it shouted "Exterminate them! Exterminate them!" when Doolittle asked what should be done with the Native Americans.[42]

Emotions over Sand Creek ran so high in Denver that few dared criticize the massacre. Captain Silas S. Soule, who refused to follow Chivington's order during the massacre, was gunned down in the street after he testified before a court of inquiry that women and children were shot without mercy. His murderer, Private Charles W. Squires, was caught and housed in a military brig but escaped. Evidence indicated that the soldiers who guarded Squires were Sand Creek veterans and helped him get away. Even a year after the massacre, Denverites denounced their new governor when he criticized the behavior of the troops at Sand Creek.[43]

The distaste that easterners and officials felt about Sand Creek was slow to die, and Colorado boosters were aware of its negative impact. Writing to Hiram Bennet, Colorado's delegate in Congress, warned, "Unless something is done to settle this trouble [Sand Creek], we are virtually killed as a territory. . . . This must be attended to immediately, or our prospects are blasted for some time to come, and the development of a rich mining country indefinitely postponed."[44]

Despite the problems Colorado faced, its boosters persisted in their efforts to improve and advance the territory. Because of their faith in Colorado's potential they came with a determination to succeed, and they persuaded others to share in their expectations. Among the territory's chief boosters were John Evans and Bela Hughes, whose major interest lay in railroad building, and editor William Byers and Walter Cheeseman, two of Colorado's major land and town site speculators. Another booster, Jerome Chaffee, Denver banker and member of the first territorial legislature, persuaded his fellow lawmakers to petition Congress for a branch of the U.S. Mint in Denver. The name *branch mint* was a misnomer, as it served merely as an assay office and no coins were struck there until 1906. The director of the U.S. Mint in Philadelphia refused to supply the necessary machinery, citing freighting expenses and "the hostility of Indian tribes . . . and bad white men" when coins were being transported to the East. Still, the branch mint was one of the more imposing structures in Denver because the federal government purchased the facilities of Clark, Gruber and Company, a private banking and assay firm, rather than construct its own building.[45]

Chaffee continued to show his faith in Colorado's possibilities when he and David Moffat secured a charter for the First National Bank of Denver in 1865. In their application, both men admitted that Denver's population was smaller than that of eastern cities with national banks, but stated a federal facility was necessary to stabilize the currency and stimulate the city's rebuilding following the flood and fire. The next year Charles and Luther Kountz, members of a prominent eastern banking family, established the Colorado National Bank in Denver as well as the Rocky Mountain National Bank in Central City.[46]

While these individuals acknowledged setbacks, they took steps to build a brighter future. They looked forward to the coming of the transcontinental railroad and had a strong faith that gold could still be found in the hills and only advances in mining technology were needed to flush it out. They also hoped for a new influx of immigrants, maybe even the arrival of families to balance out the predominantly male population and bring social stability to their raucous frontier.

Visitors, too, saw potential in the territory's future. Among them was Samuel Bowles, one of the more astute observers of early Colorado. He visited the territory in 1865 and then again in 1869. During his first visit he noted the shrinking population, the abandoned mines, the drying up of eastern capital, and the general malaise. But on his second visit he found "a new order of things." The problems were still there, but Bowles felt that the postwar years would prove the most important to the territory's development. "These were the kernel years of Colorado; they proved her, they have made her," he wrote.[47] Before the war the mining frontier had established itself at the base of the mountains but the vast plains to the east remained mostly untouched. With the Civil War over, Americans would again turn westward to conquer the High Plains that lay before the mountains.

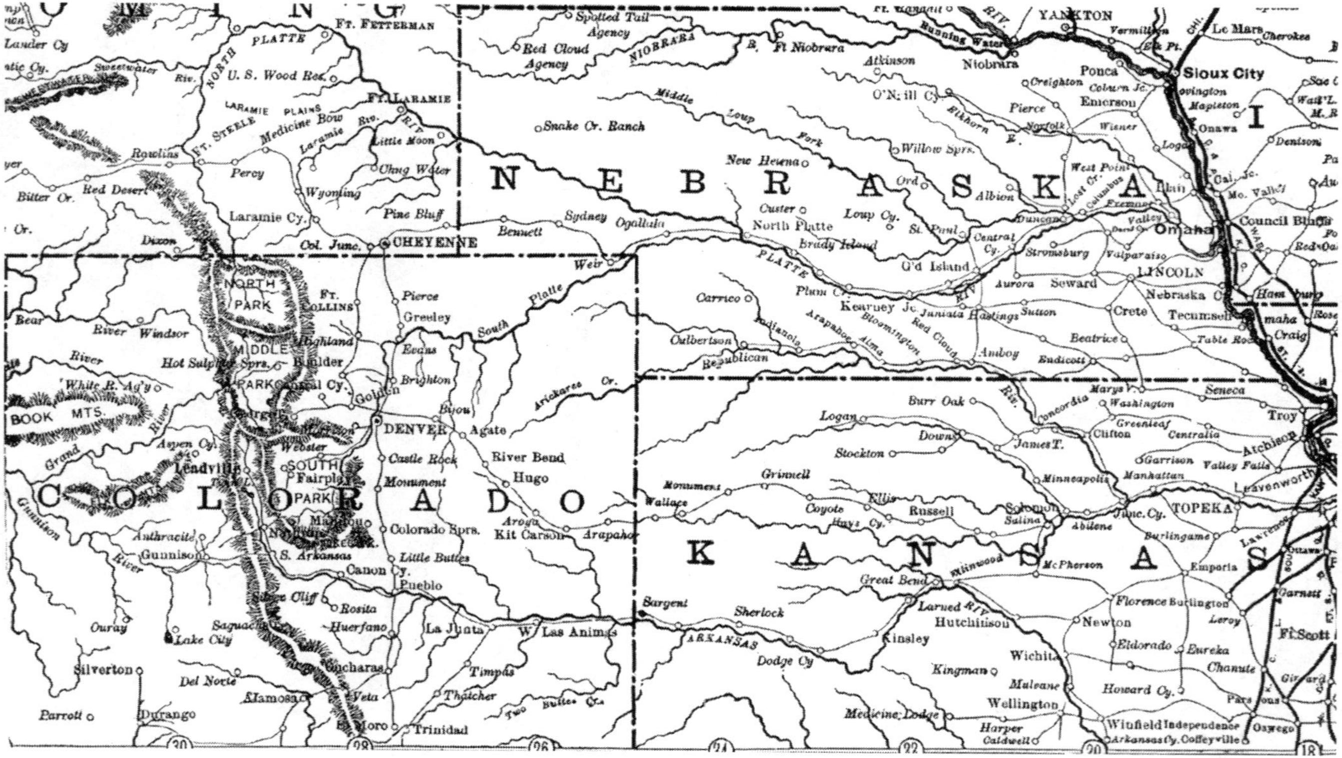

1. Map including parts of Kansas, Nebraska, and Colorado The Central Great Plains, 1883. From Henry Jacob Winser, The Great Northwest: A Guidebook and Itinerary for the use of Tourists and Travellers over the Lines of the Northern Pacific Railroad *(1883).*

2 *Subduing the Natives*

Retaliation for Sand Creek came quickly. Within days after the massacre, November 29, 1864, Southern Cheyenne leaders sent a war pipe to Arapaho and Sioux allies and by the end of December warriors from the three tribes had assembled on Cherry Creek, a branch of the Republican River near the Kansas-Colorado border. They began attacking white settlements almost immediately. Between January 7 and February 2, 1865, Native Americans struck thirty-five ranches, farms, and stage stations in the South Platte River Valley. In addition, they captured a number of wagon trains between Julesburg and Denver. In the parting days of the campaign, January 28 to February 2, they attacked every ranch and stage station between Julesburg and Valley Station, a distance of about twenty miles. Viewing the destruction at Valley Station, Colonel Thomas Moonlight, the local military commander, wrote: "The Indians are bold in the extreme. They have burned . . . nearly all the property, driven off the stock . . . and have complete control of all the country." An unofficial account listed forty-one whites killed—twenty-two soldiers and nineteen civilians. By the end of the campaign, "the stage line [between Julesburg and Denver] was broken up and no coaches were running," wrote George Bent, "every station for a distance of nearly one hundred miles had been burned and the stock run off; the Overland Telegraph had been destroyed and the government was cut off from all communication with Colorado, Utah, Nevada, and the Pacific Coast. All of this trouble was the result of Col. Chivington's 'great victory' at Sand Creek."[1]

Raids throughout the valley followed a similar pattern. Small war parties struck ranches or stations at dawn or dusk when an attack was least expected. They took any items or livestock they considered of value, ran off the rest of the livestock, and burned all buildings and haystacks. They made a special effort to seize all good range horses. According to A. R. Ross, Native Americans were excellent judges of horseflesh and "God pity anyone caught between them and a good saddle horse." Ross, among others, believed the Native Americans were mainly intent on acquiring booty and destroying property rather than murdering settlers because often they did not pursue fleeing civilians. Soldiers were not so fortunate. On January 7, two miles from Moore's ranch, Native Americans encountered two soldiers whom they identified as having participated in the Sand Creek Massacre. They tortured the men before killing them and then dismembered their bodies. Still, torture and dismemberment were rare. Canada McCollough, who witnessed the raid on the American ranch, recalled that the Natives preferred killing their foe quickly, and an experienced Native American could dispatch and scalp an enemy in less than one minute.[2]

The assaults against Julesburg were the major coordinated efforts of the South Platte Valley campaign. While small bands of warriors carried out the raids against farms and ranches, the attacks on Julesburg involved large numbers of Native Americans and were well organized and executed with military-like precision. Early in January 1865, about a thousand warriors, along with women and extra ponies, evacuated their base camp and marched northward toward the settlement. On the night of January 6, they pitched camp in the sand hills just south of Julesburg and Fort Sedgwick (then called Fort Rankin). The fort was garrisoned by fifty men of the Seventh Iowa Cavalry under the command of Captain Nicholas O'Brien. To restrain the younger braves, who were anxious for a fight, the chiefs kept them under guard to prevent them from taking any action that might reveal the Native Americans' position. At dawn a small group of warriors used the classic Native American maneuver, feigning an attack on the fort and then retreating slowly toward the hills in order to draw out the soldiers and annihilate them. Unaware that they were being led into a trap, the soldiers followed but then fell back when a contingent of excited young braves charged over the hills. Realizing that the enemy force was much larger than they had anticipated, the soldiers scurried back into the fort.[3]

As the soldiers and Native Americans were skirmishing, the westbound stagecoach approached Julesburg. Seeing the young braves charge over the hills, the travelers along with the village residents fled to the fort, arriving at the same time as the retreating soldiers. With the whites holed up in the fort, the Native Americans got down to the immediate objective of the attack: to plunder Julesburg. The women brought up the ponies while the men broke into the warehouse and raided the store.[4] Underlying the entire campaign, however, was the Natives' anger about Sand Creek and their frustration over the white man's encroachment upon their homelands.

For the remainder of the day the Native Americans hauled away guns and ammunition and most of the foodstuffs, but left the canned goods because they were unaware the cans contained food. Younger warriors found bolts of fabric, which they unfurled while riding their horses around the settlement. A U.S. paymaster on the stagecoach forgot to grab a strongbox containing $30,000 in greenbacks when he fled to safety. This the Native Americans found and, not knowing what it was, scattered the green paper to the winds. In the days following the attack, soldiers searched for the money but without much success. At the stage station some of the Native Americans ate the food that had been prepared for the arriving passengers. When the raid was over the ponies were so loaded down with booty that the Native Americans had difficulty traveling back to their base camp. Many of the items taken were totally unfamiliar and George Bent spent the next several days explaining how to use them. The Native Americans, for example, had never seen oysters or candied citron and had no idea they were edible.[5]

Soldiers and civilians watching from the fort were surprised that the Native Americans did not burn Julesburg as they retreated. But they never intended to burn the town; they planned to raid it again and hoped it would be restocked. When the second attack came on February 2, the Native Americans found much less to plunder because all wagon trains heading west had been stopped in Nebraska. Nor could they lure the soldiers out of the fort by feigning another attack. In a last attempt to entice the soldiers, the Native Americans finally began to burn Julesburg in "a most tantalizing manner, each building being consumed separately, the Indians firing one and then waiting to see the effect; then another, and so on until all were consumed." After firing the last building, the Natives suddenly left when they noticed the soldiers setting up mountain howitzers.[6]

The raids in the South Platte Valley understandably caused panic in Denver, and many believed that the city itself would soon be attacked. The *Rocky Mountain News* only strengthened such fears when it reported that 7,893 Native Americans were amassed on the plains waiting to attack the city either that evening or the next morning. But the attack never came. In fact, the strike on Pierson's Station, just fourteen miles north on the South Platte River, was the closest the Native Americans came to Denver. Their preferred method of warfare consisted of moving quickly and striking isolated targets where the odds were in their favor. Even though the Native Americans threatened to attack Colorado villages and towns, except for Julesburg they never carried out the threat during the 1865 raids.[7]

Still, the possibility of an attack demoralized citizens because the city was virtually defenseless. The Third Colorado Cavalry, whose principal service had been at Sand Creek, had been mustered out in December 1864. When the raids began, Acting Governor Samuel Elbert issued a call for volunteers to quell Native American activities but few men responded. Even the territorial legislature's offer of increased military pay failed to encourage enlistments. Finally, in desperation Col. Moonlight declared martial law and practically closed Denver down until enough volunteers could be secured. But the effort came to nothing. By the time the men received minimum training, the Native Americans had left the South Platte Valley, and the troops did not engage in a single battle before they were mustered out in April 1865. It was the last Colorado citizen-soldier unit organized to engage in warfare against Native Americans.

The lack of troops also hampered the response of federal forces. Ordered to move against the Native Americans, General Robert Mitchell, commander of the District of North Kansas, organized all the troops guarding the stage line and those at Camp Cottonwood in Nebraska Territory into one unit; still, he had only about five hundred men. Mitchell hoped a quick, surprise strike would compensate for his small force but his plan failed because the Native Americans kept eluding him. Finally, after he learned that they had moved out the valley entirely, Mitchell returned to eastern Nebraska in frustration.[8]

During their month-long campaign, the Native Americans focused on the South Platte Valley, in northeastern Colorado. Several reasons account for this. The telegraph lines and stage routes into Denver as well as most of the wagon trains followed the South Platte River. Cutting the lines and attacking passengers and supplies heading into the city would cause panic that might work to the Native Americans' advantage. The valley also contained ranches, farms, and stage stations, all of which provided articles for plunder. But most important, the Southern Cheyennes considered the land along the South Platte as well as the western branches of the Republican and Smokey Hill rivers in Kansas to be their ancestral homeland.[9] The abundance of grass, water holes, and an ideal climate had made the region a grazing ground for buffalo for hundreds of years, and the buffalo was basic to the life of the Plains Indians. In addition, the Cheyenne force engaging in the raids consisted mainly of Dog Soldiers, and they rarely ventured into southern Colorado. Opposed to the reservation established by the Treaty of Fort Wise, Dog Soldiers felt whites might interpret their presence there as tacit approval of the treaty. According to John Wesley Prowers, who ranched along the Arkansas River, Dog Soldiers also avoided the Arkansas Valley because they did not get along with the other Cheyenne tribes living there.[10]

Most white contemporaries presumed the Native American force raiding in the South Platte Valley consisted of a large portion of the Cheyenne, Arapaho, and Sioux nations. In reality, only small groups were involved: Brulè Sioux from Kansas, Arapahos from Colorado, and Cheyenne Dog Soldiers. Amanda Mary Fletcher, captured by a Cheyenne band during the outbreak, recalled the situation correctly: "The Arapahoes [in Little Raven's band] had been at peace with the whites for a long time and were friendly. I wish to state in this connection that the main tribe or band of Cheyennes were also peaceable. It was only a small band of Cheyennes, comparatively speaking, that was committing these depredations and to distinguish them from the peaceable Cheyennes, they were known at that time as Cheyenne Dog Soldiers."[11]

After Sand Creek, Black Kettle, the most important chief of the Southern Cheyennes, moved most of the tribe to southern Kansas. While the massacre left him angry and resentful, Black Kettle refused to join the Dog Soldiers in their quest for vengeance and openly criticized their activities. Black Kettle feared resistance to the whites would lead to further retribution and that the entire Cheyenne nation would be punished "for what the Dog Soldiers had done." Despite these objections, many of his younger warriors did join the Dog Soldiers.[12]

The Dog Soldiers were one of six warrior societies of the Northern and Southern Cheyenne nations. The main function of warrior societies was to protect the people of the tribe, and to accomplish this they acted as a police force within the bands and as a rear guard during the tribes' migrations. Warrior society members lived with the tribes and were subject to the council chiefs. That had also been true of the Dog Soldiers until the 1830s, when their leader was declared an outlaw. From that time, the Dog Soldiers lived separately along the Republican and Smokey Hill rivers, refusing to associate with the other Southern Cheyenne bands. They became closely allied with Brulè Sioux and had strong ties with the tribe through intermarriage. Among the warrior societies, the Dog Soldiers were the most aggressive and most adamant about retaining their ancestral lands.[13]

Military personnel and civilians who encountered the Dog Soldiers generally respected and admired them as people, and esteemed their military prowess. General George Custer referred to them as "fine looking braves of magnificent physique, in appearance and demeanor more nearly conforming to the ideal warrior than those of any other tribe." Theodore Davis, a reporter for *Harper's Weekly,* called them the finest specimen of the "Indian race" he had ever seen. And according to the *Kansas Daily Tribune,* Dog Soldiers were men "in the true sense of the word."[14]

The two most notable Dog Soldiers in the Colorado Indian wars were Tall Bull and Roman Nose. The son of a Dog Soldier father and a Sioux mother, Tall Bull was the spiritual and tribal leader of the warriors. He was also known for his displays of courage when meeting whites. Captain Albert Bernitz of the Seventh Cavalry described Tall Bull's arrival at the Medicine Lodge Creek council in 1867: Tall Bull and his men "crossed the creek on our front and emerged from the woods, in line of battle, firing their guns into the air, singing and yelling! They were gaily dressed and painted . . . , and present[ed] a truly grand and formidable appearance as they came in sight!"[15]

Roman Nose, a Northern Cheyenne considered the most famous warrior of his day, joined the Dog Soldiers following the Sand Creek Massacre. Contrary to popular belief among whites, he was not a chief. American military officers at the Medicine Lodge Creek council frequently inquired why Roman Nose was absent and seemed perplexed when told that his lack of rank made him ineligible to attend councils. The officers found it difficult to comprehend that a warrior so renowned for his bravery was not a chief. General Theophilus Rodenbough, who met Roman Nose in 1866, described him as "one of the finest specimens of the untamed savage. It would be difficult to exaggerate in describing his superb physique. A veritable man of war . . . standing six feet three inches high, he towered, giant-like, above his companions. [He had] strongly marked features . . . fierce black eyes, a large mouth [and] a Roman nose, with delicate nostrils."[16]

Both Tall Bull and Roman Nose enjoyed taunting their adversaries. During the council at Medicine Lodge Creek, General William S. Harney, an old Indian fighter, advanced toward Tall Bull and extended his hand. The chief put out his hand but with his middle finger extended and the others balled up into a fist, whereupon the general turned and took no further notice of him. When Roman Nose met General Winfield Scott

Hancock, whom he disliked intensely and vowed to kill, he brought his horse along side the general's, glared at him for several moments, and then raised his hand and struck Hancock lightly on the face. Bull Bear, also a Dog Soldier, who was next to the two men, was so certain that Roman Nose might draw his gun on the general that he quickly guided him away.[17]

Following the raids in the South Platte Valley, the Native American force broke into three parties. Attacks by small groups of warriors continued in Colorado Territory, but for the next two years most of the fighting took place in Dakota and Montana territories and in Kansas. Still, it is necessary to describe what took place because the final events poured out onto the plains of Colorado.[18] And although the territory was not directly involved, Colorado officials requested more soldiers and a military base near Denver to protect the people. But William T. Sherman, commander of the Division of the Missouri, had little sympathy for such appeals. "Denver needs no protection," he wrote. "I have travelled all the way from [Fort] Laramie without a single soldier as escort. I met single men unarmed travelling along the road as in Missouri—cattle—horses—graze loose far from their owners, most tempting to a starving Indian, and though Indians might easily make a descent on these scattered ranches yet they have not done so, and I see no external signs of fear of such an event, though all the people are clamorous for military protection." Sherman avoided committing troops to Colorado by repeatedly asking for specific information about the supposed Native American threat. Even after warfare became more intense, Sherman admitted he could do little to meet the demands of Coloradans. His troops were too few and the Native Americans too scattered. It was so difficult to predict where they might strike next that developing a strategy to defeat them was "harder to plan than the campaigns of the war."[19]

In 1867 and 1868 hostilities were centered chiefly in the northwestern quadrant of Kansas. The westward building of the Kansas Pacific Railroad (then known as the Eastern Division of the Union Pacific) and the increasing number of settlers that followed was the initial spark that renewed the conflict. But the belligerent and unyielding attitude of Gen. Hancock, commander of the Department of the Missouri, intensified the situation. In April 1867, he led a large cavalry and infantry force into western Kansas and called for a council with Sioux and Cheyenne chiefs. Accusing the Native Americans of trying to stir up war, he threatened immediate retaliation if they continued their activities. Even though Tall Bull assured Hancock of the Native Americans' peaceful intentions, the general remained adamant in his assertions. At the end of the council he informed the Cheyennes that he intended to march his troops to their village on Pawnee Fork the next day. This brought strong objections from the chiefs, whose memories of Sand Creek were still fresh. Tall Bull told Hancock that his visit would do more harm than good, but the general scoffed at the statement.

Dog Soldiers confronted Hancock's troops as they approached the village. Tall Bull again asked Hancock to cancel his plan, but the general ignored the chief and continued to march forward. The Dog Soldiers prepared to fight but desisted after the Sioux refused to join them, fearing that too many of their women and children would be killed. The Cheyennes spent the rest of the day abandoning their camp, which the soldiers now surrounded trying to prevent their escape. At nightfall they set fire to the entire village and burned 250 lodges.[20]

Once the Dog Soldiers regrouped, Kansas underwent its worst summer of Native American raids: sixty-five recorded attacks between June and September. In all, 128 civilians met their deaths at the hands of the Native Americans. While most westerners were appalled by such violence, others realized that the wrongs being perpetrated against the Native Americans caused such ruthless behavior. Sir Lambert Price, an Englishman, wrote: "Often I have heard [western] men . . . say that, before God, the Indian was in the right, and was doing what any American citizens would do in his place. . . . Their territory has been annexed [and] they have been defrauded in the most shocking and scandalous manner."[21]

Unable to quell the Native Americans on both the northern and southern plains, the federal government finally called for a grand council to meet in October 1867, at Medicine Lodge Creek in southern Kansas. The tribes present included the Cheyenne and Arapaho as well as the Kiowas and Comanche. At first the Dog Soldiers refused to attend but finally relented. According to George Bent, the treaty adopted there was the most important ever signed because "it marked the beginning of the end of the Cheyenne as free and independent warriors and hunters." By its terms the Native Americans ceded the land between the Platte and Arkansas rivers and consented to live on a reservation in the northern section of the Indian Territory (Oklahoma). They also agreed not to obstruct the construction of railroads in the Platte and Smoky Hill valleys and to stop attacking white travelers and wagon trains. In return the government promised to provide rations, yearly stipends of goods, and schools for the children. The Dog Soldier chiefs signed but only after considerable pressure from more peaceful chiefs and Native American agents. One was so angry that he jabbed the quill pen entirely though the paper when he made his mark.[22]

If the government expected the treaty to solve its problems with the Dog Soldiers, it was soon disappointed. Resentment developed immediately because the Dog Soldier chiefs "had *no idea* what they are giving up," explained Capt. Bernitz, "or that they have given up the country which they claim as their own. The treaty all amounts to nothing, and we will certainly have another war sooner or later with the Cheyennes." Bernitz felt the fighting would be on a larger scale than before because the Kansas Pacific, slowly creeping toward Colorado, would enable the government to transport soldiers to the area more quickly. It was, however, the government's failure to live up to its treaty obligations that proved the last straw, and when the new commander, General Philip Sheridan, took over he found many Native Americans rebellious and contemptuous. Dog Soldiers carried out a series of raids along the Republican, Salmon, and Saline rivers during which they drove off the settlers and destroyed property they could not carry away.[23]

By August 1868, the general uprising spread into Colorado. On August 27, Arapaho warriors, allies of the Dog Soldiers, killed Henrietta Dieterman and her five-year-old son on their farm about twenty miles north of Cañon City. The Pueblo *Colorado Chieftain* reported: "The red fiends are again on the warpath. . . . Whole families are being murdered and being scalped by these devils incarnate." Shortly thereafter a group of Arapahos appeared in Colorado City, where they roamed through the town frightening the residents. Upon their departure they stole 150 horses. In Larimer County they killed John Brush and two of his workers, then stampeded Brush's cattle and drove off his horses. They also tried, without success, to persuade Arapaho Chief Friday, who was camped on the Cache la Poudre River, to join them.[24]

When the Dieterman corpses were put on display in Denver, the citizenry reacted in anger and frustration. Seizing Acting Governor Frank Hall when he arrived at the scene, they demanded to know how he planned to deal with the problem. Hall did send a group of volunteers into the area under attack but "they did more harm than the Indians," declared George Aux, "they did everything that was bad. The Indians were our sworn enemies; it took some little time to find that they were enemies too; they were generally rough, reckless fellows, gamblers." Hall also appealed to Sherman and Sheridan for military assistance. Perhaps remembering the Coloradans' tendency to exaggerate Native American depredations, Sherman questioned Hall's accounts of the danger, while Sheridan informed him that he had no reports to confirm the situation Hall described. Sheridan finally relented and ordered part of the Seventh Cavalry to Colorado when Hall telegraphed that Vice-President Schuyler Colfax and his party, who were visiting towns in southern Colorado, were in imminent danger. Apologizing for sending so few troops, Sheridan wrote, "I am extremely sorry to have been unable to relieve the distress of the people of your frontier, but the fact of the case is, I have my hands full."[25]

The Native Americans' superior knowledge of the terrain and their rapid movements made it impossible for Sheridan's forces to keep track of them. To overcome this difficulty, he established a scouting unit composed mainly of civilians experienced at fighting Native Americans. He chose his friend Major George A. Forsyth, who had served as his staff officer during the Civil War, to head the unit. First Lieutenant Frederick H. Beecher, nephew of Harriet Beecher Stowe, was selected as second in command. Beecher had some experience in Indian warfare, having been stationed at Fort Wallace, Kansas, for about a year. Forsyth had none, however. His entire military experience had been in administration. Mustered out in 1866, he rejoined the army in 1868 and was assigned to Sheridan's staff. Forsyth expressed his pleasure at being given a field command and his enthusiasm to confront Native Americans. He might have been more cautious had he known what lay ahead. On August 29, 1868, Forsyth and Beecher, along with an army surgeon and fifty-three civilian scouts, marched out onto the plains. Among the scouts were two Coloradans, Isaac Thayer and John Donovan; the remainder were all Kansans. Forsyth planned to reconnoiter the Beaver Creek area to Fort Wallace and await further instructions there. Arriving at the fort he learned that Native Americans had attacked the Kansas Pacific Railroad. Marching northward, the scouting party discovered the Native Americans' trail near the Republican River, which indicated that they were heading westward toward Colorado.

Despite warnings from Beecher and several scouts that the trail indicated a sizeable Native American force, Forsyth foolishly pushed forward. On the night of September 16, the scouting party camped on the bank of the Arickaree River, a branch of the Republican, just opposite a low island. The site is about fifteen miles south of present-day Wray. The Native Americans, a combined force of about six hundred Dog Soldiers, Arapahos, and Sioux, knew the scouts had been following them and planned to annihilate the party the next day.[26]

As dawn broke a group of young warriors, anxious to begin fighting, rushed toward Forsyth's camp and stampeded the horses. Their action served as an advance warning but the time was too brief for a withdrawal. Forsyth ordered his force to retreat to the island, which lay about fifteen feet from the bank, rose several feet above the dry bed of the stream, and was covered with a growth of tall grass, bushy willows, alders, and a single cottonwood tree. There the men secured their horses and dug trenches in order to protect themselves from flying bullets and arrows. According to Chauncy Whitney, who kept a diary during the entire battle, the Native Americans made numerous charges the first three days. Then, slowed by an all-night rain that left the ground muddy and difficult to move across, they laid siege to the island for the next six days. During the night of September 17, Forsyth asked for volunteers to sneak through the Native Americans' lines and seek aid from Fort Wallace, about a hundred miles away. Fearing that the first volunteers might not make it, Forsyth sent out several more two nights later. After harrowing experiences and narrow escapes, both sets of volunteers reached Fort Wallace. Nine days after the battle began, Company H of the Tenth Cavalry, consisting of seventy "Buffalo Soldiers," arrived within sight of the island and the Native Americans quickly withdrew from the area.[27]

Starvation was the greatest threat the scouting party faced during the siege. Rations were nearly depleted when the group made camp on the night before the battle and in the rush to the island they left behind their food supply. Aside from a few prickly pears, the soldiers were soon forced to eat the putrefied flesh of their dead horses. After four days, scout John Hurst recalled, "we had nothing to eat but the dead horses which were festering and decaying about us, and when we cut into this meat the stench was something frightful, and it had green streaks running all through it. The only way it was made at all available for eating was by sprinkling gunpowder over it while it was cooking, which partially took away the bad odor."[28]

Forsyth's command sustained the loss of five men killed and eighteen wounded. On the first day three scouts and Lieut. Beecher, serving as a rear guard during the retreat to the island, were mortally wounded. Shortly thereafter the surgeon was shot, lapsed into a coma, and died three days later. Forsyth received a number of wounds but fully recovered. In later years the Native Americans maintained that Forsyth's move to the island saved him. Had he camped away from the island and been forced to protect himself on the prairie, it would have been much easier for them to destroy the entire command.[29]

Forsyth reported that thirty-five Native Americans had been killed but the Natives disputed the claim, insisting that only six met their deaths during the battle. For the Native Americans, the greatest loss was the death of Roman Nose. Protected by the spiritual blessing, Roman Nose had never been wounded in combat. Just prior to the battle he ate food served from a metal fork, an action that destroyed the blessing. It could only be restored by certain ceremonies, but there was insufficient time before the battle to accomplish this. Several chiefs persuaded him not to participate in the early action, but toward the evening of the first day younger braves convinced him to lead a charge. When his horse made a sudden turn as it approached the island, Roman Nose was shot in the back. His colleagues buried him in an undisclosed location to keep the soldiers from defiling his corpse.[30]

The Battle of Beecher Island, as it came to be called, remained one of the more colorful engagements of Indian warfare for the next fifty years. Reporting on the battle, the commandant at Fort Wallace informed Sheridan: "Forsyth's men fought desperately. . . . there are few cases on record of more desperate fighting, and continued endurance without food except horseflesh, surrounded by the dead and dying." General Nelson A. Miles called it "one of the most remarkable affairs with Indians in the history of the American frontier." For the American press the battle became the stuff of heroism given the odds Forsyth's men faced. But the *Rocky Mountain News* saw nothing heroic in the fight. "It seems that an evil fatality rests upon Colorado," wrote editor Byers. "Indian war, the most terrible of all wars, settles upon her . . . like a burning garment. One morning the mangled remains of our citizens are paraded through our streets; [then] we learn that a command sent to our relief is corralled and all but exterminated."[31]

Native Americans, who judged the importance of battles by the size of the enemy force, regarded the Battle of Beecher Island as a minor engagement. In terms of its overall results, the battle brought no significant change in plains warfare. Dog Soldiers and their allies continued raiding along the Smokey Hill and Republican rivers in western Kansas. Hoping to quell the raids, Sheridan sent three cavalry companies into the area. Dog Soldiers retaliated by hitting the soldiers' camps, killing troopers, and running off their horses. To elude their pursuers, the Native Americans made a trail indicating they had taken shelter in Black Kettle's encampment on the Washita River. Unaware that he was being misled, Sheridan authorized Custer to attack and destroy the village. Black Kettle and the peace chiefs were killed, but the assault did nothing to harm the Dog Soldiers, who were, in actuality, camped in the northwestern part of the state. "Black Kettle," wrote one historian, "was a striking example of a consistently friendly Indian, who, because he was friendly and so because his whereabouts were usually known, was punished for the acts of people whom it was supposed he could control."[32]

In revenge, Dog Soldiers, under Tall Bull's command, began another series of depredations in May 1869. During one week they murdered thirteen settlers and derailed a Kansas Pacific train, killing most of its crew. On May 30 they attacked a German settlement in present-day Lincoln County, Kansas, burned farms, killed homesteaders, and stole or drove off the livestock. They took as prisoners Maria Weichell, described as an attractive woman about twenty years old, and Susanna Alderice and her infant son. They killed Mrs. Alderice's other three children when she tried to protect them and later strangled the baby because he would not stop crying. Ironically, Mrs. Alderice's husband, Thomas, had been a scout at Beecher Island and was in Saline, Kansas, when the Native Americans attacked.[33]

Sheridan immediately dispatched three columns of troops to search for the troublesome Native Americans. One was commanded by Major Eugene Carr, stationed at Fort McPherson, Nebraska. Unlike Forsyth, Carr was an experienced Indian fighter and well acquainted with the Republican River Valley, where the Dog Soldiers reputedly fled. Carr's force consisted of eight undermanned companies of the Fifth Cavalry, augmented by fifty Pawnee scouts under the command of Major Frank North. William "Buffalo Bill" Cody served as chief scout for the expedition. For five weeks Carr's troops followed the raiding band along a three hundred mile trail through Kansas and Nebraska and into Colorado Territory. During the first weeks the Native Americans and troops played the game of cat and mouse along the Republican River, with almost daily clashes occurring. Then suddenly at the end of June the Native Americans disappeared, but they also left numerous false trails hoping to throw off the soldiers. Finally, on July 3 Carr came across a trail at the Arickaree Fork of the Republican River indicating that the Native Americans had headed south. Although he sent a small party to scout the trail, Carr took the bulk of his force north because he suspected the Native Americans had gone in that direction hoping to escape beyond the South Platte River and into Wyoming before he could overtake them. His assumption proved correct and at noon on July 11, scouts spotted Tall Bull's camp at Summit Springs, about ten miles south of present-day Sterling. Although there are no trees or springs at the site today, it originally contained several springs, a marsh, and an large canopy of cottonwoods.[34]

Using the hilly terrain as a natural defilade and aided by high winds that prevented dust columns from forming, Carr ordered his troops to surround the Native Americans. Led by the Pawnees, the soldiers charged at 3:00 p.m. taking the Cheyennes by complete surprise. Some were still eating or resting after their mid-day meal. The Dog Soldiers had no time to grab their weapons or run to their horses, and they fled in all directions. Total confusion reigned throughout the camp. Within minutes the Pawnees were wreaking vengeance on their ancient enemy, and the soldiers were not far behind. Soldiers hunted down and killed many of the braves who were able to flee outside the camp. Tall Bull and about twenty warriors bolted into a nearby canyon for safety but were pursued by Maj. North. Tall Bull fired at North but failed to kill him. North responded by handing his bridle to one of his soldiers, telling the man to gallop away with the horses. When Tall Bull raised himself to see if the soldiers had left, North shot him in the head.[35]

The battle lasted two hours and completely destroyed the Dog Soldiers. Only one of Carr's soldiers had been wounded, but fifty-two Native Americans lay dead and seventeen women and children had been captured. The remainder of the tribe had scattered in all directions. Other casualties included Susanna Alderice and Maria Weichell. The Native Americans attempted to kill both women when the battle began but only succeeded in wounding Weichell.

The day following the battle Carr took stock of what he had captured. The booty included 9,000 pounds of dried meat, 85 lodges, 274 horses, 133 mules, 56 rifles, 22 revolvers, 40 sets of bows and arrows, and 50 pounds of powder. Troops also found $1,300 in gold, $900 of which they gave to Mrs. Weichell. Carr ordered the burning of all the supplies that could not be carried away and reported that 160 fires were needed to accomplish the task.[36]

The Battle of Summit Springs was decisive and dramatic. Native Americans regarded it as a major battle because of the large number of troops involved. Summit Springs and the massacre at Washita broke Southern Cheyenne resistance on the Plains. But it was the death of Tall Bull that had the most lasting impact. "He was the cohesive force behind the Dog Soldier band," wrote James King, "and if the Dog Soldiers had been the last major threat to the settlement of the central plains, then that threat died with him." George Bent remembered that as a result of Summit Springs, "the power of this famous society was broken and never since have they been a factor in the wars of the Cheyenne tribe." Those Dog Soldiers who escaped never regrouped. Some joined the Northern Cheyenne in their wars on the Plains, but most drifted south and, like their less belligerent brothers, accepted life on the reservation. In Denver the legislature passed a resolution of thanks, declaring the battle ended a situation that had retarded the prosperity of the territory and had caused the deaths of defenseless women and children or subjected them to a captivity worse than death. Well might the legislature have been pleased. For at little cost to the territory, U.S. military forces had accomplished what many Coloradans had desired: removal of the Cheyennes and Arapahos from their midst.[37]

Native American problems on the Plains were by no means ended after Summit Springs. As late as 1873 and 1874 Colorado officials reported raids on livestock in eastern Colorado, and small bands of Arapaho or Sioux often appeared in isolated areas and threatened the settlers "with a general 'cleaning out.'" By May 1871, however, Native American activity in eastern Colorado had become so minimal that the War Department abandoned Fort Sedgwick and turned the land over to the Department of the Interior for settlement. Two years later a correspondent to the Denver *Colorado Tribune* recalled that in 1860 the mention of Pike's Peak called up "hideous visions of blood-thirsty savages. Gazing upon [Colorado] in these days, none . . . of the ancient horror is felt."[38]

In western Colorado the Ute Indians were relatively friendly until the Meeker massacre in 1879. Traditional enemies of the Cheyennes and Arapahos, they supported the whites in the Plains wars and after 1869 hunted buffalo on the Plains without fear of meeting their foes. Their friendliness was due in part to their lack of cohesion. In Colorado the Utes consisted of three different bands: the Yampa Utes in the northwestern part of the territory, the Tabeguache Utes in the west central region, and the Southern Utes in the southwest. Each band had its own chief and council, and they did not often act in unity.

Utes were a common sight in Denver where they camped along Cherry Creek and freely roamed throughout the city. In May 1865, the *Rocky Mountain News* reported that four hundred Utes visiting the city were the "happiest, jolliest, best-natured Indians which surround us." By 1871 a special agency was established in Denver to deal with the large number of visiting Utes. Merchants who traded in buffalo hides found doing business with the Utes lucrative, but citizens often criticized their behavior because of their fondness for liquor. Oddly, they seldom mentioned the behavior of drunken white men.[39]

Homesteaders outside of Denver complained of Utes begging for food and other favors. Occasionally they left their livestock in charge of nearby farmers while they went off to trade or visit in the city. One farmer in the Boulder Valley refused to tend a flock of goats the Utes had left in his charge, which resulted in the loss of several of the animals. The Native Americans threatened to retaliate but never did. In reporting the story, the *Rocky Mountain News* wondered why the farmer did not appeal to his neighbors for help and avoid possible trouble.[40]

In the late 1860s considerable tension existed between the Utes and Mexican Americans in southern Colorado. One quarrel in the Huerfano River Valley resulted in the deaths of one Hispano rancher and three Native Americans. Partly in retaliation Utes raided Hispano settlements along the Purgatoire River and troops from Fort Garland had to restore order. Although the Utes promised to be peaceful, small bands continued raiding.[41]

The most influential Ute with respect to white-Native American relations was Ouray. He advocated cooperation with whites as the only means for the bands to retain their lands. Unlike the chiefs of the Plains Indians, Ouray had lived among both Hispanos and Americans and did not regard them as enemies. The son of a Tabeguache mother and a Jicarilla Apache father, Ouray, at the age of nine, was apprenticed to a Mexican American family in Taos, New Mexico. Taos, at the time, was a small but cosmopolitan community populated by descendants of Spanish aristocrats, Mexicans, Americans, and members of numerous Native American tribes. By the time he left the settlement, Ouray had acquired facility in the Ute, Apache, Spanish, and English languages. Back in Colorado, he soon became spokesman for the Tabeguache Utes.[42]

The Utes at first resisted the encroachment of whites into Colorado but during the Civil War Ouray met Governor Evans at Fort Garland and offered the friendship of the bands if they were guaranteed permanent possession of the Uncompahgre-Gunnison region. Conversations between Colorado officials and the Native Americans resulted in the Tabeguache Treaty of 1863. The Utes relinquished Middle Park and all of their Colorado land east of the Continental Divide. In return they were to receive $20,000 a year for supplies and rations, plus stallions for breeding stock, as well as cattle and sheep. The document also recognized Ouray as head of all Ute tribes, even though he represented only the Tabeguache band and other Ute bands were not party to the negotiations. The government ratified the treaty but Congress failed to provide promised monies and livestock. By 1867 the head of the Conejos Indian Agency reported that younger tribesmen were committing depredations, for want of food and clothing.[43]

Alexander Cameron Hunt, territorial governor in 1868, concluded a second treaty with the Utes. Although he believed they should live on reservations and become farmers, Hunt was inclined to be generous for fear the Utes, if they felt aggrieved enough, might ally with the Arapahos and Cheyennes, leaving the whites in the territory surrounded by hostile

Native Americans. His attitude resulted in the most generous treaty ever made between the U.S. government and any Native American group. The Ute Treaty, as it is called, reconfirmed the land sessions of the Tabeguache Treaty and granted additional land to each man, woman, and child. In addition, the Native Americans were to receive $60,000 annually for twenty years for the purchase of provisions and clothing, and each family was to receive sheep and farm implements. The government also promised to build schools, sawmills, and other buildings.[44]

Not long after the treaty of 1868 gold and silver were discovered inside the Ute reservation and miners rushed into the area. Instead of forcing them to leave, the government requested more concessions from the Utes. Colorado's new territorial governor, Edward McCook, along with members of the Indian Commission, met with about 1,500 Utes to discuss the issue. Negotiations bogged down because the Native Americans disliked and distrusted McCook. They refused to cede any land and demanded that the miners leave the area. "Perhaps some people will not like it because we do not wish to sell our valley and farming lands," Ouray wrote, "but we think we have good reasons. . . . We know if we should the whites would go on them, build their cabins and drive in their stock, which would of course stray upon our lands, and then the whites themselves would crowd upon us till there would be trouble. . . . We feel it would be better for all parties for a mountain range to be between us."[45]

In an attempt to persuade the Utes, several Colorado Indian agents accompanied leaders of the Tabeguache and Yampa bands on a three-month excursion to eastern cities and Washington, D.C., where they met with President Grant and other national leaders. In the national capital the Native Americans signed the Brunot Agreement, negotiated by Felix Brunot, chairman of the Board of Indian Commissions. By its terms they surrendered the heartland of the San Juan Mountains, nearly a quarter of their reservation. They were now confined to southwestern Colorado and to the White River region in the northwestern part of the territory. Tension soon arose because some Utes did not comprehend the terms of the agreement. They believed they had given up only mining claims and no houses could be built on the ceded land. By 1879, the Yampa Utes rose in rebellion, killed Indian agent Nathan Meeker and nine of his employees, and fought a pitched battle against federal troops. A few years later a military detachment removed them to the Uintah reservation in Utah.[46]

Native American activities during Colorado's territorial years indicated that the federal government had its hands full. A few thousand

Plains Indians eluded and outmaneuvered some of the most respected generals of the Civil War. While they understood the difficulties and tactics in defeating an organized army, the generals seemed at a loss in coping with the guerrilla-like tactics of the Native Americans. Still, as the Union Pacific and Kansas Pacific railroads pushed westward, settlers followed and demanded more and more land and the removal of the Natives. Eventually the government wore down the Native Americans either on the battlefield or in council. While Native American tribes remained on the Plains for several more decades, they were swept from eastern Colorado by 1869 and from much of the Western Slope by 1880.

3 *In Pursuit of Statehood*

The Indian wars on the Plains did not deter some Coloradans from aspiring to statehood. Indeed, the wars coincided with the territory's longest effort to seek admission into the Union. When Republicans in Congress first suggested statehood, advocates moved quickly, ushering in the most turbulent political period in the territory's history. Opposition came from within as well as from outside the territory. Ethnic and political groups, urged on by an obstreperous governor, produced resistance inside Colorado and, as time went on, even national Republicans lost their enthusiasm for the idea.

Early in 1864 national Republican leaders, and even Abraham Lincoln himself, presumed that he could not be reelected. For one thing, many northerners were disillusioned with the administration because of the lack of military successes. Following victories at Gettysburg, Vicksburg, and Chattanooga in 1863, the Union army bogged down on the battlefield. For another, a group of Republicans, known as the "Radicals," was working against Lincoln's reelection because he did not openly advocate their goals of punishing the Confederacy and enfranchising black men. In the end they backed Lincoln but only after failing to secure a candidate of their own choosing.

Hoping to improve Lincoln's chances, his Republican followers persuaded Congress to pass enabling acts, permissive legislation authorizing Nevada, Nebraska, and Colorado—all Republican-oriented territories—to apply for statehood. Their admission would guarantee nine more electoral votes for Lincoln. The political intent of the acts was apparent in the provision instructing each territory to complete all requirements for admission before the November 1864 election. Moreover, Congress did not extend the same offer to New Mexico, whose population, though larger than that of the other three territories, was politically Democratic. Nor to Utah because of the legislators' distaste of polygamy.

Nevada was the only territory to achieve statehood in 1864. Nebraskans declined the offer, believing their territory too immature to assume the burdens of statehood. In Colorado a convention drafted a state constitution in June 1864, but voters overwhelmingly rejected it by a three thousand vote majority. Opposition to statehood was generally strong but voters became even more hostile when the convention delegates, dominated by Denver politicians, decided to hold an election for state officials on the same day that the constitution was submitted for public approval. While they justified the move as a means of saving time and additional election expenses, people in outlying areas felt the move was little more than a ploy by Denver politicians to control the new state.[1]

But the rejection was probably more influenced by political discord and ethnic antagonism, both of which created opposition to statehood. Even though the number of Democrats in the territory was small, hostility between the two parties was intense, and Democrats were determined to oppose a state that would be controlled by their political enemy. Tension was further intensified because Colorado Republicans were quick to wave the "Bloody Shirt," accusing Democrats of supporting the Confederacy and, therefore, of being traitors.[2]

Nor were Republicans united, and their factionalism caused many rifts and disagreements. The "Denver Crowd," led by John Evans, Jerome Chaffee, and Samuel Elbert, ardently championed statehood, while the "Golden" or "Mountain Crowd" under the control of William Loveland and Henry Teller opposed the idea. The "Mountain Crowd" was centered in Golden and the mountain communities to the west, but it also gained support from smaller communities elsewhere in the territory. Smaller towns expressed concerns about Denver's political dominance. "There is little of Denver egotism about Golden City," wrote Henry Teller. "We can hope for advantages from Golden City that Denver in her exclusiveness would never grant." Not only did the two groups disagree about statehood, but they were often divided over national issues as well.[3]

The Spanish-speaking communities of southern Colorado also opposed statehood. Anglo-Coloradans in the northern part of the territory and Mexican Americans had little direct contact with each other but, even so, their antagonism toward each other surfaced occasionally during the territorial period. While religion, language, and differences in social customs contributed to the wedge between the two groups, the Hispanos still resented their separation from New Mexico. They might have favored statehood had their region remained part of New Mexico, but they adamantly opposed being a part of Colorado as long as Anglos would control the government. Moreover, the great majority of Mexican Americans affiliated with the Democratic Party, a fact that divided them further from the Republican majority.[4]

Despite strong anti-statehood feeling, advocates for statehood determined to push the issue. In June 1865, a year after the first constitution failed, they agitated for a second constitutional convention, arguing that the enabling act was still valid despite the rejection of the 1864 document. Further, they insisted, Colorado needed a congressman and senators in Washington, D.C., to exert their influence and make sure the transcontinental railroad, now starting to push westward from Omaha, would run through the new state. The "executive committees of several political parties" finally declared for statehood, and called for a second constitutional convention to meet in Denver on August 8, 1865. Within a matter of days the delegates drew up a document and submitted it for popular approval. To improve chances of success, the convention called for the election of state officials only after the constitution was approved.

Voters sanctioned the new constitution on September 5 by a vote of 3,025 to 2,870, a margin of 155 votes. As expected, strongest opposition came from the Spanish-speaking counties: Costilla, Conejos, and Huerfano. The mountain counties—Gilpin and Clear Creek—approved the constitution but they also cast large numbers of votes against it. The firmest support came from Arapahoe County, in which Denver was then located.[5]

Along with voicing their opinion on the constitution, white male Coloradans were also asked to approve or reject black suffrage. The proposition was overwhelmingly defeated by a vote of 4,192 to 476. On the black suffrage issue all parties agreed; no county approved the reform. Just before the election the *Rocky Mountain News* announced, "The idea has not been a popular one in the West, but . . . a great revolution has been gradually taking place upon all questions in which the hitherto oppressed and despised black man is concerned."[6]

Black suffrage had been an issue since 1864, when the territorial legislature passed a law specifically disfranchising blacks. The action was undoubtedly prompted by the territory's increasing black population, which rose from 46 to 456 between 1860 and 1870. During the war large numbers of free blacks and slaves fled from Missouri and Arkansas to

Kansas and farther west. Insulted by the new law, blacks publicly complained about being deprived of the vote. They claimed the disfranchising law took away a privilege they had previously exercised, while legislators insisted they were merely clarifying the intent of the original suffrage provisions adopted when the territory was organized. The original law limited the vote to citizens of the United States, to foreigners who declared their intention to become citizens, and to Native Americans who lived off the reservation and were recognized as citizens by treaty with the U.S. government. Since blacks were not citizens,[7] backers of the new law maintained that they had never voted and the new law did not take anything from them.[8]

Blacks organized to regain the ballot. Their chief spokesman was William J. Hardin, a free black from Kentucky who had arrived in Colorado during the war. Giving a series of lectures in Denver and Central City, Hardin lauded the accomplishments of blacks and argued for the right to vote. The *Rocky Mountain News* responded, "Though his deductions and conclusions in the main may be . . . correct, the country is not fully prepared for such events." Along with Henry O. Wagoner and others, Hardin also appealed to the constitutional convention of 1865 to provide for black suffrage in the new document. But the idea was not acceptable to most white Coloradans. Aware that a black suffrage clause would defeat the constitution, the delegates instead chose to let the voters decide the issue. In doing so, they used a tactic frequently employed by the northern states during the years before the war. Although a public vote was an expedient way for the delegates to avoid a troublesome issue, they could have predicted the outcome. The denial, however, only strengthened the resolve of black Coloradans to secure the ballot, and they soon began casting around for support.[9]

The appointment of Alexander Cummings as territorial governor added an extra complication to the black suffrage issue and the quest for statehood. Prior to the Civil War, Cummings had been active in Republican politics in Pennsylvania. He strongly supported the political ambitions of Simon Cameron, Lincoln's first secretary of war, who, in turn, designated him to be a purchasing agent for the army, an appointment prompted more by their close political friendship rather than by Cummings's past experience. Within a short time Cummings revealed his ineptitude and was discharged. He wasted $200,000 of the government's money on the purchase of 1,670 straw hats and 800 carbines, which the government had previously sold because they were obsolete. Indeed, the government peddled the weapons for $3.50 each and Cummings repurchased them for $15 apiece. His activities during the remainder of the war were more commendable. He recruited the Nineteenth Regiment of Pennsylvania Cavalry Volunteers and served as the unit's colonel. Eventually he earned the brevet rank of brigadier general. In 1864 he was on Lincoln's list of possible nominees for the territorial governorship of Montana, but the president, undoubtedly remembering Cummings's War Department record, passed over his name. But Cameron continued to look after his friend, and at his urging Andrew Johnson nominated Cummings for the Colorado territorial governorship following the resignation of John Evans.[10]

The new governor arrived in Colorado in late October 1865, almost two months after voters had approved the constitution and several weeks after the "state" legislature and officials had been elected. Frank Hall, who came to loath the governor, wrote that Cummings's arrival "was not hailed with enthusiasm by any class of people except the leaders of the anti-state faction." But contemporary sources contradict Hall's conclusion and give the impression that the new governor was well received. Even before he reached the territory, the *Rocky Mountain News,* mouthpiece for the "Denver Crowd" and later Cummings's greatest critic, hailed his "intellectual qualifications" and predicted he would play a pivotal role in developing the territory. Upon Cummings's arrival, editor Byers commented, "The more people see of the Governor, the better they are pleased with him." Responding to Cummings's first annual address to the legislature, the *Daily Mining Journal* in Black Hawk wrote: "Should Colorado fail of admission into the Union as a State, we congratulate her on having an able Governor. We think it not too much to say that no state document ever . . . gave so comprehensive and clear view of our condition, necessities, and prospects."[11]

Cummings spent the first weeks of his administration traveling throughout the territory and acquainting himself with Colorado and its people. The trip certainly made him aware of anti-statehood feeling. At least the *New York Times* correspondent reported, "The State movement from what I can learn by conversation with many of the most respectable citizens, is not popular. They say that the honest vote [in the September 1865 election] was against the State, but was gotten rid of by means of the able-bodied use of funds." And it was rumored throughout the territory that John Evans and Jerome Chaffee secured their election to the U.S. Senate "by use of money."[12]

Although Cummings remained silent on the statehood question, he was forced to take a stand when the "state" legislature convened in December and proceeded to act as if the territorial government no longer existed. "Certain persons" contacted members of the territorial legislature and informed them that their scheduled meeting for January 1866 was unnecessary and they would not be paid if they did assemble. Cummings could hardly let such action go uncontested. He responded with a proclamation convening the territorial legislature and informing the people that Colorado was still a territory. Further, he continued, there was no guarantee Congress would consider the statehood issue during its current session because it faced more pressing problems involving the reconstruction of the South. Until Congress formalized admission, Cummings concluded, the territorial government was the only legitimate one in Colorado empowered to pass laws and make decisions regarding the future.[13]

Cummings's argument was legally irrefutable but it undoubtedly contributed to a personal quarrel between him and Samuel Elbert, territorial secretary. The struggle, trivial as it seems, brought the governor into direct conflict with the "Denver Crowd" and evolved into a battle of wills to determine who would be in control. Further, it was the first in a series of events that began to turn public opinion against Cummings. As noted earlier, Elbert had been appointed territorial secretary in 1862 and continued in office after Evans resigned. As secretary he also served as acting governor in the executive's absence, and it is not inconceivable that he hoped to replace Evans. Elbert was a staunch advocate of statehood and once Cummings made his position known it was difficult for the two men to maintain a friendly, working relationship.[14]

The quarrel began over the location of the governor's office. On taking up his duties, Cummings found his office in a remote section of Denver that had been inundated by the flood of 1864. In fact, many of the buildings around his office had been abandoned or torn down. Consequently, he rented a building nearer the center of town and invited Elbert to occupy part of it. Elbert refused and, according to Cummings, "rented another, at additional and needless cost to the government." Considering his territorial secretary subordinate to himself and doubting his loyalty, the governor then went to Elbert's office and removed the territory's great seal. Cummings justified his action, claiming, "I do not think him entitled to it. . . . I am sure he is not worthy to be trusted with its custody."[15] He refused to return the seal when Elbert demanded but instead wrote a long, accusatory letter claiming that Elbert was negligent because he allowed the seal to sit on a table open to the public. Further, Cummings added that the executive clerk in Elbert's office had informed him that Elbert had not used the seal for at least two years. Cummings then accused Elbert of shirking his duties, claiming the territorial secretary had spent less than one hour in his office during the past two months. Finally, Cummings charged Elbert with attempting to falsify the 1864 vote on the constitution, when statehood had been rejected, and more recently plotting to keep the territorial legislature from meeting.[16]

Elbert responded, insisting that the governor had misconstrued the facts. He also alluded to Cummings's failure as a War Department purchasing agent, which did little more than intensify the hostility between the two men. "What I had read of your history prior to your arrival in the Territory," he wrote, "as well as my short personal association with you since you came, had prepared me to expect . . . the misrepresentations . . . which your letter contains." Elbert declared that he did most of his work at the Evans's home where a room had been set aside for that purpose, and he denied being part of any plot. Finally, he questioned the governor's authority by claiming, "I am answerable to the State and Treasury Departments at Washington, for my conduct as Secretary, and not to you. Your mistake has been, that you supposed you could order, where you should have requested, suggested, and counseled—that you could misconstrue, and falsely color, and not be corrected—that you could criminate without truth or justice, and no recrimination would follow—that you could charge 'abuse', 'neglect,' 'fraud,' and 'subversion of Government' without your dictum being questioned or disputed."[17]

Almost immediately the squabble between the two men reached all the way to Washington. Cummings quickly explained the difficulties to his immediate superior, Secretary of State William Seward, and requested Elbert's removal. Fearing that his side of the argument would be unfairly represented, Elbert rushed to Washington, D.C., late in January 1866, without requesting approval from either the governor or the State Department. In leaving Elbert violated protocol, which required territorial officials to seek permission before vacating a post. His departure also left the territory without a secretary and may have weakened his case. At any rate, once in the national capital Elbert learned of the administration's decision to uphold the governor. Having no other option, he submitted his resignation, which was immediately accepted. While Cummings was successful in ridding himself of a pesky secretary, the "victory" deprived him of any support from the "Denver crowd." Indeed, its members determined to bring about the governor's removal. They resented the treatment of one of their leaders as well as the governor's opposition to statehood. They felt that Cummings, as an outsider, had no right to take a stand on the issue. A correspondent to the *Daily Mining Journal* expressed the thought of many: "Everybody stood ready to support the governor until he began to heap insult and contempt on the state party in the territory. . . . It is not only in the worst of taste, but absolutely wrong."[18]

Cummings's relationship with his second territorial secretary, Frank Hall, was even more discordant. A New Yorker who had come to Colorado in 1860 hoping to strike it rich mining, Hall soon turned to journalism. Editor of the *Daily Miner's Register* in Central City, Hall had opposed statehood in 1864 but changed his mind because "most of my social and political affiliations [were] with the promoters of state organization whom I had no intention of antagonizing." Unconcerned that hostility between the secretary and the governor would create friction in the higher echelon of territorial government, Hall accepted the secretaryship because "if I refused, Cummings would secure a candidate in full accord with his program, and be thus enabled to work further injury on the State movement." Within a short time the two men would be at loggerheads.[19]

Already reviled in Denver, Cummings soon made himself unpopular throughout the entire territory by advocating black rights and exposing Colorado's denial of equal suffrage to officials in Washington, D.C. Frustrated by the rejection of the black suffrage referendum, blacks turned to Cummings almost as soon as he arrived in Colorado. In early December 1865, Hardin and Wagoner presented the governor with a petition signed by 137 black men and requested that he forward it to Congress. The signatories reviewed their struggle to obtain the ballot, noted the denial of equal suffrage in the state constitution, and asked Congress to deny Colorado admission into the Union until the disqualification was removed. Cummings immediately forwarded the petition. The petitioners then presented the governor with a second petition asking for the repeal of the 1864 law denying their right to vote. Cummings sent this petition to the territorial legislature along with a special message. "It seems incredible," he declared, "that such a measure [the 1864 law denying suffrage] could have been adopted. . . . The colored people . . . contributed largely to the triumph of the nation over the rebellion; and . . . this wrong was perpetrated upon them." Next, Cummings suggested that the legislature desegregate the public school system. Pointing out the iniquity of taxing black parents to support schools that their children could not attend, he declared, "Justice to the living, and gratitude to those who died that the nation might live, forbid that the state of things against which these petitioners protest, should longer prevail."[20]

Public reaction was immediate and harsh. Publishing an editorial on Cummings's opposition to statehood, the *Mining Journal* screamed, "The people of Colorado don't sustain him in his malicious opposition to the admission of the State under the guise of regard for the negroes." Cummings's attitude, claimed the editor, was prompted by "mean spite" and "a more suicidal course was never voluntarily adopted by any public man." One individual wrote an unsigned letter to the same newspaper claiming, "Old broken down political hacks sent out to the Territories have not the right to oppose our admission. None but a few soreheads and negroes" were challenging admission, he continued, "and the motive of it all being the hope of personal revenge." The *Rocky Mountain News* conceded the injustice of taxing blacks to support public education but it opposed integrated schools. With respect to suffrage, editor Byers believed that white women should be enfranchised before black men.[21]

Cummings's critics firmly believed that he, and not the blacks, had initiated the petition movement and solely for the purpose of defeating admission. "It is strange that the negroes of Colorado have never before discovered how inhumanly they were treated here" until Cummings arrived in the territory, declared one writer. But such a conclusion, however, ignores important facts. For one, blacks agitated for equal suffrage even before Cummings arrived in Colorado. And while it is true that pointing out the exclusion of black Coloradans from the polls would raise the ire of Radical Republicans in Washington, D.C., who were strong advocates of black suffrage, the governor's opposition was not based on the suffrage issue alone. Rather, he had broader concerns, which he laid before the territorial legislature in January 1867. The territory contained only 27,931 people, he maintained. It needed to build a prison and roads because most were inadequate even by the most rudimentary standards And many towns lacked public schools or the financial means to support them. As a state Colorado would receive no federal money for these purposes. The loss of federal funds and the resultant increase in taxes once statehood was achieved would place extreme fiscal hardship on the small population. The pro-statehood faction, the governor concluded, was a small minority, and he was fully "convinced that at least two-thirds of the people are adverse to the formation of a state government."[22]

Critics also maintained that Cummings was hypocritical in raising the suffrage issue, that he had no concern for black rights and was merely using the question as a pretext to defeat statehood. His prewar record and wartime activities, however, might lead to a different conclusion. As early as 1856, Cummings publicly declared his opposition to slavery. Speaking before a crowd in Williamsport, Pennsylvania, he referred to slavery as a crime against humanity, insisting the purpose of the U.S.

Constitution was to guarantee freedom and "human slavery should be no part of its purpose." Cummings avoided discussing the issue of black rights. The major question confronting the nation was the expansion of slavery into the territories, he maintained, and "it is not to be determined by any interest we may take in the elevation of the African race." In February 1864, during the war, Cummings received the special assignment of recruiting fugitive slaves and free blacks in Arkansas for military service. Despite the large number of blacks who had fled or been taken to Texas by their masters, he was still able to organize one battery of light artillery and five regiments of infantry, with a total of 5,286 men in his command. Cummings's past indicates that Colorado blacks knew the governor was a friend to whom they could appeal. The outstanding peculiarity of the 1865–66 statehood movement centered on the black suffrage question. On the one hand, white Republicans in the territory opposed giving blacks the right to vote while, at the same time, seeking support from Radicals in Congress who advocated equal suffrage for the entire nation. On the other hand, the governor supported black suffrage, while Andrew Johnson, his superior, adamantly opposed it.[23]

Republicans in Congress discussed the suffrage issue in Colorado but it was not their most important consideration. When the Senate took up the Colorado statehood bill in March 1866, Charles Sumner of Massachusetts made a forceful argument against Colorado's admission because of the suffrage restriction. He found allies among Radicals, but the majority of senators felt that Colorado's population was too small and sentiment for statehood too weak. Consequently, they rejected the bill. Within a matter of days, however, President Johnson vetoed the Civil Rights Act and full war broke out between Congress and the president. Anxious to gain votes for an override, the Senate once again took up the Colorado bill. This time Sumner found himself alone. Apparently Radicals in the Senate were willing to admit Colorado with its restrictive suffrage provision if it meant defeating the president. The upper house approved the bill on April 25, 1866, and the House concurred on May 3.[24]

In Colorado the pro-statehood faction was jubilant. Allen Bradford, Colorado's delegate to Congress, informed the *Rocky Mountain News,* "there is not the slightest danger of the President vetoing the bill." But the president was not to be fooled. Republicans made little secret of the fact they were seeking two more votes to override Johnson's veto of the Civil Rights Act, and his advisers were certain that senators-elect Evans and Chaffee would vote with the Senate majority. According to historical tradition, Johnson offered to approve admission if Chaffee and Evans would promise to support him against the Radicals, but the two men refused to commit themselves. Thus, Johnson vetoed the Colorado bill, giving as his reasons the small population and the lack of support for statehood in the territory. He did not mention the denial of equal suffrage. Reacting to the president's veto, the *News* placed the entire blame on Cummings, who it now referred to as "this piece of double concentrated scum." To make certain that Coloradans were aware of the governor's past and to present him as a dishonest and unscrupulous politician, editor Byers exposed Cummings's failings as a purchasing agent for the War Department.[25]

Still seeking to bolster support in their fight with the president, Republicans in the Senate introduced another Colorado statehood bill in 1867. The motive was so apparent that James Doolittle of Wisconsin chided his colleagues, saying, "It is a new argument in the Senate of the United States to press upon the Senators what their judgement does not approve—to strengthen a party." Again Senate Radicals raised objections because of the suffrage provision, but they dropped their opposition when the House attached a "fundamental condition" to the bill: Colorado could be admitted provided the legislature struck the restricted suffrage clause from the constitution. But Johnson vetoed the bill a second time, using much of his previous argument. Attempts to override the veto failed. Even his Republican opponents realized the validity of the president's arguments about Colorado despite their disagreements on other issues. The territory was still too immature to assume the burdens of statehood.[26]

Even though the suffrage question had little impact on Colorado's fate, it had broader implications for the territories as a whole. Influenced by the restricted suffrage issue in Colorado, James Ashley, Radical Republican in the House of Representatives, presented a bill stipulating that no territory could deny the elective franchise because of race or color. The bill quickly passed both houses of Congress, and Johnson allowed it to become law without his signature.[27]

The Territorial Suffrage Act had its first test in Colorado's municipal elections on April 1, 1867. Surprisingly there was little opposition. Soon after the bill became law, Republican newspapers began a campaign to gain public acceptance. "Let those who are opposed to the measure," declared the *Miner's Register,* "remember that they gain nothing by opposition but will act far more wisely to accept the position and not combat the inevitable." Even the Democratic *Colorado Transcript* conceded that the law must be obeyed: "We never can believe that any thing of the sort [equal suffrage] can take place here at present—but if our Congress does so enact we will bow our head to the laws and obey."

Rumors circulated that groups in Central City and Denver intended to keep blacks from the polls. Whether any overt opposition was actually planned, none took place and the elections occurred without incident. The day after casting their ballots, blacks in Denver held a mass meeting thanking white Coloradans for their acquiescence and declaring themselves in favor of statehood.[28]

Although white Coloradans accepted black suffrage, they became determined to rid themselves of their governor. Antagonism against him reached its high point during the election of delegate to Congress in 1866, when his dictatorial action gave the impression that he would take any steps to defeat his enemies.

George Chilcott and Alexander Hunt were the opposing candidates. Both men were Republicans but they disagreed on most issues. Chilcott championed statehood and received strong support from the "Denver Crowd"; Hunt opposed statehood and had Cummings's backing. The election returns gave Chilcott a majority, but Hunt contested the outcome because of fraudulent voting in the southern counties, where his greatest strength lay. It now became the duty of the Board of Canvassers to determine the winner. It consisted of the territorial auditor, the territorial treasurer, and the territorial secretary, who also served as chairman. The governor was not a member and his role was restricted to signing a certificate of election based on the board's decision. According to Secretary Hall, Cummings asked him to miscount the vote but Hall refused. During the meeting of the board, Hall and the territorial auditor voted to give the election to Chilcott but the treasurer disagreed. Thereupon, Cummings grabbed all the important papers and declared himself a member of the board. He then voted with the treasurer, creating a tie. Using his tie-breaking authority as governor, Cummings next declared Hunt elected and signed the certificate of election. A short time later, after Cummings had left town, Hall signed a second certificate as acting governor in favor of Chilcott. Thus, the House of Representatives received two certificates and would have to decide which candidate had won the election. After hearing the evidence, the House seated Chilcott in March 1867.[29]

Most Coloradans, with justification, considered Cummings's actions illegal. In declaring himself a member of the board he had exceeded his authority and openly displayed his lack of impartiality. Discussion at the meeting became so acrimonious that the auditor threatened to whip the governor, who retaliated by dismissing him several days later. This action caused Cummings to lose more public support. Further, what had occurred at the meeting became common gossip, which spread throughout Denver. James Rusling, who was visiting the city at the time, recorded public reaction: "There was a breezy time in Denver for a while. The papers savagely denounced the governor's conduct, as an outrage and usurpation, and fell into a vein of course vituperation they seemed incapable of before. The saloons were filled with excited crowds at night; knots gathered on the streets by day; and presently, one morning, out came the papers with the old-time suggestion of 'a cottonwood limb and a rope,' if HIS EXCELLENCY did not yield." The governor "has gone beyond his power," announced the *Mining Journal.* "We are in favor of forcing Governor Cummings to leave this Territory and if he must govern it, . . . let him do it from a foreign point or let the president be compeled [*sic*] to sustain him with a military force."[30]

With tensions rising, Cummings began to fear for his life. He fled to Golden with the territorial records and set up the government in a rented school house. Revealing his animosity toward Denver in his next annual address to the legislature, he recommended that Golden be made the terminus for two railroads, one running northward to meet the tracks of the Union Pacific in Cheyenne, the other eastward to connect with the Kansas Pacific. Denverites instantly regarded the suggestion as an attempt to destroy their city economically. The lack of any railroad connection with the East had already caused much concern and many businessmen were moving to Cheyenne, which they believed would be the new metropolis of the West.[31]

Reaction from Denver came quickly. A petition to President Johnson, signed by 250 citizens, stressed the low regard they held for the governor. It requested Cummings's removal because he had lied about conditions in the territory and sought to retard its development "so he might continue to hold the position which he now disgraces." Cummings, declared the signatories, was so arrogant, impudent, and overbearing that Coloradans, regardless of their political affiliation, found his presence abhorrent. His record in the War Department had been so shameful that having such a man as their governor was greater punishment than they deserved. "We solemnly declare to you," concluded the petitioners, "as an insulted and outraged people, that his occupying his present official position over us is as intolerable as would be the presence of a serpent at our hearthstones, and as American citizens we earnestly pray, entreat, and implore you to relieve us from this infamous, insolent and unbearable nuisance."[32]

To strengthen the argument for Cummings's removal, Allen Bradford, Colorado's delegate to Congress, charged him with fraud and malfeasance on three counts. First, the governor had paid John Wanless

$2,342 to transport goods from Denver to Utes in Middle Park by way of South Boulder Pass, a distance of 180 miles. It would have been less costly, claimed Bradford, to use a much shorter route over Berthoud Pass. Second, Cummings had paid his daughter $1,800 to do clerical work for the year 1866 but she left the territory in April and did not return. Finally, he had appointed a new territorial treasurer and authorized him to receive government funds before the appointee had posted the surety bond required by law.[33] Upon being made aware of the charges, Cummings left for Washington, D.C., to answer them. Cummings defended himself before the House Committee on Indian Affairs and to Secretary of State Seward. With respect to moving provisions to Middle Park, Cummings maintained, everyone, Bradford included, had agreed it was preferable to take the goods to the Native Americans rather than have them come to Denver. The price paid Wanless had been approved by the co-commissioner of Indian affairs and the Ute Indian agent before the trip was undertaken. Cummings agreed that the price was higher than usual, but the long route and the rough road into Middle Park justified the extra costs. Contrary to his critics' assertions, a wagon route over Berthoud Pass did not exist; thus, Wanless had to haul the goods through the South Boulder Pass. Even then the road was so rough that it took him three days to go one mile. Finally, the Native Americans, who had been waiting for their provisions, helped the wagons over the pass.[34]

Cummings did not deny paying his daughter $1,800 but pointed out that his son had taken her place for the remainder of the year and received no compensation for his work. The governor did not notify anyone of the change because no extra costs were involved. Lastly, he vehemently denied authorizing any public official to receive government monies before posting the required bond. "I am conscious of having executed the trust confided to one with the utmost fidelity," he wrote, "and with more care of the public funds, than if they had been my own, and I am satisfied that the closest scrutiny of my accounts will show the care with which the public money has been expended."[35]

The charges were also investigated by Pershine Smith, examiner of claims, who concluded that Cummings was not guilty of fraud or malfeasance. Three territorial officials had approved the hauling charges and "if we extend to them that favorable presumption of good faith," the government would have to concede the validity of the charges. With respect to Cummings paying his daughter for work done by his son, Smith wrote, "such family arrangements rather invite suspicion and criticism," but they were not prohibited by law. On the charge of allowing the territorial treasurer to receive funds before posting bond, Smith concluded that there was no evidence that the governor had tried to control the funds and therefore, Bradford's charge "appears to be without any foundation in fact. I think the Governor has fully exonerated himself."[36]

The petition to the president, Bradford's charges, and Chilcott's victory all contributed to Cummings's downfall. It would have been impossible for him to return to Colorado and assume executive control. He was under such a cloud of disapproval and suspicion that he had little choice but to face the inevitable. He resigned as governor on April 21, 1867, and Johnson indicated his support for the governor by immediately appointing him collector of internal revenue for the Fourth District of Pennsylvania.[37]

Alexander Cummings became the most vilified of Colorado's territorial governors. He has been labeled as "unfit for the office," "stiff-necked," "pig-headed and dictatorial," a "hack politician," and a "spoilesman." His earliest and most critical detractor was Frank Hall, who when writing his history of the state could not let bygones be bygones. It is ironic that Hall's newspaper made the most thoughtful comment upon Cummings's retirement: "With a milder temper, a more careful discrimination between the wants of his constituency and political tricksters, . . . his administration would have been not only pleasurable but politically profitable. Governor Cummings is a man of distinguished ability, and a politician . . . whose practice has embraced some of the most severely contested campaigns of the present century. With a power like this at his command, he might . . . have aspired to the highest places within the gift of his people. But he chose to regard them as barbarians, fit to be governed only by the strong hand of autocratic despotism. It was impossible that they should yield gracefully to the yoke."[38]

It is true the governor lacked political finesse and allowed himself to become involved in petty quarrels, but he was ahead of his constituents on the question of equal rights for minorities. White Coloradans regarded his every action to advance political equality as an attempt to discredit the territory before the nation. Not only did Cummings reveal sympathy for blacks, but he may also have had a similar sympathy for Native Americans. As governor, Cummings also served as superintendent of Indian affairs for Colorado. Charles A. Mix, U.S. commissioner of Indian affairs, noted that no superintendency had fewer complaints than Colorado during Cummings's administration.

Alexander Hunt replaced Cummings in the governor's office and served from May 1867 until June 1869. He proved to be a more astute politician than his predecessor, and even Samuel Elbert later admitted that he was a "good governor." Unlike Cummings, Hunt was not regarded as an outsider. He had lived in the territory since 1858, had served on the Vigilante Committee, which sanctioned a number of hangings to rid the territory of its early criminal element, and was rewarded with the post of U.S. marshal for the territory. Perhaps Hunt learned from Cummings's mistakes, for he never let himself become involved in political quarrels. He avoided the statehood issue by turning the reins of opposition over to Henry Teller. When in February, 1868, Senate Republicans, looking for additional votes to convict Andrew Johnson on the eve of his impeachment trial, introduced a third bill to admit Colorado, it was Teller who led the open opposition. Even though the pro-statehood faction presented petitions from both white and black citizens in favor of statehood, Hunt worked privately with Roscoe Conkling, senator from New York, to make senators aware that most Coloradans had grown weary of the whole issue. Those Republican senators who supported Colorado statehood finally realized the futility of their effort and dropped the bill. The statehood question would not be raised again until the eve of the election for 1876.[39]

Hunt also spent little time in Denver, thus avoiding politicians with whom he did not agree. In one sense there was little reason to be in the city because the legislature met biannually, and during Hunt's two-year governorship it met for only forty days. Hunt absented himself during the entire session. The only major piece of legislation passed by the lawmakers moved the territorial capital from Golden to Denver and Hunt played no role in the change. He was willing to let Frank Hall handle many of the details of governing because of his own concern for achieving peaceful relations with the Utes. He feared that if the Utes became antagonistic toward the whites, they might ally with the Plains Indians, thus leaving the settled portion of Colorado caught between two hostile forces. During 1868 he spent almost seven months away from Denver. From January to April he escorted the Utes on a trip to Washington, D.C., where they signed the Ute Treaty. From August to October he traveled in western Colorado to obtain the Native Americans' consent to changes the Senate had made in the document.

Hunt also spent considerable time in 1868 meeting noted dignitaries and escorting them around the territory. After the Union Pacific Railroad reached Cheyenne in November 1867, Colorado became a focal point for tourists. Noted visitors during Hunt's administration included William Sherman, Ulysses S. Grant, Vice President Schuyler Colfax, former Secretary of State William Seward, and their parties. Their visits included side trips to the mountain communities and extended from several days to a week or more.[40]

The struggle for statehood at the end of the Civil War was the first of two turbulent political periods in Colorado's territorial history. It was brought about by the clashing of two strong-minded forces, neither of which indicated a willingness to compromise. Their only agreement centered in their opposition to officials appointed from Washington, D.C. Coloradans fervently believed that no outsider could understand them. They insisted that democracy and the concept of popular sovereignty entitled them to the right to choose their own leaders or, if not that, at least have men in authority who came from their own ranks. Cummings's attitude and actions only strengthened this belief. The Hunt administration served to relieve the resentment against outside rule, but resentment would surface again even stronger than before. Before then, however, territorial development would give Coloradans a much stronger argument for the right to be admitted to the sisterhood of states.

4 A Rebounding Economy

Colorado's economy began to recover during the late 1860s. New methods of extracting gold from refractory ores brought changes in the mining process and the discovery of silver deposits revived fading mining towns. By 1870 the range cattle industry was becoming a major element in the territory's economy, with cattle barons dominating the trade. Immigration and the development of towns on the once barren Plains brought substantial increases in agricultural production after farmers from the East learned to adjust to the arid, high-plains climate and lack of abundant rainfall. But it was the coming of the railroads that stimulated Colorado's economic growth. They provided a rapid means for Coloradans to ship their goods beyond the limits of the territory; they reduced the journey from the East from weeks to days and stimulated immigration; and they all converged on Denver, ensuring the continuance of the city's cultural and economic predominance of the Rocky Mountain region.

Coloradans had long been aware that railroads would lessen their isolation from the rest of the country. Unlike the states and territories along the Pacific coast, which could rely on the sea for communication and trade, Colorado was landlocked and weeks from its nearest markets. As early as 1859 citizens memorialized Congress, urging federal support for a railroad from the Missouri River to the base of the Rockies.[1] But animosity over the question of slavery in the territories and the unwillingness of either the North or South to support projects that might benefit the other prevented consideration of Colorado's request. During the war, with the majority of southern representatives now gone, Congress, in 1862, passed the Transcontinental Railroad Act, authorizing the Central Pacific Railroad to construct a line eastward from Sacramento, California, and the Union Pacific Railroad to lay tracks westward from Omaha, Nebraska. To assist in financing the undertaking the government offered land grants and loans for each mile of track laid.

Coloradans eagerly followed the progress of the bill through Congress and hailed its final passage. Boosters and newspapers encouraged the Union Pacific to come through the territory. The *Rocky Mountain News* described the mountains west of Denver as mere hills, minor obstacles for the railroad to surmount. Within a short time the excitement was dampened by delays in construction from the eastern terminus. The Central Pacific began laying track in 1863, but the Union Pacific was unable to begin building until 1865. The North's preoccupation with the war, the shortage of labor, high costs of materials, and the inability of the Union Pacific to market its securities all contributed to the delay. Coloradans encountered further disappointment when Grenville Dodge, chief engineer for the Union Pacific, recommended running the railroad through Wyoming. As a result, Julesburg would be the only Colorado city on the Union Pacific line, as it dropped out of Nebraska and then proceeded toward Cheyenne. Some Coloradans contended that Dodge's decision was prompted by his dislike of Denver. He had previously said that "in a few years [the city] would be a deserted village, the grass growing in its streets, and only abandoned buildings left to indicate its fate."[2]

But Dodge's decision was influenced by Union Pacific officials, not his personal antipathies. They were demanding that the line be pushed west as rapidly as possible so the company could receive larger government subsidies and land grants. They had little interest in Colorado and were more concerned about connecting with the Central Pacific in order to secure an outlet to international trade. Even though Denver was the most promising source of business between Omaha and the Pacific coast, the mountains to the west could bring construction to a standstill. During 1866 a surveying party examined ten Colorado mountain passes and decided against each one in turn. The chief surveyor informed Dodge, "I learned enough to satisfy myself that no railroad would—at least in our day—cross the mountains south of the Cache la Poudre." Even as late as 1879, engineers for the Colorado Central Railroad found it impossible to extend their line over Berthoud Pass.[3]

Dodge's decision had an immediate impact in Denver. Believing that Cheyenne would become the new "Queen City of the Plains," tradesmen started closing their businesses and moving north. To keep the city from being completely bypassed, boosters suggested a branch line from Cheyenne to Denver. Unfortunately, the Union Pacific did not receive federal subsidies for spur lines and it lacked the financial ability to undertake such a venture on its own. City leaders, however, were not dissuaded. Denver's citizens had subsidized a telegraph line from Julesburg in 1861, and now they expressed their willingness to finance a railroad. They quickly discovered a competitor in the city of Golden.[4]

W. A. H. Loveland, one of the leaders of the "Golden Crowd," had obtained a charter from the territorial legislature in 1865 for the Colorado Central and Pacific Railroad, and in 1867 Union Pacific officials encouraged him to construct a spur to connect with the main line in Wyoming. If the Colorado Central would grade the roadbed, the Union Pacific agreed to lay the track, supply all rolling stock, and operate the new line when it was completed. The terminus was to be Golden and from there the road was to run north through Boulder and on to Cheyenne. The estimated cost of construction was $600,000. Excited about the project, counties along the proposed route agreed to float bond issues to finance construction. Each county's contribution was determined by the size of its population, and Arapahoe County, in which Denver was then located, was apportioned $200,000, or one-third of the entire cost. But when Denver railroad promoters and Arapohoe County officials learned that their city was to be served only by a branch line connecting it to Golden, they immediately withdrew their support. They had no desire to assume a financial burden that would make Golden the economic center of the territory. With their withdrawal, the project fell apart and the Union Pacific abrogated its agreement with the Colorado Central.[5]

The Union Pacific's favoritism toward the Colorado Central caused Denver promoters to turn to the Union Pacific Eastern Division, soon renamed the Kansas Pacific. Originally it had planned to run the line into the Arkansas Valley and then into New Mexico and on to the Pacific coast. But the railroad had run out of money by the time it reached the Kansas border, and Congress's failure to provide further subsidies and land grants brought an end to construction. Kansas Pacific officials then decided that extending the line to Denver might ease their financial problems. Not only would it give better access to the mining regions west of Denver, but if the Union Pacific failed to gain a spur into Colorado, the Kansas Pacific, with its eastern terminus in St. Louis, would be the only major line between Denver and the Mississippi River. However, when railroad officials demanded a $2 million advance to extend the line, Denver promoters requested time to consider the matter.[6]

Aware of what was happening and fearful of being squeezed out of the Colorado trade altogether, Union Pacific officials now sent an agent to Denver to propose the creation of a separate company to build a line from Denver to Cheyenne. Five days after the Union Pacific reached the Wyoming city, in November 1867, Denver businessmen organized the Denver Pacific Railroad and Telegraph Company. Bela Hughes headed the company and served as its president. John Evans persuaded Congress to grant the company a forty-mile strip of land in alternate squares along the road's 106-mile length, which enabled it to secure loans and raise capital. Within days investors quickly subscribed $2 million to the project, and in a subsequent special election Denver and Arapahoe County voters approved a special $500,000 bond issue to aid the enterprise.[7]

In April 1868, Evans signed a preliminary agreement with the Union Pacific. The Denver Pacific agreed to grade the roadbed and lay the ties while the Union Pacific would install the tracks, provide the rolling stock, and operate the trains after the line was completed. The Denver Pacific was also obliged to turn over to the Union Pacific any future land grants it might receive from Congress, and in return it would receive 8 percent annual interest on the stock of the local company. Denver would have its railroad but the terms came high and worked to the future advantage of the Union Pacific. Despite the unfavorable terms, the Denver company began grading operations in May 1868.[8]

Following the pattern established by the Union Pacific as it built across Nebraska, Evans laid out towns approximately forty miles apart to serve as supply bases for construction and personal needs of the workers. All of them were named for influential members of the Denver Pacific or Union Pacific and included Hughes (now Brighton), Evans, Pierce, and Carr.[9]

Disturbed by the arrangement between the Union Pacific and Denver Pacific, officials of the Kansas Pacific applied for congressional authorization to extend their line to Denver. Next they approached Evans and worked out a cooperative agreement. The Denver Pacific gave the Kansas Pacific a perpetual right of way over its tracks in return for the transfer of 900,000 acres of a land grant that Congress had recently awarded the Kansas line. The arrangement angered Union Pacific officials and they refused to fulfill their previous commitment. Their decision left the Denver Pacific with a graded roadbed but no rails or rolling stock to complete the line.[10]

At this point the Kansas Pacific stepped in and provided track, cars, and locomotives to finish the Denver-Cheyenne spur. Two years after construction began, the first train from Cheyenne rolled into Denver on

June 20, 1870, and four days later the city commemorated the event with a silver spike ceremony. Within two months the Kansas Pacific completed its extension to Denver. In order to finish the line in record time, William Palmer, its chief engineer, hired Mexican Americans to bring ties down from the mountains and to help construct the line itself. When grading was completed, two track-laying crews, one from Denver the other from Kit Carson, raced toward each other laying, on average, one mile of track every hour. One crew beat that record by laying a mile in fifty-five minutes![11]

By the autumn of 1870 Colorado Territory was connected by rail to California, St. Louis, and Omaha. In March 1872, the Union Pacific opened a bridge across the Missouri River, giving Coloradans direct access to Chicago and cities farther east.[12] The effect was striking. In two years, between 1870 and 1872, the territory's population jumped from 39,864 to an estimated 80,000 people. In the decade between 1860 and 1870, Denver's population had increased by only ten people, from 4,749 to 4,759. By July 1872, 10,822 new residents lived in the city. Denver grew so fast that municipal authorities found it difficult to extend services to recent arrivals. One booster claimed that by 1872 the city had "a dash and animation . . . along with a finish and elegance that suggests prosperity, wealth, and Eastern stability, as well as the progressive and aggressive frontier." Reduced prices in the cost of travel between the Missouri River and Colorado encouraged this population growth. Whereas William Crawford paid $100 for a stagecoach ticket from Omaha to Denver in 1864, a rail coach ticket between the two cities in 1871 cost $65; from Kansas City the price was $44.[13]

The increase in population caused an upsurge in land values. The total valuation of property in Denver increased from $4 million to $15 million between 1870 and 1874. In Boulder it doubled, from $1,122,000 to $2,547,000. Lots on Larimer Street that had sold for $100 or less at the end of the Civil War were worth "tens of thousands" by 1873. Some Denver property owners who could hardly pay their taxes in 1865 were by 1873 "some of the biggest millionaires in the city."[14]

More noticeable to the average Denverite was the decline in the prices of consumer goods. They began to drop as the Union Pacific approached Colorado, but the most significant dip came after trains began arriving in Denver on a regular basis. The price of flour fell from its high of $25 a sack in 1865 to $2.50 in 1875; similarly hay from $70 to $25 a ton and candles from $15 to $6.25 a box. Prices also declined throughout the territory; still, they were higher in towns not on the railroad line because goods arriving in Denver had to be transported to them by wagon or cart.[15]

The coming of the railroads brought an end to the large wagon freighting operations. The yearly amount of freight brought to Denver by wagon in 1865 totaled 100 million pounds; by 1873 railroads were bringing over 2 billion pounds of freight to the city annually. And while most of the goods imported at the end of the war consisted of life's necessities, luxuries were now demanded and quickly purchased. A French bakery in Denver advertised that in addition to its usual breads and pastries, it also offered imported wines and liqueurs for the discriminating customer. Supplying such goods proved profitable for the railroads; the Union Pacific's gross earnings for the Omaha-Denver route in 1873 totaled $2,205,000.[16]

The most important line between Denver and the East, according to Frank Hall, was the Kansas Pacific because it "opened sources of supply from the rich corn, hay and grain fields of Kansas which filled our wants until our own farmers were prepared by increase of numbers . . . to meet the deficiency of agricultural products." Least important was the line westward from Cheyenne. As Hall recalled, "We had little or no trade with the West, nor marked identity of interest with that region."[17]

The first phase of railroad construction focused on the successful completion of interstate rail lines into Colorado; the second would extend lines within the territory and witnessed battles for domination. These chiefly involved the Union Pacific against its chief rivals.

Still irritated by the close working relationship between the Denver Pacific and the Kansas Pacific, Union Pacific officials sought to reduce the importance of the Denver Pacific by cutting off its trade. They again turned to the Colorado Central and worked out several schemes to isolate Denver. First, they encouraged the Colorado Central to build a connecting line from Golden to the Denver Pacific tracks north of Denver. A previously agreed upon rental arrangement allowed the Colorado Central, once it reached the Denver Pacific, to run its trains on Denver Pacific tracks to Cheyenne. Next, they devised a plan to construct a railroad between Golden and Julesburg along the South Platte River. Colorado-bound passengers and goods could alight at Julesburg and arrive in Golden, circumventing Denver completely. But the scheme failed. The Colorado Central laid tracks as far as Longmont and then halted construction during the Panic of 1873. When it resumed in 1877, the railroad turned north toward Fort Collins and on to Cheyenne.

To cut off Denver from the south, the Colorado Central negotiated a contract with the newly completed Denver & Rio Grande Railroad for a connection at Littleton but, again, lack of money terminated construction. Slowly the Colorado Central fell under the domination of the

Union Pacific, and in 1879 the larger company took control of all Colorado Central properties.[18]

Nor was the Union Pacific satisfied with attempts to squeeze out the Denver Pacific. It also began to attack the Kansas Pacific directly. The original agreement between the Union Pacific and Denver Pacific stipulated that the Union Pacific would carry Denver Pacific goods at a reduced rate beyond Cheyenne. But Union Pacific officials refused to pro-rate Kansas Pacific goods, arguing that only commodities shipped by the Denver Pacific were entitled to the reduction. Attempting to overcome the problem, Hughes resigned as president of the Denver Pacific in 1872 and turned the operation over to the Kansas Pacific, which ran both lines as a single system. But the Union Pacific was still not satisfied. Rate wars between the two forced the Kansas Pacific into receivership by 1874 and five years later the Union Pacific obtained control and incorporated the entire line into its own system. Thus, by the third year of Colorado's statehood the Kansas Pacific, the Denver Pacific, and the Colorado Central were all part of the Union Pacific system.[19]

The second phase of railroad building focused on capturing the mountain trade. In 1872 the Colorado Central laid a narrow-gauge line to Black Hawk and in 1877 continued the track to Georgetown. Even though the railroad gave mountain towns quicker access to goods and services, the system was cumbersome. Because the Colorado Central used the standard gauge (four feet, eight and one-half inches) east of Golden and the narrow gauge (three feet) to the west, all goods had to be transferred to different boxcars in Golden, thus consuming time and increasing the price of transport.[20]

The Denver & Rio Grande Railroad, projected to take the trade from the Santa Fé Trail and send it north to Denver, was the most unusual line built during the territorial period. The brainchild of William J. Palmer, surveyor and chief engineer for the Kansas Pacific, the Denver & Rio Grande was designed to be a north-south link between Denver and El Paso, Texas, and then, hopefully, on to Mexico City. Palmer adopted the narrow gauge so trains could more easily maneuver sharper curves and steeper increases in elevation. In addition, his was one of the few western railroads built in the post–Civil War years that did not receive land grants or loan subsidies from the federal government. Most of the funding was obtained by floating bonds in England and Holland. Palmer also established town sites along the route and developed mineral resources.[21]

Work on the road began in Denver in March 1871, and approximately sixty miles of track was completed by October. Here through a subsidiary, the Colorado Springs Company, Palmer laid out the town of Colorado Springs at the base of Pike's Peak, anticipating that the city would become a stylish summer resort. "My theory of [Colorado Springs]," he wrote, "is that it should be made the most attractive place in the West for homes—a place for schools, colleges, literature, science, first-class newspapers and everything the above imply." From there he pushed on to Pueblo and established the new town of South Pueblo. At that point the line divided, one branch going west to Florence and Cañon City, and another continuing south to Trinidad.[22]

The Denver & Rio Grande turned out to be less profitable than Palmer had anticipated. Its gross earnings in 1873 amounted to only $200,000 for carrying freight and $190,000 for passengers. The prolonged depression following the Panic of 1873 made it difficult for Palmer to secure loans outside of the territory, and major construction stopped during the remainder of the territorial period. Trinidad became the southern terminus for the line, and this prevented Palmer from capturing the New Mexican trade.[23]

Nor did local traffic produce must revenue. The railroad suffered from its policy of developing town sites near villages that already existed. Colorado Springs, South Pueblo, Labran, and El Moro were all within sight or close to established towns: Colorado City, Pueblo, Florence, and Trinidad. This offended local residents and when the Atchison, Topeka and Santa Fé Railroad reached the Arkansas Valley, they cooperated in diverting trade from the Denver & Rio Grande. Merchants in Denver failed to secure orders for goods from towns to the south because, remarked a correspondent to the *Colorado Tribune,* "the people will not purchase from [them] as long as the Denver and Rio Grande is the only road to carry the goods on. They will not patronize a railroad that was doing everthing [*sic*] to injure them by building up a rival town." Citizens in Trinidad, Pueblo, and Bent County even floated bond issues to assist the construction of the Santa Fé through their area even though it was more costly than constructing spurs to connect with the Denver & Rio Grande. Failing to capture the trade of southern Colorado, Palmer turned his "baby road" westward after silver was discovered in Leadville and became the first railroad to cross Colorado and reach Utah.[24]

The Denver, South Park and Pacific was the last railroad incorporated during the territorial years. Because the route ran through a thinly populated area, it failed to generate much revenue. Construction was halted during the depression following the Panic of 1873 but eventually it was extended to Gunnison in the 1880s.[25]

By 1877 Coloradans could travel along the Front Range of the Rockies on a series of intrastate railroads. The Colorado Central united cities from Fort Collins to Golden with the mountain towns, and the Denver & Rio Grande connected the southern and northern portions of the new state. The Atchison, Topeka and Santa Fé entered Colorado in 1873 but did not reach Pueblo and La Junta until 1876 because of delays in construction.

The long-range consequence of the railroad's coming to Colorado was its impact on the territory's economy. Within a decade the economy became more highly diversified and farming, ranching, and industrialization took their places alongside mining to round out the territory's economic future. In the 1860s farming had been limited to subsistence agriculture or crops that sold locally because of high shipping costs. But by the eve of statehood, Colorado grains were being recognized throughout the nation for their quality. While ranching developed during the territory's first decade, it was the railroad that made it feasible to move cattle from Colorado ranches to eastern markets. A decade after the railroad arrived in Denver, industrialization came to the city. Most of the early industries were associated with mining and transportation, but they laid the basis for further industrial development in the years of statehood. Railroads even made mining remunerative. Added to primitive mining methods, high shipping rates by wagon train kept mining from paying off during the 1860s. But in the next decade the development of the smelting process plus lower freighting rates made mining profitable. As Robert Athern so aptly put it: "Colorado, except for a few gold mines, was practically valueless until reached by rail."[26]

The mining industry began to revive shortly before the arrival of the railroads. The years 1865 to 1868 represented the lowest point in Colorado's mining history. By 1868 placer mining had dwindled to small-scale operations. Only $320,000 of placer gold and $1,690,000 of lode gold was produced in that year, while California produced $17,500,000 in gold. Even as late as 1871, after mining techniques had begun to improve, a visitor still noticed lingering evidence of the mining collapse: "Crumbling walls and tottering chimneys of 'played out' reduction works; ponderous, broken, and rusted machinery and curious shaped furnaces, whose fires had been extinguished for years, meet the eye everywhere and chill the hearts of capitalists anxious to invest in the rich mines of these mountains. The fact that mining has survived these terrible trials and disasters is proof of its inherent vitality in Colorado, and a pledge of its future prosperity."[27]

These unproductive years were marked by the so-called process mania, in which pseudo scientists and charlatans devised various ideas and devises to extract more gold from the refractory ores. Most of them failed to work and cost more than the value of the gold they extracted. In one process, the miner "had a concern something like a big ice cream freezer. The ore, after being pulverized, was forced by hydraulic pressure up through a syphon at the bottom of the machine and passed out the top. It worked first rate but did not save any gold and required a tank of quicksilver (worth $200) every fifteen minutes." Extravagance and pet processes, one Coloradan concluded, used up greenbacks and netted most miners very little profit.[28]

New developments, all coming in the late 1860s, helped to revive the industry. Several mining entrepreneurs hit upon the scheme of sending ores to the Paris Exposition of 1867 in order to attract European money. The French government awarded the ores a gold medal, and Napoleon III sent Louis L. Simonin to examine mines in the territory. The recognition and Simonin's positive report made eastern investors reevaluate their attitude toward Colorado mines. They also stimulated the immigration of European miners to the mining districts. In Gilpin County, where most mining occurred, highly professional Cornish or Irish miners took the place of American amateurs. With their long experience in underground work, Cornishmen especially contributed much to the improvement of mining techniques. In 1870 the county contained 1,493 immigrants of British extraction, the largest number of foreign-born in the territory. By contrast Arapahoe County had 792 immigrants from the British Isles.[29]

The second stimulus came with the consolidation of mining properties into more efficient units. Miners also reconstructed stamp mills that gave the refractory ores a finer crushing and exposed the crushed rock to interaction with the mercury for a longer time. This reduced the daily tonnage that the stamp mill could crush but resulted in the recovery of more precious metal. But most significant in reviving the industry was the development of the smelting process to separate gold from refractory ores.[30]

James E. Lyon had employed the smelting process on a small scale in Central City, but it was Nathaniel P. Hill who refined the process and made it profitable. A professor of chemistry at Brown University, Hill was lured to Colorado in 1864 by William Gilpin. The former governor, who had extensive land holdings in the San Luis Valley, employed Hill to find gold deposits there. Gilpin contacted Hill because, besides teaching, the professor also conducted scientific investigations and was well regarded in the East as a man of integrity, thoroughness, and sound judgment. After visiting the valley, Hill decided that the real potential for mining lay in the Central City and Black Hawk area. Torn between retaining his position at Brown and giving his full attention to mining, Hill resigned his teaching position when he learned that "certain gentlemen of the faculty" were concerned by his long absences for the "base motive of getting money." In 1865 he organized the Hill Gold Mining Company at Central City. He soon became convinced that the stamping process was too unprofitable and decided that smelting would be more practical. This involved using a high heat process to collect and hold precious metals to copper matte from which they were later extracted.[31]

Hill concluded after further research that the Swansea process would best fit his needs. Developed at Swansea, Wales, the center of the British copper industry, the process had become famous enough to attract entrepreneurs from around the world. Hill traveled to Swansea, where he toured factories, visited mines, and talked to metallurgists. Next, he crossed over to the Continent to inspect ore dressing machinery and learn more about mining and metallurgy at Freiberg, Saxony, a Mecca for top-caliber mining engineers the world over. While there he hired Hermann Beeger, a metallurgist, who had worked at smelters in Germany and Swansea. Hill also employed a number of skilled workers in Wales and paid their transportation costs to Colorado.[32]

By 1867 Hill obtained financial backing from a number of eastern investors and organized the Boston and Colorado Smelting Company. Located near the site of Lyon's defunct smelter in Black Hawk, Hill's company began commercial operations in February 1868. Initially he employed ninety-four men who could process about twenty-five tons of ore daily at a cost of about $35 a ton. In comparison to stamp mills, which charged between $2 and $3 a ton, smelting was expensive but it recovered about 97 percent of the gold. Because of the expense, however, only the more valuable ores were sent to the smelter for the extraction process. Most ores continued to be treated in stamp mills, despite the waste. Nevertheless, Hill's business proved to be so successful that he built additional smelters in 1869 and 1871. By 1872 Central City, Black Hawk, and other mining towns in the locality began to take on a show of permanence.[33]

When he began his operation, Hill sent the copper matte to Swansea, where the gold was separated from the copper plate. In 1873 he completed his own separating works, making the trip to Swansea unnecessary. To supervise the process he hired Richard Pearce, a Cornish-born metallurgist who had studied at both the Royal School of

Mines and Freiberg, and had been manager of the Swansea Smelting and Refining Company. Pearce was much more of a scientist than Hill and he successfully combined science and engineering to solve the problems presented by the complex nature of Colorado's mineral ores.[34]

The final step in expanding Hill's operation came with the opening of the coal fields in southern Colorado. Toward the end of the territorial period Hill decided to relocate his operations in Denver because labor costs were cheaper and he could use coal instead of wood. The major difficulty involved moving the ores from the mountains to the city. The Colorado Central was impractical because it utilized the narrow gauge from Black Hawk to Golden and standard gauge east of that point, requiring ores to be transferred to different boxcars in Golden. Hill tried to persuade the railroad to convert its entire line to standard gauge but without success. The Colorado Central finally capitulated when Hill threatened to build his own railroad. To save time and money it simply laid an extra track along the narrow-gauge line. Still, by the first year of statehood, Hill had moved his operation from Black Hawk to Argo, a district in north Denver.[35]

In the early 1870s silver created a second boom in Colorado mining. It started with the discovery of the Caribou Mine in Boulder County in 1869, but by 1871 shifted to Georgetown in Clear Creek County, the first of the "Silver Queens." For years miners looked for gold in areas rich with silver never realizing the wealth they were passing up. Nearly 75 percent of the silver mined in the Georgetown area before the silver boom began was washed down streams to irretrievable waste. Miners paid little attention to silver because prices declined on the open market after 1867 and it was undervalued by the federal government. While silver was used for coins of small denomination, miners generally presumed that the United States was committed to the gold standard and had no use for large amounts of silver. Until 1869 little silver ore was produced and smelting facilities were minimal. By 1870 production jumped to $600,000 and to $3,000,000 in 1874, when silver output exceed that of gold for the first time. But the real heyday for silver came when the mines at Leadville were opened in the later 1870s.[36]

Explorations for both gold and silver were carried on in western Colorado during the territorial period, especially in the San Juan Mountains. As previously noted, this caused difficulties with the Utes and ultimately resulted in a sizeable reduction in their reservation. In 1872 the village of Del Norte was laid out, followed by Silverton in 1874. But the lack of passable roads over the mountains and the high cost of freighting kept the towns isolated until the coming of the Durango and

Silverton Railroad in 1882. Even then a trip into western Colorado could be a rugged undertaking.[37]

Agriculture, like mining, made strides in the early 1870s. Actually, farming appeared in eastern Colorado simultaneously with mining. Colorado's early isolation and the difficulties of transporting foodstuffs and goods across the plains encouraged unsuccessful miners to turn to farming. Yet, until the coming of the railroad agricultural development was slow and in 1870 there were only 1,728 farms and ranches in the entire territory. Growth was also retarded by limited markets, grasshopper infestations, and inexperience in high country farming. Traveling through eastern Colorado in 1871, George W. Pine commented on the agricultural potential of the territory. In the southern portion, formerly part of New Mexico, agriculture was limited to the upper section of the Arkansas River Valley and to the San Luis Valley. Despite the fertility of the soil, farmers used antiquated agricultural methods and raised mainly corn. Pine also noted that the population was older, many people having resided there even before the gold rush. To the north, farming in the South Platte River Valley and the river's tributaries, according to Pine, was far more progressive. Because the region was more recently settled, farmers used modern methods of agriculture and the crops were more varied, including barley, oats, potatoes, hay, alfalfa, and vegetables.[38]

Railroads did much to improve the territory's agricultural potential. To make their routes more profitable railroads encouraged the development of towns with the result that Colorado's population increased 387 percent between 1870 and 1880, from 39,864 to 194,327 persons. In the same decade the number of farms increased from 1,728 to 4,506. Railroads also offered rapid transportation for surplus crops, and Colorado changed from an importing to an exporting region. By 1873 farmers were shipping excess produce to the East and no longer importing foodstuffs from the Missouri–Mississippi River Valley. And they quickly adapted to the new transportation method. The first Kansas Pacific train that traveled east from Kit Carson in 1869 carried a carload of cattle headed for St. Louis.[39]

Contemporaries disagreed about the value of Colorado Territory's agricultural production in the early 1870s. Frank Hall admitted that agriculture expanded with the coming of the railroads but the value of the total output could only be estimated because of the lack of accurate records. He calculated the value of crops in 1871 to be $4 million but made no estimate for the later years. Frank Fossett, whose tourist guide was designed to make Colorado appealing to outsiders, claimed that farmers produced close to 3 million bushes of wheat, corn, oats, barley, rye and potatoes and 50,000 tons of hay in 1878. Their garden produce was valued at $250,000 and dairy products at $350,000.[40]

The rapid growth of agricultural production is remarkable in light of the two major problems farmers had to contend with: adapting to High-Plains, arid farming techniques and fighting grasshopper infestations. Most pioneer farmers in Colorado came from the humid East and were accustomed to farming in a region with twenty or more inches of annual rainfall. Moreover, depending upon the region, the growing season in the East varied from six to seven months. On Colorado's plains, by contrast, rainfall averaged fourteen inches annually and the season lasted from four to five months. While there was little farmers could do to adjust the growing season, they compensated for the lack of rainfall by building more and larger irrigation canals.

The first irrigation canals in Colorado were narrow and short and designed to irrigate small plots of land. Many were also close to the mountains because they depended on descending mountain streams to provide the water. Few extended more than one-half mile from their water source. Also, these early ditches were built by individuals or small groups.[41]

The settlement of towns farther out on the Plains brought changes in the system, most notably in Weld County. Almost immediately upon their arrival, settlers in Greeley began constructing an irrigation canal, which drained off the Cache la Poudre River, to provide water for lots and gardens in the town. The canal proved so successful that it was enlarged three times during the next two years. Next they built Canal #2, as they called it, to irrigate the farmlands around the town. It was a far more revolutionary concept; when completed Canal #2 was thirty-six miles long and thirty-two feet wide on the bottom. Taking their cue from Greeley, most towns along the Front Range made canal building one of their first priorities. These later canals were distinguished from the earlier ones by their length and depth and by the fact that they carried enough water to irrigate fields farther from the main source of supply. They were also built by towns rather than individuals, and were maintained and owned by the community. At the same time the germ of the stockholding irrigation company was emerging along the Arkansas River, where George Swing and his neighbors built a sixteen-mile canal and incorporated it as the Rocky Ford Ditch Company.[42]

Lack of water sometimes led to hard feelings between towns, as seen in the quarrel between Greeley and Fort Collins in the summer of 1874. Sparse rainfall caused farmers around Fort Collins, higher up the river, to take so much water from the Cache la Poudre that there was not enough left to fill Greeley's irrigation canals. Greeley farmers protested that their rights were being disregarded, and leaders of the two towns met to discuss the issue. No agreement was reached because heavy rains temporarily solved the problem. By 1878 other communities with similar problems convened in Denver and suggested laws to deal with them. As a result, the next year Colorado became the first state to assert public control over the diversion of streams used in irrigation.[43]

Irrigation was an important enough topic for Samuel Elbert, territorial governor in 1873, to convene representatives from the western states and territories to discuss the issue. The convention memorialized Congress to grant the states and territories half of their arid land so they could use the proceeds to build and maintain irrigation canals. The proposal seemed ludicrous to eastern lawmakers in 1873, but growing knowledge of western conditions encouraged Congress to accept a modified proposal in 1889.[44]

While Colorado farmers reduced the problems caused by lack of rainfall though irrigation, they found coping with grasshoppers more difficult. Although small numbers of the pests could be detected during every summer, the worst infestations occurred in 1874, 1875, and 1876, and were brought about by relatively mild winters. During the summer mature grasshoppers laid their eggs in the soil as they ravaged farm fields but the subsequent winters were not severe enough to destroy them. And according to James Harlow, "myriads of the pests" emerged the following spring and "they begin eating as soon as they can walk." In 1875 the number of grasshoppers "was so large that it baffled comprehension. They ate everything in sight; invaded towns, in which the streets and sidewalks were alive with them. The destruction of millions seemed not to affect their numbers. They even impeded the movement of trains because their crushed bodies caused the wheels to whir rather than turn." In 1874 and 1875 hundreds of farms in the South Platte Valley lost between three-fourths to seven-eighths of their crops, and many families were without food for themselves or their animals the following winter. By 1876 ex-Governor Evans lamented the third year of infestation, concluding, "Grasshoppers are the worse plague Colorado has to contend with."[45]

Pioneers often referred to grasshopper plagues in their letters and memoirs. Amelia Block, who lived near Boulder, recalled that her neighbor, Mrs. Hauck, and her children were attacked by a wave of grasshoppers while on an early evening walk. All of their clothes were covered with brown spots where the pests had spit on them and Mrs. Hauck's dress was full of small holes. Upon arriving home, the family immediately noted that the trees around the house had been stripped bare of leaves and the baby's clothes, which had been hung out to dry, had completely disappeared. John Hall informed his father that he saw his first grasshopper on July 16, 1874. Within a week there were "millions, until they cover everything. I think there are ten or a dozen in our wheat patch to every stalk of wheat thus far."[46]

Most farmers attempted to destroy the pests by pouring kerosene on the water in their irrigation ditches and driving the grasshoppers toward them. Once the task was accomplished they set the ditches on fire. Other pioneers simply gave up farming rather than continue to face grasshopper infestations. Near Fort Collins, James Harlow could not understand why anyone would purchase land, pay for water rights, build a home and out buildings, plant a crop only to see it "eaten by the grasshopper," when the same amount of money would purchase a larger and more productive farm in New York State. Mollie Stanford and her husband abandoned their family farm "when the grasshoppers came, and in a few short hours destroyed the work of weeks, and about all the hopes we had." Fortunately, Mr. Stanford was able to find employment at the Denver Mint but the change required them to take up a more urban lifestyle. "We could not stay and starve," wrote Mrs. Stanford, "and it was too late to plant again, but I loved my country home."[47]

The economic hard times caused by grasshopper infestations and the depression following the Panic of 1873 caused Colorado farmers to become strong supporters of the Grange. Established as the Patrons of Husbandry following the Civil War, the Grange was designed as a social outlet for isolated farm families. Grange chapters in the Midwest soon evolved into pressure groups that persuaded legislatures to pass legislation regulating railroads and grain elevators. Chapters also formed cooperatives, purchasing products in quantity and selling them at lower prices than farmers had to pay on the market. At least one Colorado farmer living in Southwater, near present-day Monument, hoped the Colorado Grange would become powerful and effective. "This grange system is going to knock Monopolists in the head," wrote N. Z. Cozens, "and do away with the middle men. A Cooperate Store will be in full bloom on the divide by spring so that we can by [*sic*] our produce a little cheeper [*sic*]. . . . The present state of affairs must be changed, and we are going to try it."[48]

By 1874 there were sixty-one Grange chapters in Colorado, most of them in the South Platte River Valley. Yet, the organization lacked unity. One of its leaders attributed the lack of cohesion in the territory to the isolation of chapters and their separation from more organized units in the East. It may also have been due to the failure to seek political support. Colorado grangers welcomed politicians to their conventions but refused to let them speak or raise political issues. As a result, the most coordinated effort Colorado grangers made to regulate railroads came at the constitutional convention in 1876, when they proposed giving the state supreme court original jurisdiction over railroad controversies and the right to order and decree just and reasonable rates. But the proposal alarmed business and railroad interests, who argued that it would prevent outside capital from investing in the new state, and it was voted down in committee, even before it reached the convention floor for debate.[49]

The proposal also failed to receive strong support because, except for farmers, most Coloradans did not feel the effects of the depression until the eve of statehood. According to contemporary accounts mining was on the upswing, and even the valuation of property for purposes of taxation increased by $35 million between 1873 and 1875. A correspondent to the *New York Times* reported that business was slow in Denver, but none of the banks had failed and public confidence in their soundness was high. He also noted that except for Greeley, newly established towns were doing very well.[50]

In Colorado and throughout the central Great Plains, a more profitable enterprise than farming was cattle raising. Cattle barons and cowboys have long been the featured characters in plots of western romantic fiction and advertisements. The Marlboro man lounging by the open fire may give the impression of a colorful, idyllic occupation that in reality involved long hours in the saddle, coping with dust created by throngs of moving cows.

According to legend Colorado's range cattle industry began almost by accident when a government trader (in some accounts he is a miner) encountered a snow storm on the Colorado Plains and abandoned his cattle, thinking they would perish during the winter. Returning the following spring, he found the cows in better condition than when he left them. This, the legend continued, made settlers aware that cattle were capable of thriving on the native grasses. Whatever the truth of the legend, most Colorado pioneers realized that if buffalo survived on the Plains there was little reason why cattle could not. As late as 1869, Charles Dilke, an Englishman, observed as he passed through Colorado, "nothing, short of violence or special legislation can prevent the Plains from continuing to be forever that which under Nature's farming they have ever been—the feeding ground for mighty flocks, the cattle pasture of the world."[51]

Three prospectors near Castle Rock brought the first cattle raised for sale in Colorado. They found their fortune not in gold but in cattle. Significant expansion of the industry came in the postwar years after Charles Goodnight brought cattle up the Pecos Trail and several of his cowhands established ranches near Trinidad and Pueblo. The high price of beef in the North encouraged Texans to drive their cattle to western railheads for shipment to the East, but they soon found their route cut off when Missouri and Kansas passed laws prohibiting cattle drives through their states. Texas cattle were infected with "Texas" or "Spanish" fever, which was fatal to cattle on the northern ranges and killed between 50 and 90 percent of those that came into contact with it. Consequently, cattle drivers drove their herds north by way of the eastern plains of Colorado.[52]

By 1879 the number of cattle in Colorado was estimated to be 855,000 with a total value of $13,000,000, while there were 2 million sheep valued at $4,200,000. The largest cattle raising counties were Bent, with 125,000 cattle, and Weld (95,000) and the largest sheep raising counties were El Paso (230,000) and Las Animas (210,000). Sheep raising remained popular in the southern region because, according to Rufus Tarbox, he could hire a Mexican American for $30 a month, "plus grub," and always know where his sheep were. With cattle it would take days to "ride around and round them up."[53]

While cattle raising was generally profitable for everyone engaged in it, some cattlemen turned small initial investments into fortunes. John Wesley Prowers began his cattle business in 1861 with a $234 investment and died a millionaire in 1884. When John Wesley Iliff, Colorado's best known cattleman, died in 1878, his heirs sold $250,000 worth of cattle and hardly made a dent in the herd. What made the business profitable was the minimal upkeep costs once the initial investment had been made. Cattlemen merely moved their herds onto the public domain where the grazing land was free. Iliff estimated that during the season each cow cost him between 62 and 75 cents to maintain and he could sell the animal for $30 or $35. Nor was the cost of labor expensive. Monthly salaries for cowhands ranged from $25 to $30, plus board, but even these costs fluctuated during the year because most cattlemen reduced their crews by more than half during the winter months.[54]

For cattlemen the most important necessity was access to water. Cattlemen understood that they had to control the water resources and that the location of the land they owned was more important than the amount. While they appropriated land under the Homestead Act, their greater interest was in securing water holes and stream banks. Prowers, for example, owned eight thousand acres but its location along the Arkansas River and its tributaries gave him de facto possession of half-million more. Iliff held title to only 15,558 acres in a number of different parcels but because each bordered a river bank or contained water holes, he controlled a land area sixty miles wide and one hundred miles long, stretching from Greeley to Julesburg along the South Platte River.[55]

Unquestionably, the two principal cattle barons of Colorado Territory were Iliff and Prowers. They were both expert managers and shrewd businessmen who took advantage of the open range before others thought of doing so. They gained the respect of both Native Americans and whites by their fair and honest treatment. When they purchased private land, for example, both men often hired the previous owners as cowhands. Neither ever suffered heavy losses due to Native American depredations. Iliff purposely made friends of Native American chiefs in his area and allowed them to kill his cattle for food. Prowers learned the local Native American language and married Amache, daughter of a prominent Southern Cheyenne chief. He also permitted the band to camp on his land whenever they wished. Both men left their mark on Colorado. Iliff's heirs endowed the Iliff School of Theology in Denver, and the state legislature created Prowers County in 1889, five years after the cattleman's death.[56]

Iliff learned the cattle trade from his father, a farmer who specialized in breeding and raising fine stock on the family farm near Zanesville, Ohio. He attended Ohio Wesleyan University but left without graduating and came to Colorado during the 1859 gold rush. He may have tried mining for a while, but he soon began raising vegetables to sell in the mining camps. With his profits he established a cow camp near present-day Fort Morgan and began importing Shorthorn breeding bulls from Iowa and Illinois. By 1863 he set up a second cow camp at Freemont's Orchard, about forty-eight miles from the future site of Greeley. He also purchased or bartered trail poor, lame, and footsore cattle from people who were crossing the Plains and let the animals fatten themselves on the prairie grasses around the camp. As the Union Pacific Railroad approached Colorado, Iliff contracted to provide cattle for the construction gangs and the troops guarding them. In 1868 he purchased $40,000 worth of cattle from Charles Goodnight and hired Edward F. Bishop to run the operations with the Union Pacific. After the completion of the transcontinental railroad, he established his main headquarters at Riverside, near present-day Iliff, and spent the remainder of his life improving the quality of his stock. Iliff married twice. His first wife, whom he met in Kansas, died in 1865 due to complications of childbirth, and in 1870 he married Elizabeth Fraser of

Chicago. When Iliff died in 1878, the *Cheyenne Leader* lauded him as the "most successful cattle merchant that the West has ever produced. Texas may have seen ranchmen who owned as many cattle, . . . but no man [in Texas] had Mr. Iliff's genius for handling cattle and conducting successfully large operations."[57]

Little is known about Prowers's childhood. His biographer hints that his relations with his parents were difficult. At least, he came west to Colorado, in 1856, while still a teenager and worked at Bent's Fort, after which he became a freight hauler for the government, transporting supplies between Leavenworth, Kansas, and Fort Union, New Mexico. In 1861 Prowers bought six hundred head of cattle in Missouri, and grazed them along the Arkansas River prior to shipping many of them to the mining camps. The results were so profitable that he added a hundred more stock cows to the herd the following year. "Mr. Prowers," wrote the *Colorado Chieftain,* "has done more than any person residing in this territory to improve the breed of cattle." By the end of the territorial period, Prowers controlled half-million acres of river frontage along the Arkansas and owned over ten thousand cattle. Not only was he an astute businessman, but his election to the territorial legislature in 1873 indicates that he was well respected by his neighbors.[58]

Almost from the beginning of the industry, cattlemen found themselves facing common problems: exorbitant railroad rates and losses from rustling. According to the *Colorado Tribune,* it cost more to ship cattle from Denver to Kansas City than from Chicago to New York. Cattlemen in northern Colorado drove their stock to Cheyenne to avoid the high rates charged by the Denver Pacific Railroad. To remedy cattle losses, cattlemen formed a stock-growers' association in Bent County in 1870 and two years later the Colorado Stock Growers' Association organized. It required cattlemen to brand their stock in order to identify them in roundups and as protection against cattle rustlers. In Weld County officials registered brands to sort out the multiplying herds along the South Platte River. By the end of the territorial period the legislature passed laws controlling herding, branding, and ear-marking of cattle on the range. Although the Colorado organization became powerful, it was never as politically dominant as the Wyoming Stock Growers' Association because it had to compete with mining and agricultural interests in the legislature.[59]

Colorado underwent a remarkable development in the post–Civil War years. A number of factors contributed to this transformation. The war was now over, and the desire of Americans to move west was renewed. Veterans discontent with life on the old homestead, northerners looking to improve their economic circumstances, and southerners wanting to escape the uncertainties of Reconstruction headed for Colorado as well as other western regions. Successful treatment of refractory ores gave added impetus to mining development. The agricultural resources of the territory, which had been demonstrated during the war, now invited further development. But the catalyst behind it all was the railroad. Prior to the railroad the chief industry was mining. Once the railroad arrived attention was turned to agriculture and livestock raising. The few individuals and groups who arrived in Colorado between 1865 and 1870 seemed to have no particular destination or purpose in mind. Travel across the Plains had been hard and they needed time to recuperate before deciding their next move. But travel by rail brought settlers ready to take up the task they had come to accomplish. Not all who came fulfilled their dreams or remained in the territory, but enough survived the initial hardships to begin the settlement of a grassland wilderness.

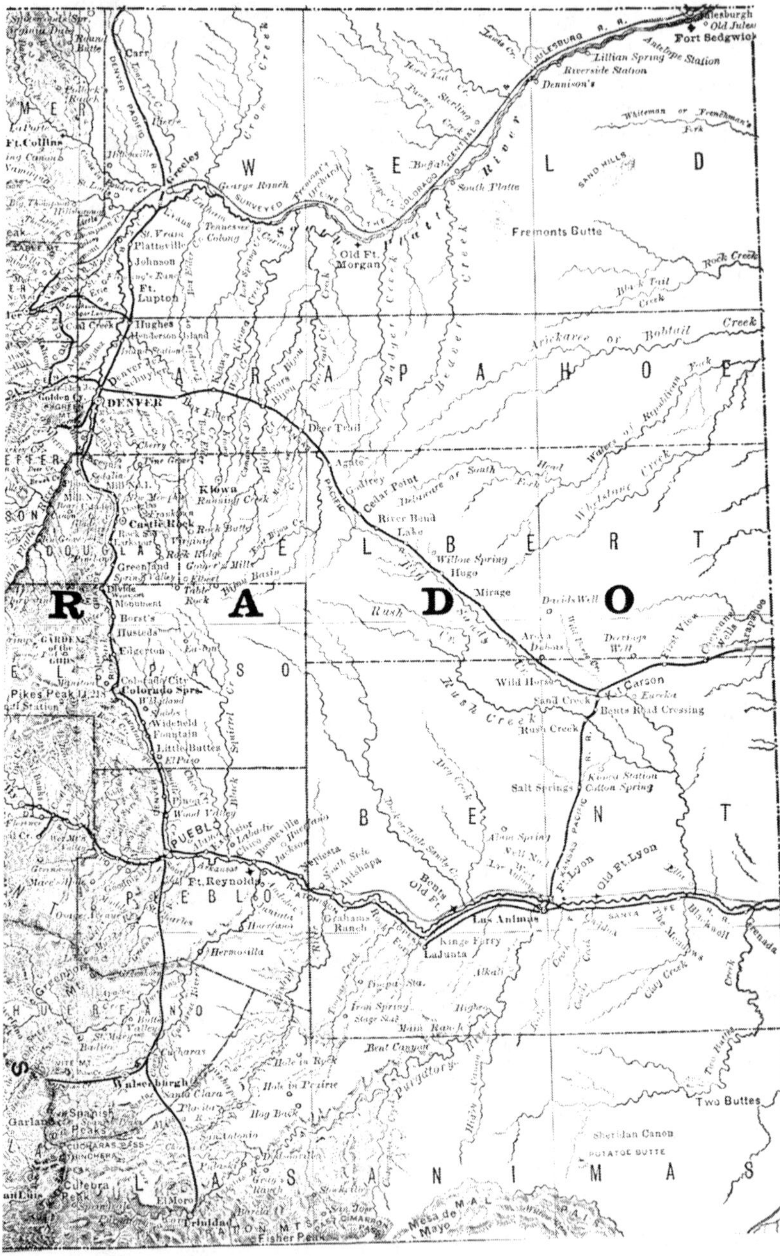

2. *Map of Colorado. Colorado Business Atlas of 1876. From* Rand McNally's Business Atlas of the Great Mississippi Valley and the Pacific Slope *(1876–77).*

5 *Settling the Plains*

"Hell on Wheels," some called it. Others referred to Julesburg as the "most debauched and most bloodstained little moral pesthouse the Far West ever saw." Founded by Jules Beni in 1859, Julesburg, for a brief time, served as a relay station on the Pony Express and then as a transfer point on the stage line for travelers going to Denver or on to the West Coast. The town rebuilt following the devastating Native American raids of 1865, and for six months in 1867, from June to November, it served as the terminus for the Union Pacific Railroad. During those months its population was estimated between six thousand and seven thousand, making it the largest town in the Colorado Territory.[1]

Ugly by day and dangerous by night, Julesburg contained some 1,200 shanty structures, most of them dedicated to vice. Its population consisted of a mixture of soldiers, Native Americans, gamblers, railroad workers, ranchers, dance hall girls, prostitutes, and derelicts who defied description. The only law was the gun, the knife blade, and the rope, and almost no night passed without a gunfight. Gambling and vice became so notorious and corrupt that Grenville Dodge, chief engineer of the Union Pacific Railroad, sent two hundred armed men to clean up the town. When he arrived later to inspect their work, they showed him a new graveyard that contained the remains of those who refused to change their ways.[2]

When the Union Pacific entered Cheyenne, the railroad workers and their camp followers dismantled Julesburg and moved on. Within several years the population had dwindled to fifteen people and the town, according to one source, consisted of "about three and a half dilapidated board shanties stuck down in a treeless waste of yellowish-brown buffalo grass, which spread on every side to the horizon."[3]

Julesburg had little in common with other Colorado towns that would be established during the next decade except for their reliance on railroads. The success or failure to acquire a railroad could make or break newly established hamlets. If settlers located their cities along existing rail routes or if the rails came shortly after the town was settled, success was almost guaranteed. Villages that failed to attract railroads early in their existence either languished until one arrived or became ghost towns.

But if towns needed railroads, they, in turn, depended upon towns to ensure or increase profits. As a result, railroad entrepreneurs were as anxious to establish towns as they were to construct rail lines. Even before the Denver Pacific was completed, John Evans entered into a contract with the National Land Company to encourage immigration. The Land Company acted as the selling agent for Denver Pacific and Kansas Pacific land grants and the railroad received 10 percent of the gross receipts from the sales. In addition to publishing circulars praising Colorado's agricultural potential, the Land Company assisted immigrants in their move west, helping them select town sites and arranging transportation for settlers and their possessions, often at a reduced rate. In Colorado, William Byers served as the local agent, and he employed Colonel C. N. Pratt of Chicago to travel throughout the Midwest and East and publicize the virtues of the territory. To encourage easterners, Colorado newspapers published notices informing potential settlers that it took only sixty-eight hours to travel from Chicago to Denver, fifty-six hours if one discounted stops to load and unload passengers and freight. The territorial legislature also assisted the effort by creating the Bureau of Immigration, which promoted the territory's economic and agricultural potential.[4]

Encouraged by such endeavors, various groups in the eastern part of the nation were attracted to Colorado, and the early 1870s saw the establishment of a number of colonies, communities whose economic basis was farming. "The completion of the railroad into Colorado and to the City of Denver in the summer of 1870," wrote one historian, "marks the end of the pioneer period and the beginning of the period of colonization." Because of Byers's efforts and the prices offered by the Land Company, all of the colonies, except one, were located in the northeastern part of the territory on land belonging to the Denver Pacific.[5]

The colony type of settlement held many attractions for people unfamiliar with Colorado. Often, but not always, colonists came from the same area in the East and from similar socioeconomic backgrounds, so they were familiar with their new neighbors' values and mores. Colony settlers arrived in groups; thus, they did not have to endure the isolation so common on the frontier. Colony leaders gave particular attention to town building, which immediately offered the benefits of community life, schools, and churches. In most of the colonies families lived in town and farmed in the surrounding area, and neighbors were close at hand in time of need. Colony leaders also made the construction of irrigation canals one of their main priorities, and for farmers the availability of water for their crops was an attraction. While the cost of land was cheaper for community members than for lone settlers, it was offset by various dues and expenses incurred in joining the group.

In return for the advantages, colony members gave up some independence. In addition to building their own homes, they were required to assist in constructing town buildings and irrigation canals. Moreover, members had to agree to abide by the community's rules, usually abstention from alcohol. But, still, various reasons compelled settlers to undertake the new venture. Many war veterans found it difficult to readjust to their prewar lifestyle and took off for new adventures. Southerners sought to distance themselves both physically and psychologically from the changes occurring in the postwar South. And as the benefits of Colorado's dry climate became widely known, not a few came to escape the fever and ague (malarial fever) so common in the Mississippi Valley. Finally, many were attracted simply by their desire to own land.[6]

Colonies were either cooperative or semi-cooperative. In the one fully cooperative venture—the German Colonization Society in the Wet Mountain Valley—capital and labor was pooled and all members were expected to labor for five years, after which they were to share the profits of their undertaking. The Union Colony at Greeley and the Chicago-Colorado Colony in Longmont are examples of semi-cooperative colonies. Members built the irrigation projects and town buildings, but they worked their own farms and kept the benefits of their own labor.[7]

While many of the new settlements established in Colorado between 1870 and 1873 called themselves colonies in order to attract settlers, only a few met the three characteristics of a true colony. First, a colony was organized outside the territory, usually in an eastern city, where members were recruited and officers elected. Second, the members elected a committee to travel to Colorado and choose a site for the new community, which the members agreed beforehand to accept. Third, the committee, with assistance from Land Company officials, arranged transportation for the settlers and undertook to organize the initial building of the town and irrigation canals. In Colorado, only four communities met all three characteristics: the German Colony, the Union Colony, the Chicago-Colorado Colony, and the St. Louis Western Colony. But by 1872 the term *colony* became so widely used that small groups often referred to themselves as colonies. One example was the Kentucky Fountain Colony organized in Cynthiana, Kentucky, during the summer of 1870. The chief aim of its members was to gain a reduced rate for transportation and to settle as a group. No membership fee was required and leaders never purchased land or laid out a town. Among town developers the most disingenuous were those who used the term *colony* merely to induce settlers to purchase town lots under the guise of admitting them to membership in a colony.[8]

The German Colonization Society, founded in Chicago in 1869, established the first colony in the territory. Carl Wulsten, a Prussian who had served in the Union army and was editor of the *Staats Zeitung*, organized the society to provide better living conditions for poor Germans working in greasy, ill-ventilated factories in the Windy City. Members had to be between twenty-one and forty-five years of age, pay a $250 membership fee, and agree to work for the benefit of the community for five years, after which all profits would be divided equally. Wulsten and two other members traveled to Colorado, where they acquired forty thousand acres of land in the Wet Mountain Valley as the future home of the colony. The isolated area, approximately forty miles southwest of Pueblo, was unoccupied and ranged in elevation from seven thousand to nine thousand feet.

In February 1870, some three hundred men, women, and children, along with their personal possessions, plus tools, implements, and livestock, traveled by rail from Chicago to Fort Wallace, Kansas. Planning had been so inept that no arrangements had been made for the settlers to transport their goods to their new home. Thus, the U.S. Army loaned them wagons, and provided troops to escort them to their destination and to protect them against Native American attacks. Governor McCook shipped the settlers three boxes of rifles and two thousand cartridges when he learned that they lacked any arms for defense against Native Americans or wild animals.

The colonists immediately began building temporary cabins and clearing thirty acres for a community garden. In addition, they planted over four hundred additional acres in wheat, rye, oats, and barley. By summer the settlers established a town and constructed a community center, which also served as a general store. They named their village Colfax in honor of the vice president of the United States.[9]

By fall events took a turn for the worse. Congress rejected Wulsten's petition requesting 160 acres of land for every man in the colony. The petition was denied because the land would be owned by the group and not the individual. An early frost destroyed many of the crops, and in December the community center burned, destroying all the records. Cooperation among the settlers had been weak from the beginning but the troubles brought further dissension and forced Wulsten to resign as president. Although many of his followers regarded Wulsten as "hot-headed, arbitrary, and impracticable" in his dealings with the settlers, his successor proved less able. By the spring of 1871 many families had left the colony and relocated in Pueblo, Denver, or Cañon City.[10]

Besides internal dissension, the colony also encountered criticism from the outside. Samuel McBride, editor of the Pueblo *Colorado Chieftain,* was especially displeased that federal troops had accompanied the colonists from Kansas to the Wet Mountain Valley and that Governor McCook had supplied weapons. He could see no reason why the federal government furnished "escort of troops, arms and rations, to the march of these Teutons . . . through the peaceful cornfields of Pueblo and Fremont counties." He pointed out that other settlers did not get an escort and the government ignored them when they complained about the Native Americans. McBride became angrier after Wulsten announced that he and all of his followers were Republicans and would carry Fremont County for the party at the next election. He regarded the colony as a plot to overturn the Democratic majority in southern Colorado.[11]

Other editors soon came to the defense of the colonists. The *Colorado Chieftain* "lets out another sad wail this week about the facilities this colony had in coming to our Territory, which is very amusing," wrote one editor. They all agreed that most of McBride's comments were exaggerated and politically motivated. He would not have complained, they concluded, had the new arrivals been Democrats instead of Republicans.[12]

Antagonism between the two men became more intense after McBride and Wulsten encountered each other one evening and angry words passed between them. According to McBride, Wulsten became violent and used language "too filthy to publish." When the two accidentally met again the following morning, McBride demanded an apology and when it was not forthcoming, he shot Wulsten in the arm. McBride alleged, in his defense, that Wulsten had pulled a gun first, but none of the witnesses supported his claim. At the trial, held in July 1871, the judge discharged McBride after he promised to stop publishing derogatory editorials about the German colony. The concession hardly mattered because by then the colony was on the verge of collapse.[13]

The German Colony was short-lived for many reasons. Most of the settlers were inexperienced as farmers. They had immigrated from German cities and worked in factories in Chicago. They had little familiarity with farming or with frequent weather changes at high altitude. As a result, they delayed harvesting the first crop and an early frost killed it. Some were more skilled and ambitious than others and objected to sharing equally with those who did less work. As one of the surviving members expressed it a few years later: "There was too much *Kommunismus.*" Reflecting on additional reasons for failure, the *Greeley Tribune* claimed the site chosen was totally inappropriate for an agricultural community. Seven thousand feet in elevation was just too high because "where [cold] fronts come in July, no great results can be expected." Moreover the settlers had built a brewery and that, according to editor Nathan Meeker, "was enough to ruin any Colony."[14]

Meeker's readers may have considered his opinion definitive. Not only was he president of the Union Colony at Greeley, Colorado's most successful colony town, but he also had long experience with agricultural utopian societies. In 1844 he and his family joined the Thrumbull Phalanx in Bracewell, Ohio, a cooperative community patterned on the teaching of Charles Fourier, a French socialist. When it failed, the Meekers affiliated with a Campbellite phalanx. During the Civil War Meeker became a reporter for Horace Greeley's *New York Tribune* and rose to the position of agricultural editor by 1869. Following a tour of the West, Meeker determined to find a cooperative community in Colorado. With Greeley's support, he called a public meeting in New York City, where the Union Colony was born.

Membership in the colony was open to men of good character who agreed to abstain from using alcohol. In return for a fee of $155 each member received a town lot for his residence plus 150 acres of farming land. The town lot had to be improved within one year in order for the owner to gain title. Members also agreed to cooperate in building a town center and irrigation canals. Meeker and a committee traveled to Colorado, where after looking over several sites in South Park and the Pike's Peak region, decided to establish their community near the confluence of the South Platte and Cache la Poudre rivers. "The valley of the [South] Platte," Meeker wrote, "is probably the finest body of wind land to be found anywhere in the world." The group purchased 12,000 acres from the Denver Pacific Railroad for $31,000 and made an initial filing for sixty thousand acres of public land.[15]

The first colonists, consisting of about fifty families, arrived in the spring of 1870 and immediately began designing the town. They surveyed lots, laid out streets, and planted trees. Within several months a community center and public school were built, and plans made for a library, a lyceum, and a farmers' club. Colony officials also donated land for a church. During this time the settlers lived in tents or were housed in the "Hotel de Comfort," a building transported from Cheyenne, Wyoming, and made into a lodging house. By June the *Rocky Mountain News* reported that the community had between 400 and 550 residents and contained 70 houses, a general store, 2 bakeries, several boarding houses, a hotel, and a bank. In addition a post office, train depot, and telegraph office were soon to open. On the eve of statehood Greeley boasted of nearly 2,000 residents, spacious homes, thriving business blocks, and the appearance of a long-established community.[16]

While most early residents came from New York, Ohio, and Indiana, letters to Meeker indicate that the colony sparked widespread interest in other states, for various reasons. Some wanted to escape the cold winters of the Great Lakes region, while others hoped to locate in a place were summers were cool. A number of southerners wrote expressing their interest in leaving the turmoil of the South.[17]

Not everyone, however, found Greeley to their liking. No statistics were kept on the number of people who left the community, but contemporary accounts indicate that it was a considerable number. One group of young men arrived, walked through the town, and took the next train back east. No longer used to dealing with frontier conditions, many potential settlers complained that improvements were not occurring fast enough. Nell Brown Propst related an amusing account that might have applied to immigrants heading for Greeley or any other Colorado town: "In 1873 Sidney Propst, a 27 year old native of Palmetto, Alabama, and a number of Kentuckians came to Colorado. The family got off the train at Julesburg and proceeded to Buffalo, which was about half way to Sterling. As they proceeded toward the new colony, a dandy from Kentucky said, 'Boys, when we get to Buffalo, let's go to a private house. It will be cheaper than a hotel.' Sid said that when the young man saw Buffalo, he and two others left for Kentucky the very next morning. There was not only no hotel, there was only one private dwelling; a part dugout, part soddy that had been constructed by the Ramus Nelson family, who were Danish immigrants."[18]

Other residents left Greeley because they felt the town was being controlled by wealthier members who had purchased more than one membership. Moreover, speculators were buying memberships hoping to make a profit on the resale of their land. Most colonists also objected to a provision of the colony's by-laws that entitled a person to one vote for every membership he possessed, thus allowing multiple members to outvote those with single memberships. Other settlers came to regard Colorado as a "dreary looking place" and Greeley located "on a barren, gravelly, sandy plain . . . bounded chiefly by prickly pears . . . and a crop of anything else is totally out of the question." Especially critical was Augustus Hobbs, who returned to Illinois after a short stay in the colony. "That is the last place on the face of this terrestrial ball that any human being should contemplate a removal to!" he wrote, "Greeley, C. T., is a delusion, a snare—it is a fraud, a cheat, a swindle."[19]

Nor were Greeley's neighbors more charitable. Local stockmen referred to the town as "Saint's Rest" and its inhabitants as "Saints." When the town officers voted to build a forty-mile fence around the town to keep roaming cattle from destroying gardens, local cattlemen insisted the real purpose was to keep the Saints in and not restrain the cattle. The idea gained further credibility when the legislature refused to allow gates across the road that were to be closed at night, and town leaders responded by posting guards after sunset.

Friction between Greeley and Evans, which was four miles to the south, existed from the beginning and became stronger as Greeley sought to wrest the Weld County seat from Evans. Union colonists argued that the saloons in Evans offended them when conducting official county business in the town. Greeley petitioned the county commissioners three times and lost three elections to change the county seat. The other towns in the county supported Evans because of their dislike of Greeley. Finally, the growth of Greeley and the decline of Evans caused a reversal and in 1877 Greeley became the permanent seat of Weld County.[20]

Perhaps outsiders ridiculed the town because Meeker's editorials revealed a certain smugness that seemed out of place for a frontier community. Writing about the town's unmarried men, who were required to live in Bachelor's Hall, Meeker declared it would be impossible to find so many men who could read, write, and run businesses, and "So far as our knowledge extends, the conversation of our young men is free from oaths or vulgarity nor is rough ungentlemanly language of any kind used." Referring to the people generally, Meeker declared, "They are educated, cultivated and have taste for the refined. . . . They have a sprightly, often a spiritual look, making some of them quite beautiful. We should say then, that this colony or town is composed of men and women who form the best part of society . . . leaving much that was abhorred, wicked and immoral behind." On another occasion he conceded, "As to our fanaticism . . . we do . . . acknowledge it, and we boast of it," When the Georgetown *Miner* dubbed Greeley the dullest town in Colorado, Meeker replied that it was dull because of its strong sense of morality.[21]

Less successful than the Union Colony was the St. Louis Western Colony founded by the Reverend Andrew C. Todd in November 1870. The colony was located at Evans, four miles south of Greeley. Originally a terminus on the Denver Pacific Railroad, Evans had been a rip-roaring railroad town but had declined rapidly by the time Meeker founded the Union Colony. Indeed, many of Greeley's early buildings were moved from Evans. "Your correspondent has been informed," wrote one individual, "that nearly every house in Evans is for sale and can be purchased by the Greeley colony. Cities rise and fall like bubbles on the water, and as Greeley rises, Evans falls."[22]

Perhaps hoping to stop further decline of the town that was named in honor of his friend John Evans, William Byers persuaded Todd to establish his colony at Evans. Todd acquired forty thousand acres in the surrounding area and brought the first settlers in April 1871. But the St. Louis colony failed to thrive, and at its height in 1872 there were only 750 inhabitants. Todd lacked leadership qualities but more important, the older residents of Evans and the colonists found themselves at odds over the character of the town. On the one hand, saloons and gambling halls flourished in the town before the colonists had arrived, and the older residents could not be persuaded to close them. On the other hand, most of the new settlers were Presbyterians who strongly disapproved of alcoholic beverages and the evils associated with them. Discontented with the quality of life in the community, many colonists returned east or moved to Greeley, where they found society more agreeable.[23]

While the St. Louis colony floundered, the Southwestern-Tennessee Colony, better known as Green City, collapsed soon after it was established. David S. Green of Memphis organized the effort merely for the purpose of land speculation. He obtained two sections of government land, located twenty-seven miles down the South Platte River from Greeley, for $1.25 an acre. He divided it into twenty-five-foot-wide town lots and sold them to members of the colony for $100 each. In addition a member received the privilege of pre-empting 160 acres of government land. This was hardly a "privilege" because he could have filed for the land under the Homestead Act even without purchasing a town lot. To entice settlers, Green advertised the city as a commercial center for a prosperous farming area and even included pictures of steamboats at a wharf in his advertisements. In addition, he announced that the projected Colorado Central line from Golden to Julesburg would pass through the city.

Approximately two hundred families joined the Green City venture but many soon left in disgust. An irrigation ditch, meant to provide water, was so long and ran through such sandy soil that the water disappeared before it reached the city. Construction of the Colorado Central ceased with the Panic of 1873 and when it resumed the line changed directions and never came near the settlement. Within two years after being established Green City contained very few families, most of the others having resettled in other Colorado towns. Those who stayed renamed the town Corona, "not wishing to be reminded that the name of the founder was the only thing about the place that was green."[24]

Unlike the St. Louis and Tennessee colonies, Longmont weathered its difficult times but eventually became a permanent community. Originally known as the Chicago-Colorado Colony, it benefited from strong encouragement when it was organized in November 1870. C. N. Pratt, Byers, and Meeker all attended early organizational meetings in Chicago to encourage the project, Illinois politicians actively promoted the colony, and Robert Collyer, a well-known Unitarian minister, served as its first president.

For a fee of $155 members received from five to forty acres of land, depending on the land's distance from the town. They could also purchase town lots at a cost of $25 or $50, price being determined by location and size of the lot. Membership was limited to a thousand families of "temperate habits and good moral character." As with the other colony ventures, a committee traveled to Colorado to select a location.[25]

In Colorado, Byers suggested sites near the Denver Pacific Railroad, but the committee rejected them. In the end they chose land in the Boulder Valley, along the St. Vrain River. "They seem to be averse to getting far away from Denver," Byers wrote. But others thought the committee's reasons were based on sounder considerations. "I think the location the best of any colony in the territory," declared John Tice," since it is contiguous to the mountains, where it must eventually find markets for its products [and] is convenient to coal both at Erie and Boulder, is supplied with lumber from the mountains, and is well watered." The major difficulty in obtaining the site was that some of the land lay with the limits of Burlington, a community of about 150 people, which was little more than a post office and stage stop on the Overland Trail. The obstacle was quickly overcome, however, when about half of Burlington's residents agreed to join the colony, opening the way for the committee to purchase thirty thousand acres of private or railroad land and lay claim to an equal amount of government acreage.[26]

The first settlers arrived in March 1871, and by June the population reached 415 residents. By July twenty-three miles of irrigation canals had been dug and seventy-five buildings, including a town hall and library, were erected. Land was also set aside for schools, parks, and churches. One correspondent wrote, "To say I was much surprised would but faintly express my astonishment as I witnessed the agricultural development in all directions. The rolling prairies were dotted with farm houses as far as the eye could reach." Almost as soon as it was founded, the town began to serve as an outfitting post for travelers to Estes Park and Long's Peak.[27]

But the initial energies began to fade. The ditches proved inadequate to water all the land under cultivation and a plague of grasshoppers decimated planted fields. Conflicting land titles created dissatisfaction within the community, and the *Boulder County News* thought the "prospects of the town and colony were anything but flattering." When settlers began to leave the community, Warren Blinn, a former Burlington resident, assumed leadership and provided direction for those who had no experience with High Plains living. Possibly because few of the Chicago organizers actually came to the community, the residents lost interest in remaining a colony. In 1873 they petitioned the Boulder County Board of Commissioners to incorporate the colony as the city of Longmont under existing territorial statutes. Shortly after, the Colorado Central Railroad steamed into the community and a broader market and easier access to the outside offered a new beginning. Longmont, in effect, abandoned the vestiges of its colony experiment in order to thrive, and the move proved successful. Longmont's action had an impact on Greeley. After the Union Colony's charter expired in 1880, Greeley was incorporated as a city and there were no longer any true colonies in Colorado.[28]

Several factors determined the success or failure of colonial experiments: location, financial support, spirit of the settlers, and leadership. Lack of leadership worked against the German Colony. Neither Wulsten nor his successor was able to hold the colony together, although that would have been a difficult task because of its unfavorable location. While there was excellent grazing land, the short growing season of the Wet Mountain Valley made it difficult to sustain an agricultural economy based on crops that were not frost hardy. Lack of fortitude worked against the success of both Green City and the St. Louis-Western Colony at Evans. When the residents of Green City realized that David

Green had duped them and that none of the promises he made were forthcoming, they had little choice but to abandon the project. Loss of spirit on the part of the Presbyterian settlers brought the Evans experiment to an end, but poor leadership and location were also factors. Rev. Todd lacked the magnetism to persuade Evans's older residents to change to a teetotaling community or to keep his flock intact when his efforts failed. Moreover, Evans's closeness to Greeley made it impossible for both communities to thrive as market centers for the surrounding agricultural region, and Greeley had the advantage of being larger and better known.

Longmont and Greeley thrived for many reasons. Longmont had the backing of a number of philanthropists and businessmen who wanted to help the less fortunate. For example, Elizabeth Thompson, wife of philanthropist Thomas Thompson, purchased twenty-five memberships, which she then distributed to people who expressed interest in settling in Longmont but were financially unable to join the colony. She also endowed the town library on condition it would be one of the first buildings constructed. The absence of the colony's organizers may have worked to the community's advantage. They had little familiarity with frontier living, whereas the Burlington residents who took over leadership had lived in the area for over a decade and knew how to cope with its difficulties.[29]

Greeley's greatest advantage was its strong leadership during the first year of its existence. While historians credit Meeker with the town's success, it was more likely due to Robert A. Cameron. Indeed, Cameron had a broader influence on town building in Colorado Territory than any other individual. At least that was the opinion of the *Colorado Tribune:* "He impresses us as a man of solid worth whom it is well to tie to, and we doubt not but that he is destined to become an influential citizen of the Territory." Born in New York in 1828, Cameron graduated from Indiana Medical College and later served in the Indiana state legislature. During the Civil War he fought at Vicksburg and in the Red River campaign and received a brevet rank of major general by war's end.[30]

As vice president and superintendent of the Union Colony, Cameron did all the practical planning and kept the experiment from falling apart in periods of discouragement. He brought in E. S. Nettleton, an engineer, to supervise the building of the irrigation canals and William E. Pabor to publicize the colony outside of the territory. Cameron personally thought Meeker too puritanical and imperious to understand the day-to-day requirements of town building. While he approved of the ban on liquor, he did not personally abstain and irritated Meeker when he gave speeches while under the influence. And when the townspeople destroyed a tavern that had been built within the town limits, Cameron fought with Meeker to prevent him from destroying the liquor. The two men fell out further after Cameron advocated establishing a woolen mill within the town limits. At a meeting to discuss the matter, "the venom was mainly personal and directed solely against General Cameron and associates," according to a reporter for the *Rocky Mountain News.* Meeker said very little but he had a "jumping jack" who at a touch from "the chieftain of the clan" would spring up and "play his part." After Meeker published an editorial criticizing Cameron for "leaning to the side of the liquor sellers," Cameron accepted an offer from William Palmer to build Colorado Springs on the model of Greeley. That task completed he then organized the Fort Collins Agricultural Colony when the area was opened for settlement.[31]

Not only was Greeley successful, but it also spurred several communities in northeastern Colorado. Groups who left Greeley settled around Fort Lupton and Fort Morgan. But growth was slow and these areas did not see an increase in population until after statehood. More important was a group of southerners from Mississippi and Tennessee who arrived in Greeley in 1873. Many of them had been slave holders and were Confederate veterans. One family even brought a former slave to serve as a maid. The southerners felt unwelcome after their leader reported overhearing a number of Greeley residents express dismay at their arrival. The older residents feared the former Confederates would not be law-abiding. Even after the southerners established their own community some Greeley residents referred to it as a "small whisky town" where "cow boys" could hold their "carousals" instead of going to Cheyenne or Denver.[32]

When the southerners learned of the projected Colorado Central Railroad line along the South Platte River they established Sterling. Although they engaged in agriculture themselves, they sought to ensure a more varied economy by offering the railroad eighty acres of land to build shops near the town. Word of the community's success spread and in 1876 a group of southerners, who had settled at Sidney, Nebraska, joined the Sterling community.[33]

To the west of Greeley, Fort Collins soon began to develop into a permanent settlement. Before 1872, a small community of houses and a number of ranches had clustered around Camp Collins, a military post established to protect travelers on the Overland Trail. The government closed the camp in 1867 but continued to hold the land as a military reservation. In 1872 Jerome Chaffee, Colorado's delegate, persuaded Congress to open the area for settlement. Immediately Robert Cameron organized the "Fort Collins Agricultural Colony." Both city lots and farm land were made available for fees ranging from $50 to $250. By 1873 the town built a large irrigation canal, established local government, a bank, and a newspaper. The initial growth spurt ended with the Panic of 1873 and the town languished for the next four years. The Colorado Central Railroad brought another spurt of development after 1877, and by 1880 Fort Collins was the largest Colorado town north of Boulder.[34]

Immigration also occurred in southeastern Colorado but fewer towns developed. Walsenburg, La Junta, and Las Animas were agriculture service centers rather than towns during the territorial years. Because of the lack of inexpensive and reliable transportation, commerce in southeastern Colorado flowed east and south using older routes, such as the Sante Fé Trail. Groups migrating to the region tended to be from the southern states and established farms rather than cities. As a result the southern region took on a more isolated look until the coming of statehood.[35]

Some settlers in northern Colorado tended to look down upon their southern neighbors. Writing to the *Colorado Tribune*, "forward" referred to residents of southern Colorado as "butternut-clothed loungers" who kept "their languid eyes on me until to have followed further would have inaugurated the necessity of turning their heads, which they seemed to [*sic*] lazy to do." He concluded that "nothing short of a fire, an earthquake, . . . could get them to move over the speed of a snail."[36]

The largest group in southern Colorado were settlers from North Carolina and Georgia, who settled in Huerfano County in 1870. The first group consisted of two hundred people, followed by four hundred more the following year. The *Rocky Mountain News* reported that Green Russell of gold rush fame headed the groups, but both the *Colorado Chieftain* and the *Colorado Tribune* mentioned Samuel Patterson as the leader. If Russell did not return in 1870, he was back in the territory in 1872. Martha Russell Marshall, his daughter, wrote that the Russell party, consisting of about 120 people, left Georgia in May 1872, and arrived in Huerfano County the following October. Like most of his neighbors, Russell engaged in stock raising. Unable to settle down, he moved to the San Luis Valley in 1874 and in 1876 to the Indian Territory (Oklahoma), where his wife and children were entitled to take up land because of their Cherokee Indian ancestry.[37]

Colorado Springs was an exception to most Colorado towns in several ways. Founded by William J. Palmer, builder of the Denver and Rio Grande Railroad, it was the territory's first planned residential and tourist community. Unlike most towns established in the 1870s, it did not rely on agriculture or manufacturing. Mills, smelters, and manufacturing establishments were prohibited within the town limits. Citizens were permitted to have gardens and livestock but with limitations. Cattle were not allowed to roam in the streets as in most other places, and the town employed a herder to see that they did not. Each morning he rounded up the cows and drove them to a pasture outside the city limits and every evening he returned them to their owners. Animals left in town to run at large were impounded and sold. Apparently the law caused some negative comment, for "A Citizen" wrote: "The town will never be a popular stock-range or hog-yard; and any man who cannot see the necessity for restricting stock from running at large in a place like this had better go down on the Arkansas and take up a ranch."[38]

Palmer became attracted to the Pike's Peak area while surveying for the railroad, and he purchased ten thousand acres at the confluence of Monument and Fountain creeks plus an additional 640 acres at Manitou Springs. Explaining his plans, he wrote, "My theory for this place is that it should be made the most attractive place for homes in the West, a place for schools, colleges, science, first class newspapers, and everything that the above imply."[39]

To assist him in the venture, Palmer hired Robert A. Cameron and a number of his associates who had supervised the early development of Greeley. Cameron remained for only one year. He left when his contract ran out and Palmer refused to raise his salary. Palmer also attracted William Bell to the project. A London doctor who was attending a series of lectures on homeopathy in St. Louis, Bell became intrigued when he heard about Palmer's new town and joined the project as a photographer. He would play an important role in financing the project.[40]

Hoping to lure settlers to his new city, Palmer formed the Fountain "Colony," and publicized features that he thought would make it attractive. He planted trees and staked out roads and streets a hundred feet wide. He donated land for churches of different denominations and twenty acres for a college. He also arranged for the building of a lyceum and library. Like most other Colorado towns, Colorado Springs prohibited the sale of alcoholic beverages. To encourage the purchase of town lots, Palmer allowed buyers to discharge their debt over a period of years rather than purchase a membership as was common in the other towns.

He also sought financial backing from his friends in the East, while Bell made appeals to wealthy Englishmen.[41]

Colorado Springs grew more rapidly than other towns. The *Colorado Tribune* reported that one year after building began, the city contained, besides residences, ten stores, three hotels, two livery stables, a tailor shop, a printing establishment and newspaper, a railroad station, and a telegraph office. The newspaper continued, "Many may object that the town has nothing but scenery to support it but given its location it will become the main trading post for the South Park region." By 1873 Colorado Springs boasted of 850 buildings and a population of 3,200. Nor did the depression of the 1870s hinder its growth. By 1880, 4,226 people lived in the city, making it the second largest in the territory.[42]

In seeking new residents, Palmer and Bell appealed to wealthy Britons, hoping to attract people of more genteel breeding "not withstanding the remoteness and rather wild repute of this frontier." Bell encouraged those not interested in living within the city limits to invest in land in the surrounding area, and one historian claims that Englishmen owned one-third of the ranches in El Paso County. Hoping to impress potential British settlers, Palmer encouraged the building of three first-class hotels, conspicuous among them the Colorado Springs Hotel, which offered the finest amenities of any hotel in the territory.[43]

The response was perhaps more successful than Palmer expected. So many Englishmen came to Colorado Springs by the end of the territorial period that some Coloradans referred to the city as "little London." R. B. Townshend, himself an Englishman, described the place as "a very high-toned sort of new town indeed. . . . It was run by a very tony [*sic*] Company, on teetotal lines." The newcomers introduced golf, cricket, polo, and fox hunting. Afternoon tea became a traditional ritual for many, and Boxing Day was celebrated with more enthusiasm than Christmas. One individual noted that more Union Jacks flew from flagpoles on Queen Victoria's birthday than Stars and Stripes on the Fourth of July. Because of the lack of industry or large-scale agriculture, Coloradans in other towns came to regard Colorado Springs as a city for the wealthy. In Greeley, Nathan Meeker remarked that towns in which people did not work were no better than red light districts. "While the people of Greeley are engaged in creating wealth," he continued, "the people of Colorado Springs are spending it."[44]

Colorado Springs also became a haven for individuals suffering from tuberculosis and other respiratory aliments. In 1875 Dr. Samuel E. Solly, who had just recovered from a serious illness, published a pamphlet urging people with ailments to seek the restorative powers of the waters at

Manitou Springs. Others praised the climate as beneficial for those suffering from any variety of infirmities. As one resident put it: Colorado Springs "is the only region that combines the sky and climate of Italy, the air and scenery of Switzerland, the water of Ems and the society of nature." During the winter of 1873–74 some eight hundred visitors came to the city, most of them invalid. Recovery rates were so successful that James Muirhead wrote, "two-thirds of them come to die, and they can't do it." The *Colorado Tribune* declared physicians' salaries in Colorado Springs were higher than other parts of the territory because of all the people who went there to get well. After Solly established medical facilities for long-term patients, individuals dubbed the city the "consumptive's home of America" or "the great American sanitarium."[45]

While new towns were being established on the plains, older cities began to take on new importance. By the early 1870s Trinidad, Cañon City, and Pueblo all served as commercial centers for ranchers and farmers. Pueblo also became a major livestock market. For a short time the economic interests of Denver and Pueblo complemented each other and territorial legislators cooperated in passing bills that benefited both cities. But synergy ended after Pueblo officials blamed Denver for the Denver & Rio Grande's decision to bypass their city and believed Denver was attempting to control the territory's entire economy.[46]

Excluding the population of Denver, 38,000 people moved into Front Range counties between 1870 and 1880, joining the 15,000 already there. By the standards of many, however, the new settlements were extremely crude. Isabella Bird, an Englishwoman who traveled extensively throughout the region in the 1870s, visited the new towns and found little about them to admire. Bird referred to Colorado Springs as "a queer embryo looking place," and to Boulder as "a hideous collection of frame houses on the burning plain." She lauded the lack of saloons in Greeley but described the town as a place where nothing went on "except irrigation and irritation" because of flies and mosquitoes. She found Longmont a "wretched little town" and Fort Collins "a bare and burning plain, altogether revolting."[47]

The Western Slope, too, began to witness some development. A land apart, almost nothing was known about the region until Ferdinand Hayden surveyed it in 1873. Even the three major population centers—Breckenridge, Montezuma, and St. John's—contained a total of only 144 people in 1870. William Byers tried to encourage settlement in Middle Park, where he owned land and had built a rustic resort at Hot Sulphur Springs. But the severe winters discouraged settlers who ventured into the park and there were only 417 people living there by 1880. Sylvester

Richardson founded Gunnison in 1874 but the town did not take shape until 1879. Silverton was established in 1874 and languished until 1882, when the railroad steamed into town. Still, the population fluctuated with the seasons; prospectors moved in during the summer but only the more hearty braved the winter. Del Norte was the most successful Western Slope town with nearly two thousand inhabitants in the winter of 1874. But it served principally as winter quarters for miners and a local business center for the region.[48]

Immigration declined during the depression following the Panic of 1873, which impacted the East more severely than Colorado. While many may have been interested in relocating in the West, they found themselves without the means to do so. But exaggerations about the territory's potential influenced others to stay away. One correspondent to a Kansas newspaper declared that the South Platte Valley was "the nicest farming valley . . . I have yet seen, capable of producing everything common at this latitude" while another claimed that the "Arkansas bottoms will yield abundantly." But it was the Territorial Board of Immigration that painted the most idyllic picture of the territory. Established by the legislature in 1871 to encourage immigration, it sent agents to both the East and to Europe and printed about 77,000 pamphlets extolling Colorado's physical beauty, its healthful climate, and overstating its agricultural potential. Its literature said little about the lack of rainfall, the grasshoppers, and the rugged conditions of frontier life. The board's major drawback, however, was its lack of funding to assist needy immigrants once they arrived. As a result, many returned to their former homes and, according to Frank Hall, "the Territory was vindictively denounced from one end of the Union to the other. It [would have been] better to have no Board of Immigration at all, better not to waste time and money in advertising and entreating" than to lure settlers to the territory under false pretenses.[49]

In terms of population increase, growth in the Rocky Mountain West was slow in the 1870s. Harsh winters plus the presence of a large number of hostile Native Americans discouraged settlement in northeastern Wyoming and eastern Montana. Except for the heartiest, Idaho was simply too isolated. Despite it nearness to California, Nevada began to lose population during the 1870s, and Arizona with its thirty thousand Native Americans was too isolated and dangerous. The dislike of most eastern Americans for both Mormonism and polygamy made them avoid Utah, whereas the culture and language of the Spanish-speaking population of New Mexico made the territory seem both foreign and unwelcoming.[50]

Only Colorado gained a substantial population during the decade. Without doubt, the rapid transportation provided by railroads encouraged individuals and families to move there, but other factors made Colorado attractive. The territory's diversified economy provided opportunities not only for miners and farmers but for ranchers, businessmen, and laborers as well. The removal of the Native Americans, the expansion of agriculture, changes in mining techniques, and the growth of industry all stimulated population growth. Still, the overwhelming majority of the new immigrants were farmers. It is estimated that in the 1870s one of every two persons in the Colorado labor force worked at some form of agriculture. In the last decade of the territorial period immigrants came chiefly to the agricultural counties, especially those in the South Platte and Arkansas river valleys. While the number varied from county to county, the population increases in each ranged from five thousand to nine thousand.[51] And the newcomers, along with the older residents, whether from other parts of the United States, Mexico, or Europe, began to merge the different aspects of their cultures and create a High Plains, frontier society.

Fort Collins, 1877. Photographer unknown. Courtesy Western History Department, Denver Public Library.

Boulder, 1870. Photographer unknown. Courtesy Western History Department, Denver Public Library.

Main Street, Longmont, 1872. Photographer unknown. Courtesy Western History Department, Denver Public Library.

Greeley, 1870. Photographer unknown. Courtesy Western History Department, Denver Public Library.

Santa Fe Avenue, Pueblo, 1870. Photographer Theodore Anderson. Courtesy Western History Department, Denver Public Library.

Tejon Street, Colorado Springs, 1882. Photographer William Henry Jackson. Courtesy Western History Department, Denver Public Library.

Early Denver. Artist James F. Gookins. From Harper's Weekly (October 13, 1866).

William Gilpin, 1861–62. Courtesy Colorado State Archives.

John Evans, 1862–65. Courtesy Colorado State Archives.

Alexander Cummings, 1865–67. Courtesy Colorado State Archives.

Alexander Hunt, 1867–69. Courtesy Colorado State Archives.

Edward McCook, 1869–73; 1874–75. Courtesy Colorado State Archives.

Samuel Elbert, 1873–74. Courtesy Colorado State Archives.

John Routt, 1875–76. Courtesy Colorado State Archives.

6 *Town and Country Society*

Murder, robbery, and general lawlessness were common enough during Denver's early years for Horace Greeley to write that there were "more . . . brawls, more fights, more pistol-shots with criminal intent in this log city of one hundred and fifty dwellings . . . then in any community of equal numbers on earth." Nor were other parts of the territory less ruckus. Contemporaries described most mining towns as "the favorite haunts of desperadoes and abandoned women, from whose doors crime stalked with a bold front to spread death and destruction upon the streets."[1]

As the population declined during the Civil War, the crime rate and violence dropped but picked up again during the later territorial period. Of the 102 lynchings in the territory between 1859 and 1876, 74 took place after 1865. Most lynching victims were accused—but not always convicted—of murder, robbery, or livestock rustling. In 1868 a mob lynched L. H. Musgrove, who headed a gang of horse thieves in the northern part of the territory. Some years earlier the members of the Reynolds gang met an even more ghastly fate. Known as Confederate sympathizers, the gang had terrorized the region from Denver to the New Mexican border. Finally captured by a unit of the Third Colorado Cavalry, the prisoners were ordered under guard to Fort Lyons for trial. But they never completed the trip. The guards shot the gang members before they reached the fort. Although the soldiers claimed the prisoners had tried to escape, one critic noted that the corpses were still restrained by leg shackles.[2]

Southern Colorado was considered the most crime-prone section of the territory. Lack of statistics, however, makes the assertion hard to verify. Nevertheless, David J. Cook, head of the Rocky Mountain Detective Association, believed the large number of "tough characters" in Pueblo and southern Colorado made it a place of refuge for criminals from the surrounding region.[3]

Denver newspapers seldom reported robberies and lesser crimes in outlaying areas but often gave murders full coverage. Of those reported, the most grisly homicides during the territorial years were the Italian murders in 1874. Filomeno Gallotti and members of his gang slit the throats of a fellow Italian immigrant and three boys and hid their bodies in the cellar. The crime was not discovered until neighbors complained to police about the horrible stench coming from the immigrant's house. Apprehended and brought to trial, the criminals avoided the death penalty by pleading guilty. The law stipulated a prison sentence for accused individuals who confessed to the crime of murder. Gallotti received a life sentence and was the 179th person admitted to the Colorado Territorial Prison, which had only been open for three years.[4]

Murders occurring outside Denver also received attention. In 1870 William DuBois killed Edward Kinney near Burlington (later Longmont) after Kinney identified him as one of several bandits in a stagecoach holdup. DuBois was later mortally wounded as he attempted to stand off the posse sent to arrest him. Four years later, in 1874, Griffith Evans shot Jim Nugent, a well-known mountain man and local guide in the Estes Park area. Although authorities charged Griffith with murder, he was never punished because the only witness to the shooting fled the territory before the trial began.[5]

On one occasion murder led to civil disobedience in the so-called Lake County War. In 1874 Elijah Gibbs killed his neighbor George Harrington in an argument over water rights. At the trial, held in Denver because authorities believed that Gibbs would not receive a fair hearing locally, he was acquitted. Still, many Lake County residents wanted Gibbs punished and persuaded Harrington's wife to request a warrant for his arrest for assaulting her husband prior to the murder. Gibbs shot two officials when they attempted to serve the warrant and later assassinated the judge who issued it. He fled the territory, but Harrington's friends were not satisfied. They convened a People's Court and ordered Gibbs's supporters to leave the county. One individual who refused was later found dead. When Governor John Routt sent detectives to Lake County to investigate, local residents threatened to kill them. Lacking funds to establish a military force to quell the disturbance, Routt, in desperation, appealed to General Sherman to station federal troops in the county "to allay the fears of the timid [and] to protect the law abiding citizens." Although no troops were sent, Routt's action quieted the whole affair.[6]

Despite the evidence of crime, many Coloradans and visitors believed criminal activities were infrequent occurrences. Some even portrayed Colorado as "a paradise of quiet and repose." James Meline and Rose Kingsley concluded that "the days of danger are past," and Denverites "behave with a decorum and self-respect, which . . . we could hardly expect to find universal." One optimist went so far as to assert that baggage left outside all night was less likely to be stolen in Denver than in any New England city.[7]

James Rusling, visiting Denver in 1866 at the height of the opposition to Governor Cummings, expressed surprise that people did little more than gather on street corners and voice their concern. "The mob spirit of [Denver's] early days could not be revived over the political row now in progress." he wrote. Attempting to explain the change, Rusling concluded that even though Denver citizens liked lynching, they "liked English capital and English immigration better, and would do nothing to offend either."[8]

Boosters praised the mining towns, too, for having lost their earlier rowdiness. Central City and Black Hawk were described as almost "puritanical." Public drunkenness was frowned upon and gambling was conducted quietly. Even "ladies of the night" behaved with decorum in public. The Clear Creek towns," wrote one Coloradan, "were known throughout the mountains for their relative sobriety and want of violence." Georgetown, Colorado's first Silver Queen, contained more saloons than most mining towns; still, public drunkenness was uncommon, and miners crowded the churches on Sunday morning expecting to hear inspiring sermons. Even Trinidad, noted historian Morris Taylor, was not the town of hovels and violence it was reputed to be.[9]

Individuals who insisted that crime was less prevalent in the later territorial years than it had been previously attributed the change to two factors: the harsh punishment meted out by People's Courts during the earlier years and the arrival of more women and children in the 1870s. The presence of the fairer sex, wrote Frank Hall, "softened and put the brutal instincts of misguided men to shame." Remarking on the attitudes of Coloradans toward women, William Dixon concluded, "the lady is a power in this country. From the day when a silk dress and a black shawl were seen in Main Street, that thoroughfare became passably clean and quiet; oaths were less frequently heard; knives were less frequently drawn; [and] pistols were less frequently fired."[10]

Besides being influenced by the standards of the Victorian Age, male behavior was also prompted by the scarcity of women. In 1870 the territory contained 9,774 more adult males than women, 24,173 men to 14,399 females. Despite the development of towns in the 1870s and the rapid growth in the general population, the sex ratio widened dramatically by 1880. The census of that year recorded only 37,852 women eighteen years of age or older while the number of males in the same age bracket was 100,803.[11]

Women who commented on men's behavior noted that "they were invariably polite and well-behaved to a degree that struck one in sharp contrast to their uncared-for appearance." In the cities men removed their hats when a woman entered an elevator and did not put them on again until she alighted. In the mining towns, miners would step in the mud "in order that [women] might pass dry-shod." If a woman spoke to them, miners removed their hats and took their pipes from their mouths. Deference toward women also gave them an advantage in other ways. Trying a case between a husband and wife in 1876, Irving Stanton demanded a jury trial when he learned that the judge had recently immigrated from the East and might not render a decision in the wife's favor. The husband had brought suit against his wife, asking that she be evicted from their home on the grounds that his money had paid for it. True to Stanton's expectation, the jury refused to evict the woman. Had the judge decided the case, Stanton was certain a different decision would have been reached.[12]

Their small number also gave women an advantage in the job market. Perhaps at his wife's urging, William Byers wrote an editorial lamenting the high wages paid to domestic help. Servants usually received a monthly salary of $40 or $50, plus room and board, making the total monthly expenditure for each servant nearly $100. Noting that this was a higher salary than most laborers earned, Byers concluded the short supply of women was the cause. He also claimed that scarcity of women created an unstable labor market. No matter how high the salary, households that could afford a female servant faced the added problem of keeping her. Unmarried women, according to some accounts, were courted immediately upon arriving in the territory. "I have seen young girls of thirteen and hideous old girls of fifty snapped up eagerly as soon as they arrived in the country," recalled Isabelle Randall. William Dixon lamented the lack of female servants in public inns: "When you call for the chamber-maid, either Sam puts in his woolly head, or Chi Hi pops in his shaven crown. Hardly any help can be hired in these waste; Molly runs away with a miner, Biddy gets married to a merchant."[13]

Women who could not afford servants found homemaking a full-time job. Most complained about the dust and insects and the time it took to maintain their homes. For Ellen Pennock cooking was a laborious chore. Her only cooking utensils consisted of a kettle on a hook over a fire and a bake kettle. It took her an entire day to bake a batch of cookies and two pumpkin pies because she could only bake four cookies or one pie at a time. She felt that her efforts amounted to very little because the men in the family ate everything she had baked in one meal. Missouri Propst had a good cook stove and equipment, but she tired at the sameness of the diet—"buffalo meat and bread, bread and buffalo meat, a pudding now and then to keep from forgetting how such things taste."[14]

Women who lived in rural areas often remarked on the crudeness of their living conditions. Most of their furniture was homemade, often consisting of benches or chairs and tables. It was not uncommon to sleep on tables. On the day her husband purchased a bed and installed it in their cabin, Sarah Hively recorded in her journal, "I guess that I will not have to sleep upon boxes anymore." More often than not a rural residence consisted of one room which served as kitchen, parlor, dining room, and bedroom. And the residence itself might be either a tent, a wood structure, or a sod house. Missouri Propst considered the tent her husband purchased on their way to Colorado to be "their salvation." Beside it Propst had constructed an eight by eight sod addition with a slanting roof, which Missouri used as a kitchen and storage room. Mournfully she wrote, "and my trunks full of fine marseilles quilts, embroidered pillow cases, silks, laces, etc., stowed away in a leaky sod shack. Don't think I am making it out worse than it is, not *half so bad,* believe me."[15]

Encountering Native Americans was the greatest fear of pioneer women. Nearing the completion of his journey to Colorado in 1866, George Buss decided to leave the wagon train at Fort Morgan and push ahead to Denver. He failed to anticipate his wife's opposition, however. While Amelia willingly endured the hardships and inconveniences of the trek across the plains, she refused to leave the safety of the wagon train. "I am so afraid of indians [*sic*] I can not bear to go," she wrote. Similarly, Sarah Hively wrote in her journal, "Oh I do hope that they [the Native Americans] will behave themselves and mind their own affairs . . . if I can only get home once I don't think that I will ever come out here again."[16]

While pioneer women feared death at the hands of Native Americans, they had a greater dread of sexual assault. According to H. Slate, braves on the warpath often raped their victims and many women committed suicide rather than endure violation. Some, however, fought off their attackers. In Burlington, Mrs. David Taylor drove off a Native American brave with a stick after he grabbed her and "offered her indignities of an outrageous sort."[17]

There are many contemporary comments to suggest that Native American men were attracted to white women. Molly Sanford, Mrs. Daniel Witter, and Mary R. Reithmann all recalled that their husbands or fathers were offered livestock or Native American women in exchange for their wives or daughters. In Mary Reithmann's case the chief, White Cloud, made the offer on numerous occasions and finally returned with forty ponies and blankets and insisted on a trade. Despite the father's refusal, White Cloud remained friendly and later interceded to prevent braves from attacking the family farm. Clark Secrest reports that Native American men willingly let their wives "satisfy the needs of white men." If such was the case, they saw nothing wrong in expecting the arrangement to be reciprocal.[18]

Evidence also indicates that braves appreciated the cooking of pioneer women. From Sterling to the San Luis Valley, women recorded instances of Native Americans coming to their homes and demanding food. According to Mrs. Mote, "Old Washington," who lived in the San Luis Valley, had an extreme dislike of white people. That dislike, however, did not extend to her. "Old Washington" periodically appeared with his wife and demanded "bees-keet," and Mrs. Mote, fearing personal harm if she refused, immediately began making biscuits. So voracious was "Old Washington's" appetite that he often ate his wife's portion while waiting for the next batch to arrive. Mrs. Sven Magni, a Swedish immigrant, recalled spending an entire morning making bread and just as it came from the oven several Native Americans arrived at her cabin and took every loaf.[19]

Amelia Buss, who often expressed her fear of Native Americans, seemed to have more encounters than most pioneer women. She recorded three such incidents during the autumn of 1867. In each case braves or Native American women came to her door asking for food or water, and Buss was not harmed in any way. But given her fear of Native Americans, she found each instance disturbing.[20]

Loneliness was the chief complaint of women who lived in rural areas. Ellen Pennock remembered spending days weeping and longing to be with her friends back East. But she refused to make her husband feel guilty for separating her from her family, so she put on a brave front whenever he was near. Sarah Hively lamented in her journal, "Oh how lonely I do feel here all alone with no one to keep me company . . . but I will put my trust in god [*sic*] he will never forsake me, if I will only trust in him." Similarly Mrs. J. A. Davis wrote, "It was not easy for me to adjust myself to the new conditions . . . but the most difficult was the intense loneliness that not only surrounded, but almost seemed to suffocate me at times." The sense of loneliness was especially intense during the absence of a husband. Several times a year George Buss went to the mountains to cut wood and left Amelia in charge of their farm. On those occasions she found her best friend to be her diary, where she recorded her innermost thoughts. Buss arrived in Colorado during September 1866, and it took a year before she could write: "Now I have settled down with the belief that here I shall and [end?] my days & the sooner I make it home the better my prospects look."[21]

Despite the distance between farms, there was much socializing among rural families. It was common for several farm families to celebrate major holidays, such as Christmas, together. There were occasional parties, too, but "as girls were rather scarce, it was often quite a serious thing with the boys as to who should engage the girls first." Nor was there a rigid social distinction between small farmers and ranchers. Farm families "translated into 'women' and in some cases marriageable young women," wrote Nell Brown Propst. "Any excuse for a dance would do. Even a corn shucking could turn into a party for both ranch hands and settlers."[22]

While social stratification was not evident in rural areas, egalitarianism, according to Gunther Barth, fell by the wayside in larger cities. True, acceptance into elite social circles might come faster in frontier communities, still individuals or families could not expect immediate entrée. One of the most important events for Denver's upper class society was Margaret Evans's annual reception. Yet, her guest list was limited to her husband's business and political associates, members of the Methodist Church, or those who worked with Mrs. Evans in her various social causes.[23]

Among the least acceptable in white society were mountain men who had married Native American women, or "squaw men" as they were derogatorily referred to. By 1870 most had left the cities for rural areas where they were not looked down upon. A case in point is William McGaa. He settled in Denver in the late 1850s and often mediated disputes between Native Americans and whites. He was well regarded enough to have a street named in his honor. By the end of the Civil War, McGaa's marriage proved to be a social hindrance, so he left the city for more rural LaPorte. After he died in 1867, Denver authorities renamed McGaa Street to Holladay Street, and later, after it became the most notorious red light district in the region, to Market Street. As Elliott West wrote, "As a road to status, a man's marriage to an Indian was a dead end at best."[24]

Class distinction aside, cities offered a greater variety of entertainment than rural areas for the average citizen. Ice cream socials and dances were especially popular in Denver during the territorial years. Often young men organized a dance and invited families with marriageable daughters. Such affairs were usually held in hotels, Alice Polk Hill recalled, and concluded with supper served at midnight. Occasionally a circus came to town and attracted large crowds. Grace Greenwood admitted enjoying circus performances but found it shocking to see "women in horrible undress, swinging, and tumbling and plunging heels over head out of their sphere." Visits to fortune tellers or attendance at séances attracted the more adventurous. Deciding that such "low brow" entertainment was a fraud, a *Colorado Tribune* reporter attempted to expose both fortune tellers and mediums. He concluded that having one's fortune told was a "pastime for the gullible," but the séance left him shaken. Miss Overton of St. Louis, the medium, did not impress him until she called out his name and informed him that his dead sister-in-law was standing in the corner. While the spirit admitted to being happy, she was waiting for a member of the family to join her. The reporter had never seen Miss Overton before attending the séance and was certain she was unaware of his intentions. He admitted that he left the séance and sought spirits of another kind.[25]

Many families enjoyed evening drives into the country and excursions into the mountains. "Every man who can afford it has his carriage & horses, with which he drives out every pleasant afternoon upon the long smooth and perfectly level roads," Frank Hall informed his mother. After the completion of the Colorado Central Railroad from Denver to the mining towns, excursions became very popular, especially among church groups. "Excursion season is upon us again," commented the *Colorado Tribune* in 1873, noting that an excursion had been planned for almost every day in the month of July. The most popular were those to Idaho Springs, Black Hawk, or Central City. The party left Denver in the afternoon and arrived at its destination just before dinner. Evenings were taken up with dinner and some type of entertainment, usually a dance or play. After breakfast the following morning, the party returned to Denver. While excursions were popular, one individual noted that they were not always pleasant. Railroad cars were often crowded, hot, and late, and ladies parasols poked everyone around them.[26]

The largest excursion occurred in 1875 when William Holly, secretary of the Colorado Stock Growers' Association, invited six hundred guests to watch cowboys at work in Elbert County. The guest list included newspaper men, businessmen, politicians, and debutantes. After observing the cowboys, the guests attended a barbecue and dance. At night they slept outside under blankets and buffalo robes. That everyone had a good time was attested to by the liquid refreshment consumed: "seventeen gallons of brandy, two barrels of whiskey, plus cigars, pipes, and pickles."[27]

Many Coloradans found diversion from their daily lives by attending the theater, although the type of dramatic productions offered and the facilities they were performed in seemed crude to newcomers. Dramatic companies occasionally presented Shakespeare's *Othello* or Sir Walter Scott's *Lady of the Lake,* but audiences preferred such low comedies as *Our Girl* or *Man of the World.* Until the Governor's Guard Hall opened in 1873, Denver lacked a legitimate theater and most troupes performed in inadequate facilities, usually saloons. Drama companies in Denver played at the Apollo, a rowdy gambling casino with an amusement hall on the second floor. Noise filtering up from the first floor often made it impossible to hear the actors. Like Denver, all of the outlying communities lacked theaters. Efforts to build one in Colorado Springs did not materialize during the territorial years, and the Central City Opera House, which still presents productions in the summer, was not opened until 1878.[28]

John Langrishe operated the most popular dramatic company in the territory. His troupe performed mainly in Denver and the mountain towns, and occasionally in Colorado Springs. Among actors, Mike Dougherty drew the largest audiences, and when he announced his departure from Denver in 1866 a farewell dinner was held in his honor. But Dougherty failed to succeed elsewhere and the following spring returned to Denver, where he died shortly after. Following his death theater attendance declined because many felt no one could adequately perform the roles he had played. To lure back audiences managers promoted their shows by sending brass bands and actors to perform skits in the streets.[29]

The declining interest in theater was attributed, in part, to the small number of traveling theatrical companies that came to Colorado. Before the railroad reached Denver, they were unwilling to cross the Plains because of Native American troubles or the hardship of travel. Yet, even after railroads arrived few companies came to the territory, causing the

Colorado Tribune to lament the lack of theater performances "that should be enjoyed by all." Important, too, was the feeling among many traveling theatrical groups that they were not welcome. The *Greeley Tribune,* for instance, lambasted theater companies as morally corrupt even before they had a chance to appear. Meeker set the standards in his community and urged the citizens "to keep up this practice forever and a day. We have amusements of various kinds," he wrote, "and what is best, they are got up by our own people. Our theatrical band, and children's concerts are first rate, and the money paid out stays with us." Other newly established towns in the territory were more welcoming but for many theatrical companies the potential audience was too small to undertake the expense of performing in them.[30]

Like actors, clergymen in early Colorado Territory gave sermons wherever they could find a place, often saloons. Many of the first ordained ministers were circuit riders, who preached or performed the sacraments any day of the week. Sometimes their efforts seemed fruitless because congregations might consist of as few as four or five individuals. By the end of the Civil War, however, permanent churches began to appear in Denver and the mining towns. Organizers of the new towns in the 1870s recognized the importance of religion to the settlers and donated land for churches and made efforts to help them get established.[31]

Roman Catholicism was late in organizing in the northern and central portions of Colorado but was the largest denomination in the territory, chiefly because Mexican Americans in the southern counties were strong adherents. At first authorities in Rome planned on attaching Colorado Territory to the Kansas bishopric, but after the bishop there pointed out the distance between eastern Kansas and Colorado, the territory was incorporated into the diocese of New Mexico. In 1860 the Reverend J. P. Machebeuf was transferred from Santa Fé to Denver, and he soon became one of the strongest voices in the territory on social and religious matters. Methodists comprised the second largest denomination in the territory with 1,070 members in 1872. During the territorial years Presbyterians, Episcopalians, and Baptists all built churches in various cities but congregations remained small. In 1868 the Reverend J. M. Wilkerson organized the African Methodist Episcopal Church in Denver, and the first Jewish synagogue opened in Denver in 1872. Lutheran and Christian Scientist congregations were not established until after Colorado achieved statehood. On the whole, though, congregations remained small and church attendance spotty.[32]

A number of circumstances influenced an individual's social life, among them financial ability and location. Denver, with its larger and more diverse population, offered a greater number of choices than did the towns on the Plains, whose population consisted chiefly of farmers and merchants who served their needs. Another limitation was race. Anglo-Coloradans, whether they had lived in the northern or southern states before immigrating to the territory, brought their prejudices with them and like most other white Americans they tended to look down upon non-Anglo races.

According to the 1870 census, 457 blacks lived in Colorado, and over half of them, 237, in Denver. The mining towns of Central City and Georgetown contained the next highest number, with 54 and 17 blacks respectively. By 1880 the black population increased to 2,435, with most residing in Denver. The remainder lived in Leadville, Colorado Springs, or Pueblo. The number of blacks in other cities was extremely small, ranging from a dozen or less to none at all.[33]

The census takers' reports for 1870 indicate that blacks in Denver held the more menial jobs or worked in professions relegated to minorities. The 230 blacks in the city included 105 males over 18 years of age. Of the 104 who listed their employment, 49 were "laborers." The remainder worked as domestic servants or porters, cooks or waiters, even painters. Some 14 blacks were engaged in barbering—a typical black trade in nineteenth-century America—although it is unclear how many of them were self-employed. There was also one school teacher, one minister, and a single restaurant-hotel owner. These figures reveal that while unemployment among black men appears low, they were primarily confined to the unskilled positions.[34]

Discrimination was evident in areas other than employment. Saloons and other public establishments ostracized blacks. While saloon keepers were willing to tolerate blacks as waiters, janitors, and cooks, they would not allow them as patrons. As a result, blacks established their own bars located mainly near the railroad tracks on Twenty-third Street, a rowdy neighborhood commonly referred to as the "Deep South." For those who did not want to venture into the area, Henry O. Wagoner maintained a tavern on Blake Street. Nor did white hotel owners cater to blacks. Maurice Morris, staying at the Tremont House, claimed the only "qualification for admission," besides the ability to pay, was "being Caucasian, for I do not think the President of Hayti himself—the greatest man of the proscribed race I can at the moment recall—would be admitted to its fellowship."[35]

While excluded from public places, blacks did not encounter discrimination in housing during the territorial period. Their residences were dispersed throughout the city until the 1890s. Then as whites moved out of Five Points, just northeast of the downtown, and relocated in the more fashionable Capitol Hill area, blacks moved into the vacated Victorians homes and established their own neighborhood.[36]

There was a small cadre of black leadership during the territorial years. William J. Hardin, Henry O. Wagoner, Edward Sanderlin, all barbers, and Barney L. Ford, owner of the Interocean Hotel, took the lead in speaking for the black population on matters of public interest or helping the less fortunate. In 1871 when a group of destitute, white colonists from Georgia arrived in Denver on their way to the southern part of the territory, it was Barney Ford, himself a former slave in Georgia, who provided dinner for the group. Black leaders also formed their own Masonic Lodge, known as the Rocky Mountain Lodge No. 7.[37]

Colorado's blacks also played an important role in the territory's political affairs after Congress passed the Territorial Suffrage Act in 1867. Indeed, it was the black vote in Arapahoe County that enabled the Republicans to win the election for delegate to Congress in 1868. The Republican candidate secured a mere seventeen-vote margin over his Democratic opponent—a victory made possible only by the 120 Republican black votes cast in Denver. Hoping to retain the support of black voters, white Republicans welcomed their participation in territorial party conventions. Hardin, known for his oratorical ability, often spoke at political conventions until he moved to Cheyenne in 1872. From then until 1875 Wagoner and Ford openly participated in political affairs. In March 1875, Wagoner, president of the Central Political Equal Rights League, forwarded a resolution of appreciation to U.S. Senator Charles Sumner for his work in bringing about the Civil Rights Act of that year.

On the eve of statehood, however, Colorado Republicans began to reflect the attitude of the national party, which had begun to lose interest in the plight of blacks and their participation in politics. In 1876 both the *Colorado Chieftain* and the *Colorado Tribune* focused on crimes committed by blacks. It may have been merely a matter of reporting the news, but given the limited size of each newspaper and the fact that most of the reported crimes occurred outside the territory, it appeared as if a firmer discriminatory attitude toward blacks was developing.[38]

Anglo-Coloradans seldom encountered Mexican Americans because they did not move north from the southern counties until the twentieth century. Still, most expressed a dislike for Spanish-speaking people and discriminated against them. White Coloradans assumed that Hispanos were lazy because of their more relaxed lifestyle, they considered their eagerness to hold fandangos as indicative of lack of seriousness, and they were suspicious of their Roman Catholicism. Almost without exception

English-language newspapers used the phrase "degraded and ignorant" before the word *Mexican.*[39]

Such attitudes, of course, were not universal. John Lawrence farmed in the San Luis Valley and his diary indicates a close relationship with his Mexican American neighbors. Lawrence boarded Hispano farmhands on his ranch, and mentioned Hispano friends. He also arbitrated difficulties between Mexican Americans and Anglos. James Rusling considered Mexican Americans "to be honest, simple folk, who took life as it came, without fret or worriment." A number of observers noted that despite Anglo criticism of the Spanish language, a number of words were creeping into their own language: Anglo-Coloradans called an animal enclosure a corral, a mud house an adobe, and often referred to a farm as a ranch.[40]

Non-landowning Mexican Americans, like blacks, held low-paying, service jobs. Sheep farmers hired boys as herders because they worked for as little as $50 a year. Men preferred higher-paying jobs as freighters but Anglos usually owned the companies they worked for. A. B. Legard reported that even though wages paid to Mexican Americans in Colorado were not high, they attracted men from both Mexico and New Mexico who also considered their treatment from Colorado employers to be better than it was back home.[41]

Landowning Hispanos were held in higher regard and Democratic politicians sought their support for party candidates. The staunch Democratic vote in the southern counties was needed to offset the usual Republican majorities in the north. U. B. Holloway expressed the general attitude when he wrote: "Whatever one may think of them as a people, one must count their votes." Political influence also allowed some Hispano men to become important in the territory's political affairs. For example, among the three Archuleta brothers, Donaciano served as a legislator, Marcelino became the first judge in Archuleta County, while Preciliano remained at home and ran the family's stock raising business. But on the whole Mexican Americans felt alienated and as more Anglos moved into their area, they left the territory.[42]

The chief complaints of Mexican Americans focused on two issues. First, they were exasperated by the failure of the territorial legislature to publish the statutes in Spanish despite repeated requests to do so. Second, they insisted that Mexican Americans who committed crimes were punished more severely than Anglo offenders. Even the *Colorado Chieftain,* which revealed no great sympathy for Hispanos, felt the former complaint was valid. Both California and New Mexico printed laws in Spanish and English, the editor argued, and if the Hispano people were required to meet the obligations of citizenship, they needed to be able to read and understand the laws that governed them.[43]

Two cases proved the argument about punishment. In 1873 two Mexican Americans and an Anglo were suspected of murdering a rancher and his wife near Trinidad. The vigilantes lynched the Hispanos but allowed the Anglo to escape. Mexican Americans in Trinidad were so enraged that they surged through the streets, vowing vengeance. Their anger subsided after they seized and hanged the woman who had named the suspects. Reports did not say whether she was Hispano or Anglo.

Earlier, in 1872, a Texas cattle herder named Baker and his party stopped at Jose Gonzales's ranch in Huerfano County and requested permission to camp for the night. Gonzales not only gave permission, but also provided dinner and breakfast for the Texans. When Baker attempted to rape Mrs. Gonzales, her husband interfered and Baker shot him. Fortunately, the wound was not fatal and Gonzales survived. But local Mexican Americans complained because Baker and his party fled and were never apprehended. Thomas Sproull, county sheriff, defended himself, claiming that his call for assistance from the Mexican American community went unheeded. Realizing that he would have to face a gang rather than one man, Sproull gave up the chase and returned home. This case contrasted sharply with a similar one in Golden in 1866. A Mexican American was hung after attempting to assault two women. In addition, several Hispano residents in the town, who did not even know the culprit, were ordered to leave the area on threat of also being hanged.[44]

Resentment between Anglo- and Mexican Americans flared into violence in the so-called Trinidad War of 1867. It began on Christmas Day when Frank Blue, a stage driver and gambler known for his violent temper, challenged anyone to a wrestling or boxing match. A Mexican American accepted but Blue's tactics were so rough that he broke the man's leg. This angered the Hispanos and a gunfight broke out during which one Mexican American was killed. Meanwhile, Blue fled to a nearby house where he was holed up until Sheriff Juan N. Gutierrez Jr. arrived and put him under guard in a separate building. There was no jail in Trinidad. For the next several nights Mexican Americans shot out the windows in the building and the sheriff made no attempt to stop them.

On New Year's Day, 1868, several of Blue's friends met at the local hotel and plotted to free him. They forced a deputy sheriff to release Blue and the group went back to the hotel. Sheriff Gutierrez laid siege to the hotel and by day's end two Mexican Americans had been killed and five wounded; there were no Anglo casualties. On January 3 Gutierrez called for troops to quell the disturbance. Even after Blue and several friends escaped, rumors spread that Mexican American bands, forming in Colorado and New Mexico, were on they way to Trinidad to join the battle. General Penrose, commander at Fort Lyon, arrived with troops on January 5 and proclaimed martial law, which temporarily calmed the volatile situation. After the lapse of a week, however, violence broke out between Hispanos and the soldiers, and three Mexican nationals were killed. The presence of the troops kept the situation under control but, even then, they were not withdrawn until spring.[45]

Acting Governor Frank Hall blamed the outburst on the "very worst class of Americans—thieves, murderers and desperadoes . . . whose daily incursions . . . kept the citizens in a chronic state of alarm." Looking at the situation with historical hindsight, Morris Taylor saw it as a "flare-up of ethnic rivalry and friction." The Anglo population, while still in the minority, was increasing, and many Mexican Americans were afraid of being driven out or suffering financially as Anglos replaced them in their jobs. Nevertheless, the whole affair made Mexican Americans leery of Anglo growth and influence and caused them to oppose statehood during the entire territorial period.[46]

Edward M. McCook, who became territorial governor in 1869, invited the first Chinese to the territory. He justified his action to the legislature, saying, "if we can first avail ourselves to their muscle, we can attend to their morals afterwards." There were only seven Chinese in 1870 but the number grew to 612 ten years later. Like Chinese immigrants to California two decades earlier, the early arrivals opened laundries in Denver or took up gold mining in areas whites considered too unproductive to be worthy of attention. One reporter described those in the mining regions as the "worst looking lot of human beings," he had ever seen. "Most of them are slim, cadaverous chaps who remind one forcibly of the grinning skeletons of an anatomical museum." But for the most part the Chinese outside of Denver caused little attention because their numbers were so few.[47]

In Denver, as in Sacramento and San Francisco, Chinese residents remained aloof from the general population but they were easily identified because of their Asian customs and dress, which they steadfastly retained. Still, the only continuous negative comment came from the *Colorado Tribune*, which had opposed the governor's efforts from the beginning. While admitting that Denver's Chinese were quiet, honest, and industrious, the editor objected to their presence because they saved rather than spent their money. When the Fairplay Gold Mining Company, unable to find white laborers, imported Chinese, the editor concluded that the jobs might help the Asians but the company's decision was bad for the economy because "they purchase less and contribute less" than any other group. During the first years of statehood Denver would witness a fierce anti-Chinese riot, but during the 1870s, with the Anglo population ever increasing, the number of Chinese was too small to cause much attention. Even the few whites who attended the celebration of the Chinese New Year in 1876 quickly grew bored with the festivities and soon left.[48]

The growth of towns witnessed changes in the society of territorial Colorado. The frontier atmosphere, while it did not disappear completely, declined to the point where foreigners and eastern Americans, alike, felt disappointed at their failure to perceive it immediately. True, crime and violence continued but the presence of women, children, schools, and churches acted as a calming influence on the predominantly male society. In racial matters, Coloradans reflected the attitudes found in other parts of the nation. The participation of blacks in political affairs became less important as the general population increased and the black vote became less influential in determining the outcome of elections. Colorado's feeling toward blacks mirrored that of most Americans, who lost interest in their plight during the 1870s. Anglo attitudes toward Mexican Americans and Chinese were similar to those held toward blacks, but Hispanos in Colorado, as in New Mexico, could not be ignored because of their numbers and their political importance. It was not the same for the Chinese. Without the right to vote and because of their small numbers, the Asian immigrants in Colorado, as in California, were regarded as a negative influence in society.

Along with the growth and development of society came social issues that some found objectionable. They sought to remove or ameliorate them and to build institutions that would improve the social climate in the territory as well as lay the foundations for statehood.

7 *Reform and Corruption*

Much of Colorado's territorial growth occurred during the Reconstruction era, 1865–76, one of the least understood decades in American history. Historians have emphasized the major national events of the period, mainly the political impasse between President Andrew Johnson and Congress and the racial and political problems in the postwar South. But less attention has been paid to events taking place in the northern states and the territories: demands for reform and growing divisions within the Republican Party. Many of the reforms predated the Civil War and included temperance, improvement in prison conditions, public assistance for the mentally and physically handicapped, as well as broader and more open education, and women's rights.

The prewar reform impetus came from the Republican Party, for during its early years the party had attracted both antislavery zealots and individuals interested in improving society. This latter group put aside their reform goals to support the war and bring about an end to slavery. When the fighting ended they began agitating again only to find that the party's more conservative element had lost interest in reform and was more concerned about retaining political power and reaping the benefits of a growing industrial society. Many of these conservatives soon acquired a reputation for being corrupt, and political infighting between conservatives and liberals became common. Indeed, by 1872 the reformers bolted the party, labeled themselves "Liberal Republicans," and joined the Democrats to oppose the reelection of Ulysses S. Grant and Republican policies generally.[1]

Colorado Territory was not immune from these trends. Reform movements and political disruption followed a similar pattern but on a smaller scale. Likewise, the reforms met the same fate; those that failed elsewhere met defeat in Colorado and those that succeeded were also adopted in the territory.

Temperance was widely advocated throughout the nation but never gained much support in the northern states. Nor was it successful in Colorado. Only the Methodists and the Christian Temperance Alliance, formed in 1872, called for an alcohol-free society. Their most notable achievement came in rural areas when, for example, 1,051 members of the Colorado Grange took the pledge in 1875 and resolved to encourage sobriety. Strongest resistance came from the cities and mining towns. In Denver the number of saloons was significant enough for visitors to comment about them. Isabella Bird described Denver as a saloon town where "whisky is significant of all evil and violence." A congressional report in 1873 estimated that twenty thousand people lived in Denver. In that same year the city contained nearly a hundred saloons.[2] South Pueblo became known for its "Dance Halls, variety theater and gambling rooms" almost as soon as construction of the town began. This situation existed because William J. Palmer designed the town as the manufacturing center for his Denver & Rio Grande Railroad and never forbade the sale of liquor. While Palmer designated Colorado Springs, where he built his home, as a temperance town, he saw no reason to restrict liquor in South Pueblo.[3]

For the predominantly male population in the larger cities and the mining towns, saloons filled a social need and both owners and patrons resisted attempts to close them. Those with dance halls offered female companionship; those without were places for friends to gather. One Englishman described saloons as the social centers of the West. In addition, saloons served the community in a number of other ways. Because of the lack of churches and theaters during the early days of the territory, religious services and dramatic performances were held in these drinking halls. Saloons were also altruistic institutions. Bartenders often contributed food to the less fortunate and offered them warm places to gather in bad weather. When yellow fever ravaged Denver in the 1870s, saloon keepers John Kinneavy and Frank Parker donated their receipts to fever victims.[4]

By custom, but not by law, Denver's saloons were segregated according to race and social standing, usually signified by the price the customer paid for beer or liquor. While anyone could enter a saloon that catered to the more socially elite, the prices charged and the general atmosphere discouraged him from staying. Moreover, the city's most prominent citizens almost never frequented public drinking establishments. Former Governor Evans and members of his political circle shunned barrooms and instead gathered weekly at his home at Fourteenth and Arapahoe streets. Evans was a staunch Methodist and may not have served liquor. Henry Teller, however, who lived in more rustic Central City, was reported to patronize Denver taverns whenever he was in town. Whether or not individuals with political ambitions frequented saloons, it was not wise to be seen in them too often. In 1865 the *Rocky Mountain News* noted that U.S. District Attorney Samuel Brown spent too much time in saloons and was noticeably drunk on occasion.[5]

Residents of Denver may not have been too concerned about the number of saloons because it was easy to avoid them; most were located in a twelve-block area on Blake, Larimer, and Market streets rather than spread throughout the city. And they remained in those locations as the city grew. While Denverites were not opposed to frequenting saloons in the city, they did not encourage them in the suburbs. Further, saloon owners preferred the downtown location because they were near other forms of vice and entertainment and the Denver Pacific Railroad station, all of which generated more business than might be found in suburban residential areas.[6]

Although the idea of temperance was more acceptable in smaller towns, especially those that banned alcoholic beverages, liquor was still available. Residents of Greeley could easily travel to Evans and those of Colorado Springs had nearby Colorado City, but the town's reputation for drunken brawls kept many Colorado Springs residents away. Even towns that banned the sale of liquor permitted drugstores to sell whiskey for medicinal purposes, and contemporary evidence indicates that druggists did not question their customers too closely. During the first year of Greeley's existence, the townspeople destroyed a saloon established by a German immigrant at the edge of town. Yet, they allowed two drugstores on the town's main street to sell whiskey. Hearing that liquor was readily available in Dr. Buchtel's drugstore, two temperance men made a purchase and then filed a complaint with town authorities. Confronted, Dr. Buchtel explained that he purchased whiskey for "up-country people" and purchased it in bulk so he could sell it cheaper. Buchtel insisted he was not violating the town's liquor ban because patrons who bought whiskey did not live in the city nor did they consume it within the town limits. Authorities dropped the matter after Buchtel promised not to sell liquor to Greeley residents except for medical reasons. Reporting the incident, the *Colorado Tribune* thought the doctor's explanation "somewhat muddy . . . but if it satisfies the Greeley colony, we, of Denver, certainly have no right to complain, . . . Naughty Dr. Buchtel!"[7]

Imbibers in Colorado Springs commonly used snakebite as an excuse to purchase whiskey in drugstores. A correspondent to the *Colorado Chieftain* wrote: "More people [in Colorado Springs] are snake bitten than in any town of its size I know of. . . . It is a little remarkable with what facility a man can get a prescription for snake bite in such a temperance town." But people did not have to fake snakebite to buy a drink. A storeroom on Tejon Street served as a kind of nineteenth-century speakeasy. It contained nothing but a wall that divided the building in half. The customer placed his money on a turntable in the wall and as it turned his money disappeared only to be replaced by the liquid of his choice. The proprietor of the LaFont House openly sold liquor in violation of the municipal ban, a situation authorities knew about. He periodically appeared in police court, paid his fine, and hurried back to his business.[8]

Individuals who disapproved of prohibition laws often attempted to overturn them. In Colorado Springs they tried to abolish the liquor ban on four different occasions during the territorial years. The editor of the Colorado Springs *Gazette,* a strong advocate of temperance, happily reported each failure. The proximity of Burlington to Longmont and the opposition of former Burlington residents to Longmont's ban on liquor caused only half-hearted enforcement. By 1875 the town council decided to issue liquor licenses so it could collect license fees and enlarge the town treasury.[9]

The situation was similar in Fort Collins. Before the town was founded, Larimer county commissioners, in 1864, granted liquor licenses for a $100 annual fee, but when the trustees incorporated the town they prohibited the "sale of vinous, spiritous, and intoxicating liquors, drug stores alone excepted." Within eighteen months citizens requested the repeal of the prohibition. When the trustees refused, the voters elected an entirely new board at the next election, and it immediately passed an ordinance permitting the issuance of liquor licenses for a $150 annual fee, later raised to $300. The *Greeley Tribune* criticized the move as nothing more than a money-making scheme. Not only would the town collect license fees, but police could also arrest and fine individuals who appeared on the streets inebriated.[10]

Along with the evils of liquor, prostitution came under close scrutiny in the post–Civil War era. Prostitutes had long engaged in their trade but during the war their numbers proliferated around military bases, making the general populace more aware of them. After the war, as many prostitutes moved to the northern cities, Republican reformers began to demand the total elimination of brothels. In most cases closure only succeeded in driving the prostitutes underground or onto the streets.[11]

In Colorado, prostitution existed in the mining camps and cities but was not an obvious problem in the new towns established on the Plains. If brothels were not located in the town, they were nearby. Colorado Springs had its Colorado City and Greeley had Evans, only four miles distant. More likely the situation in most places may have been similar to that in Fort Collins. Citizens were aware that a brothel operated on the outskirts of town but did their best to ignore it. Even in Denver, where prostitution flourished, most brothels were located in the neighborhood around Twentieth and Holladay streets, and most citizens could avoid them. Occasionally, however, some did complain. One letter to the *Colorado Tribune* blasted a certain house on Holladay Street as "a shame and disgrace upon the city of Denver and its authorities" and added that "decent people avoid the street and ladies walk several blocks out of their way."[12]

Where prostitution thrived, it took two forms. Younger and more attractive women worked in brothels where the price often depended upon the reputation of the house. Older and less appealing women plied their trade in cribs and charged much less. Women also worked in dance halls and saloons but, by most accounts, owners hired them to entertain the customers in the establishment and what they did beyond that was their own business.[13]

The *Rocky Mountain News* was the strongest voice in Denver against prostitution. Editor Byers displayed sympathy for prostitutes and blamed the existence of brothels on the men who patronized them and the authorities who permitted them to operate. Byers became especially critical when a group of men caught in a Thanksgiving eve raid in 1872 were fined only $18 each while the women were harassed and paid higher fines.[14]

While the *News* indicated a genuine interest in eliminating prostitution, its compassion was limited. In 1871 a group of Denver women, seriously concerned about the openness of the profession, suggested that prostitutes be taken from bordellos, found gainful employment, and housed with families who could provide care and set a high moral tone. Even though the flaws of such a plan were obvious, the *News* reacted in horror, predicting the destruction of the virtue of every woman in the city. "Let these fallen women stay in one quarter, as they are inclined to," wrote Byers, "and your sons and your daughters will be less likely to see their evil conduct and to be misled by it." In 1875, after physicians warned about the increasing rise of venereal disease, the Denver city council proposed an ordinance requiring prostitutes to be licensed and undergo periodic medical examinations. Again Byers complained: "to tax hard-working and virtuous people that the prostitute may be kept free from venereal disease for those who frequent her, seems not only execrable and unjust, but an open and disreputable premium to morality."[15]

After other city newspapers joined in the crusade against prostitution, Denver authorities began to raid bordellos more frequently. As in eastern cities where the same tactic had been tried, this only forced prostitutes onto the streets or dispersed them throughout the city. The city council fought back with an edict forbidding the ladies from showing "'undue prominence' upon the streets" and compelled them "to remain inside their houses while conducting business."[16]

Prostitution continued to flourish in Denver and by 1877 respectable ladies were bombarding the city council with petitions to close all brothels. Such appeals were unsuccessful. Business owners, police, and other authorities were often reluctant to put pressure on bordellos. In 1873, for example, citizens of Central City petitioned the aldermen to close a "certain house of ill repute." To avoid the issue they turned the matter over to the police, who did nothing. Brothels were a source of income for policemen who received kickbacks on a regular basis. They also brought visitors to town, who spent money in other places as well as in bordellos.[17]

Woman suffrage, of the many reforms proposed in the post–Civil War era, received considerable attention in the West. Even though Colorado's males were not won over quickly to the cause, agitation kept the question alive. Prompted by demands from the American Equal Rights Association and local lawmakers, the Kansas legislature in 1867 authorized a public referendum on voting rights for women. Although defeated in Kansas, the campaign received national attention and encouraged women in Colorado to seek the ballot. When Mrs. Gordon spoke publicly in favor of equal suffrage, she caused controversy by arguing that women were better qualified than black men to vote. Immediately Louis H. Douglass, son of the great abolitionist Frederick Douglass, angrily responded that "white women" did not have a stronger claim to the ballot than black men "because of the intelligence of the one, and ignorance of the other."[18]

The action of the Wyoming territorial legislature, hoping to stimulate immigration, again brought up the question in Colorado. In 1869 it gave women the right to vote. Not long after D. M. Richards, a Colorado territorial legislator, introduced a woman suffrage bill but found almost no support, even though former Governor Evans, one of Colorado's most respected citizens, favored the measure.[19]

Woman suffrage received a broader hearing in 1870 after Governor Edward McCook, in his annual message, recommended giving women the right to vote. Many citizens wrote letters criticizing or supporting the governor's suggestion. Negative arguments stressed women's emotional dependence upon their husbands and their stronger interest in home and children, and declared their fragile natures would be offended by the rough and tumble of politics. The strongest support came from mining communities. Willard Teller of Central City maintained that taxing women while denying them the right to vote violated the first principle of "our government." In a minority report to the legislative Council, Amos Speck and J. Wellington Nesmith, members from Gilpin County, concluded that it was not "unnatural" for women to request the right to vote. Nor did they think politics were too dirty or too difficult for women to understand. In fact, they suggested "that bringing women into politics will make politics cleaner." Even Susan B. Anthony and Elizabeth Cady Stanton, nationally known suffragists, came to Colorado to advocate the cause. Although he did not elaborate on their speeches, George Kassler thought Anthony too "strident," while Stanton's motherly demeanor made her the more effective speaker.[20]

Due partly to McCook's general unpopularity and the unwillingness of legislators to admit women to the polls, the governor's recommendation fell on deaf ears. But it would not go away. Even a month after the legislature rejected the reform, letters of support continued to appear in local newspapers. And the issue would come up more strongly during the constitutional convention of 1876.[21]

Social legislation during territorial days centered on the care of paupers and deaf, blind, and dependent children. The lack of funds, however, often caused the legislature to shift the responsibility to other agencies. When, for example, in 1865, legislators saw a need for poorhouses, they authorized counties to establish them. Unfortunately, most counties were less affluent than the territorial government and the few institutions established were inadequate and poorly maintained. The Ladies' Union Aid Society, organized by Elizabeth Byers and Margaret Evans during the war to provide clothing for militia volunteers, reorganized itself as the Ladies Relief Society in 1874. It provided a home for indigent women and arranged for men and boys to receive food and shelter in exchange for their labor. Margaret Evans, with the support of many prominent women in Denver, also opened an orphanage in 1872.[22]

The Colorado School for the Deaf and Blind was the first institution for the handicapped to receive support from the territorial legislature. Labeled "the most important benevolent enterprise of the Territory," the school was the inspiration of Jonathan R. Kennedy, the father of several deaf children. To persuade the legislature of the school's necessity, Kennedy brought deaf and blind children before the body and pointed out that most had received no education at all. In response the lawmakers appropriated $5,000 while the Colorado Springs Land Company donated ten acres for the school. The institution was patterned after the Kansas School for the Deaf at Olathe, and John P. Ralstin, from the Kansas school, became its first principal. It opened in April 1874, with twelve students and within two years the student body grew to twenty. The deaf and blind school was so successful that it encouraged the state legislature to open the State Insane Asylum in Pueblo in 1879. Before then mentally handicapped individuals were sent to the state institution in Jacksonville, Illinois, one of the outstanding institutions of its kind in the nation.[23]

Besides institutions for the unfortunate, the territory also acquired a penitentiary. Until the prison opened on June 6, 1871, offenders were housed in county jails or in military guard houses where they existed. Territorial law required counties to build and operate prisons at their own expense; thus, many were outmoded or poorly maintained. Counties without prisons sent their wrong-doers to other counties, while hardened criminals were often transferred to prisons in other territories or states.

By 1868 penal facilities had become so inadequate and the system so cumbersome that the territorial legislature authorized the construction of a penitentiary at Cañon City. The federal government contributed $37,000, and the U.S. Department of the Interior supervised construction. When completed the penitentiary contained forty-two cells, each six by eight feet in dimension. According to one newspaper account, the cells were well ventilated and furnished and each contained a moveable bed, a wash basin, a large wooden slop bucket, and a stool. Each prisoner received an adequate supply of sheets, blankets, and towels; fresh linens were supplied weekly. Prisoners exercised daily and received meals in their cells. The reporter concluded that the "prisoners are well clothed, fed and appear to be as robust a set of men as found on the outside."[24]

Public education evolved slowly in Colorado Territory. In 1861 the legislature authorized the levying of district and county taxes to support education and established the office of superintendent of common schools. Few communities, however, imposed the taxes and most education remained private. By the end of the Civil War the superintendent's office ceased to exist and only Denver, Boulder, and Golden had established public schools. The lack of interest elsewhere was attributed to "the predominance of single men in the population" but was also due to the small number of school-age children. The 1860 census listed only 1,017 children between the ages of five and fifteen, and the number did not increase substantially during the war years. In addition, parents were not required to send their children to school. Indeed, the last superintendent, noting the phlegmatic interest of many parents, suggested that education monies from the territorial treasury should be apportioned to counties on the basis of attendance and not school-age population.[25]

Events within and outside the territory sparked a new interest in education by 1870: the increase in the school-age population, the immigration of families, and an increasing concern about public education throughout the nation. These changes encouraged the legislature to reestablish the office of superintendent of public instruction and to pass a compulsory attendance law. Localities that had not previously provided public education quickly built school houses, and all the towns established during the 1870s made public education a high priority. Denver, Boulder, and Pueblo established high schools. Denver schools were segregated but resistance from black parents and demands for equal facilities brought an end to the system in 1871. Between 1870 and 1875 the school-age population in Colorado tripled, from 6,308 to 21,962, and number of schools increased to 175.[26]

Coloradans revealed an interest in higher education early; however, universities were slow to develop. In 1861 the legislature incorporated the University of Colorado but the unstable economy, Native American problems, and the declining population during the war discouraged further progress. As a result, the first classes were not held until 1877. In 1870, encouraged by the expansion of higher education in many eastern states because of the Land Grant College Act, the legislature authorized the establishment of the "Agricultural College of Colorado," which eventually became Colorado State University. The federal act gave to every loyal state thirty thousand acres of land for each senator and representative for the purpose of endowing at least one agricultural college. But Colorado did not receive the land grant until it achieved statehood; as a result, the agricultural college did not open its doors until 1879.

Pushed by both the mining interest and the city of Golden, which desired compensation for losing the territorial capital to Denver in 1867, the legislature took a greater interest in education for mining engineers.

In 1870 it appropriated $3,800 for Episcopalian Bishop George M. Randall to begin instruction in mining at Jarvis Hall, part of the College of St. John the Evangelist in Golden. Randall transferred the entire enterprise to the territory in 1874, and the legislature, after approving $5,000 for an additional building and maintenance, renamed the institution the Colorado School of Mines.[27]

Until the economy became more varied and the population increased in the 1870s, lack of money was the major impediment to furthering higher education. Not only was the territory too poor, but it lacked the ability to collect taxes. Until the mid-1870s every attempt to gain an appropriation for the University of Colorado failed. The legislature finally allocated $15,000, but only after the citizens of Boulder promised an additional $6,500. Another $15,000 grant the next year plus seventy-two sections of land as a federal grant when Colorado entered the Union ensured the university's future.[28]

Nor were other towns in Colorado ready to accept the sites chosen for the universities. Even though the legislature selected Boulder as the seat of the state university, Denver, Golden, and Pueblo each coveted the institution. The most serious threat came from Burlington (later Longmont), and as a result the people of Boulder organized a campaign under the slogan "Give Boulder the University, and the rest of Colorado may take all other institutions." Realizing they were engaging in a losing battle, Burlington's residents finally agreed to host the annual county fair instead. Cañon City hoped to lure the agricultural college away from Fort Collins, but finally opted for the prison, which was to be built with federal funds and, therefore, was more likely to be completed.[29]

Opposition to funding higher education also discouraged the legislature from being too generous. The $3,800 grant to Bishop Randall in 1870 provoked widespread protests, in part because of the school's religious affiliation. When the state legislature debated a grant to the agricultural college in 1877, a Pueblo representative declared, "I feel as if it is throwing money away, for you never can make Colorado an agricultural state. It is only fit for cow pasture and mining." More outspoken against higher education was Nathan Meeker. "There are not probably twenty-five young people in the Territory who, at present, could afford to attend a University and take the regular course," he wrote. Meeker concluded that "it would be cheaper" to provide subsidies to Colorado students to attend "some Eastern college" than to tax the public to support public institutions in Colorado.[30]

Private, church-related colleges faced an even more difficult financial challenge than state institutions. Bishop Randall offered the Episcopal college to the territorial government when he realized the futility of attempting to gain public financial backing. John Evans launched the Colorado Seminary in 1864, patterning it after Northwestern University, which he helped establish in 1855. The declining population and lack of funds forced the school to close in 1867 but it reopened in 1886 as the University of Denver.[31]

The most successful venture in private higher education during the territorial years was Colorado College, which had been incorporated into William Palmer's design for Colorado Springs. In 1874 Palmer offered seventy acres and a $10,000 grant to Congregationalists to establish the school, and he persuaded the territorial legislature to grant it a charter. Even before a campus was established the first classes opened in a rented downtown building. To ensure the growth of a student body, Colorado College's first president, the Reverend Edward Payson Tenney, encouraged local youths to enroll despite their religious or ethnic background. He also established preparatory schools in Salt Lake City, Trinidad, and Santa Fé to serve as feeders for the college. When the college seemed to be on the verge of collapse in 1876, Tenney appealed to Congregationalists in the East for funds. In 1882 the Colorado Springs *Gazette* declared that money contributed by New Englanders had paid the cost of operating the college for its first eight years. The editor also asserted, "This college year the expenses for tuition and other purposes will amount to $10,000 and all this is paid by eastern People."[32]

In addition to reform, the Reconstruction period was also characterized by political infighting among Republicans. As issues arising from the war faded after 1868, liberal Republicans found fault with the conservative element. In addition to their reluctance to correct the evils of society, conservatives seemed unwilling to curb political corruption and reduce the influence of big business over government. As already noted, these disagreements caused political disruption at the national level. Within the states, factions quarreled over similar issues and engaged in power struggles. While the Republican Party continued to dominate national politics during the late nineteenth century, their infighting allowed Democrats to regain some small measure of control at both the national and state levels.

Colorado territorial politics followed this national trend. From its inception, the territory had been a Republican stronghold. The lack of a united Democratic opposition allowed Republicans to split over issues and still retain political control. The major division was between Republicans in Denver and those outside the city. Those in Denver, dubbed the "Denver Ring" by their enemies, were led by Samuel Elbert, John Evans,

David Moffat, and Jerome Chaffee. Ring members included the territory's main boosters and some of its leading businessmen. In addition, most of them had been members of the Denver Crowd in the postwar years. They hoped to build a society where governmental stability furthered economic growth, and they were not above using their political position or friendships to achieve their goals. Although he was never seated in the U.S. Senate, John Evans spent several years in the national capital as senator-elect and made many friends to whom he appealed in later years to secure land grants for his railroad projects. While serving as territorial delegate, Jerome Chaffee corresponded with the secretary of the treasury requesting that the Denver Land Office be urged to conduct all its financial business with the First National Bank of Denver instead of the Colorado National Bank, even though the latter had twice as much money in bonds deposited with the Treasurer of the United States. Chaffee did not mention, however, that he was also president of the First National.[33]

Outside of Denver, Republicans regarded Henry Teller as their spokesman and leader, and the two groups eyed each other with suspicion during the entire territorial period. Smaller towns, especially, expressed concerns about Denver's political dominance. Irving Stanton, registrar of the land office in Pueblo, revealed the anti-Denver attitude: "Denver thinks she is the State and we frankly admit that she is a large and important part of it. . . . Denver is progressive and aggressive; she wants everything in sight and takes what she gets. Denver's singleness of purpose and generous liberality-for Denver-are well-nigh relentless." Another individual stated his feelings more personally: "About Ex-Gov. Evans and his son-in-law Judge Elbert there is much humbug. They are cold blooded mercenary men, ready to praise themselves and each other profusely, but have in reality but little patriotism."[34] And while most Coloradans expressed negative opinions of federal officials sent to govern them, opposition newspapers often found themselves defending the appointee most resented by the "Denver Ring."

With the demise of the statehood question in the late 1860s, political calm descended upon the Republican Party. It soon ended, however, when Ulysses S. Grant unceremoniously removed Alexander Hunt as governor in June 1869, and replaced him with Edward Moody McCook. Grant could not have known the future impact of his action, but McCook's appointment caused political disruption in Colorado that lasted until the eve of statehood. Reviewing the situation from 1870 to 1875, the *New York Times* concluded that "local politics in the Territory have been at times uncommonly foul."[35]

McCook had lived in Colorado from 1859 to 1861, when he returned to Ohio to join the U.S. Army as a first lieutenant. He commanded a cavalry division on the western front, where he and Grant became friends. By war's end McCook rose to the brevet rank of major general. After the war he received an appointment as minister resident to Hawaii but resigned upon Grant's election. He soon arrived in Washington, D.C., to request the Colorado governorship.[36]

Upon hearing of McCook's appointment, Coloradans raised the issue of carpetbaggerism. Overlooking the new governor's previous residence in the territory, the Republican *Colorado Tribune,* which would become one of McCook's most ardent supporters, wrote: "The great fault we have to find is that Eastern men . . . who have no claim to govern us, are given the preferences over our own citizens, as though we had no rights which the Administration was bound to respect."[37]

McCook made a number of political blunders upon his arrival in the territory. He immediately allied himself with Henry Teller, which won him no friends in the Denver Ring. Next, he appointed James B. Thompson, his brother-in-law, as private secretary, auditor of public accounts, and special agent to the Utes. While nepotism was common in political appointments, Thompson's many jobs made his influence over the governor seem unduly strong. Finally, McCook soon made it apparent that he was more concerned with dabbling in land speculation, railroad projects, and cattle ranching than in governing.

The first year of McCook's administration passed without achievement. He failed to persuade the legislature to pass a woman suffrage bill. He also asked the legislature to remove the voting restriction against blacks from the territorial voting law on the grounds that the Territorial Suffrage Act and the Fifteenth Amendment made the restriction inoperative. The lawmakers ignored his request.[38]

The beginning of McCook's downfall came with the election of Jerome Chaffee as delegate to Congress in 1870 and in his dealings with the Utes. A leader in the Denver Ring, Chaffee had no sympathy for McCook and became his chief critic once he arrived in the national capital. McCook had no sympathy for the Utes, described them as "indolent savages," and condemned the treaty of 1868 for setting apart a large portion of western Colorado for their exclusive use. His attitude was unfortunate because as governor, McCook also served as superintendent of Indian affairs for Colorado and was required to carry out the provisions of the 1868 treaty. He soon figured out that he could observe them and profit at the same time.[39]

Among the provisions was a stipulation that the Utes were to receive periodic shipments of cattle and sheep, and that the cows had to be superior American cattle. In 1869 McCook accepted a bid to purchase 750 "good American cows" for $45.75 each. The bid immediately raised the suspicions of Hiram Bennet and George Chilcott, members of the Denver Ring who had also submitted bids, and they undoubtedly let them be known. Subsequent investigations by detectives and records from the First National Bank in Denver indicated that McCook was cheating the government out of thousands of dollars. The successful bidder was C. F. Holt, a relative of McCook's by marriage, and the cows, described as "a very poor lot of scrawny Texas cattle," had originally been purchased by McCook for $7.50 apiece. Indeed, the cattle were so puny that the Utes refused to accept them. The government made a payment of $30,000 to Holt but the money was deposited in McCook's account. Deducting the original amount paid for the cattle and the $800 McCook paid for Holt's services, the governor netted a profit of between $22,000 and $23,000.[40]

Further investigations implicated McCook in a number of questionable money transactions. In one instance, he extorted $1,000 from the surveyor general of Colorado for using his influence to save the man's job. In another, McCook refused to pay a supplier $5,000 for goods supplied to the Utes and the man settled for $2,000. McCook, however, billed the federal government $5,000 and deposited the $3,000 in his own account. And the governor was careless about discharging his duties. In 1870 the legislature granted a divorce, which only it, and not the courts, had the power to grant. By law McCook was required to sign the divorce decree within ten days of the legislature's adjournment. When seven months later the couple requested a certified copy of the bill from the territorial secretary's office, they discovered the decree had not been signed. Since the man had remarried in the interim, he was legally a bigamist. Leaving the office for a brief time, the couple returned to find the bill freshly signed by the governor and predated to the day of its passage.[41]

By December 1872, Denver Republicans were determined to prevent McCook's reappointment for a second term. Using the same tactic they had used against Governor Cummings in 1867, they began circulating petitions exposing McCook's crimes and requesting his removal. These were then sent to Washington, D.C., where Chaffee pressured Grant to remove the governor and nominate Samuel Elbert in his place.

The *Rocky Mountain News,* mouthpiece of the Denver Ring, insisted that the petition drive was a spontaneous, popular movement, but James Thompson thought otherwise. He informed McCook that

Elbert, Bennet, and Byers were heading the "drive for your removal." The group had traveled throughout the territory to collect signatures, and even Frank Hall was "not attending to duties as Acting Gov." Determined to replace McCook with Elbert, the group "is telling his friends and those who will listen that you have resigned and have recommended him for the Governorship." Perhaps not to appear too anxious, Elbert spread a rumor that Bennet initiated the petition drive, a rumor that Thompson denied: "I know that [Elbert] was in the caucus that got up the thing and I also know he was very active in Pueblo, Greeley and Evans putting forth his claim for the governorship."[42]

Faced with the petitions and the charges against McCook, Grant removed the governor and appointed Elbert, whose governorship lasted only ten months, from March 9, 1873, to January 27, 1874. During that time McCook, determined to regain his office, remained in Washington, D.C., where he had gone to defend himself, and exposed every scandal that erupted in the territory. While Elbert was not directly involved in any of them, they indicated that his supporters were venal and unscrupulous. The first scandal was minor; yet, it strengthened the general impression of rampant political corruption.

Upon assuming office, Elbert had appointed Anson Rudd of Cañon City as superintendent of the new penitentiary. It also happened that Rudd was part owner of an unfinished irrigation ditch that ran through prison property. To complete the ditch a tunnel needed to be cut through a solid rock formation. Whatever Rudd's plans before becoming superintendent, he now used convict labor to complete the ditch, without compensating the territory or paying the prisoners. The work increased the value of the ditch by $2,500. When the matter was discovered, Rudd produced a contract between the prison directors and the ditch company that granted the penitentiary fifty inches of water a year for irrigation purposes in return for the prisoners' labor. But the *Colorado Tribune* remained suspicious of the arrangement. First, the land on which the prison had been built was so infertile, the editor surmised, that, even if irrigated, it would produce nothing but sagebrush. Second, the contract was not drawn up until four weeks after the work began and only after Rudd discovered that the matter was being investigated. The *Tribune* concluded its own investigation by writing: "When Colorado gets a new governor, we will get an honest warden."[43]

The second scandal, known as the Las Animas land grab, involved 4,800 acres along the Arkansas River in southern Colorado. The land was initially part of two Mexican land grants, and farmers had lived on it with the consent the owners. In February 1873, Congress opened the land to pre-emption and homestead claims. In fairness to those living there, Congress gave them one year to file their claims before any others could be filed. But before the farmers filled out any papers, one D. W. Hughes informed the Pueblo Land Office, through his lawyer, that he held previous rights to 4,800 acres of the land. His statement automatically prevented the residents living on this land from filing their own claims. Hughes's statement was immediately suspect because the land he claimed lay along the projected route of the Atchison, Topeka and Santa Fé Railroad and would greatly increase in value when the railroad was completed. Hughes withdrew his claim several months later but by the time the farmers found out, a year had passed and other claims for the land had already been filed, approved, and patented. Investigating the matter, the residents learned that no one had ever seen or heard of the new claimants and that they had transferred their titles, through a third party, to David Moffat and Robert E. Carr. Moffat and Carr were political cohorts of Governor Elbert and also trustees for the Arkansas Railroad Company. The angry farmers petitioned both Congress and the territorial legislature to investigate the matter, insisting that the scheme was nothing more an attempt to grab off large chunks of the public domain at little or no cost.[44]

In January 1874, the commissioner general of the General Land Office sent M. B. Robinson to investigate the charges. Robinson found no evidence to implicate Carr or Moffat, but his report insinuated that Charles A. Cook, a land office employee, was involved. "Someone connected with the Pueblo Land Office did know the character of these transactions and aided and abetted the fraud," Robinson concluded. He pointed out that the claims had been filed under false names and none of the claimants actually existed. It "is the belief of everyone I have met. . . . that the preemptors were prepared in Denver" and "Cook was in Denver when the preemptors were made out." Robinson also noted that "Cook was at one time partners with Moffat and Jerome B. Chaffee in the banking business in Denver. He spends most of his time in Denver [and] is on intimate terms with Moffat." Both Robinson and the commissioner general recommended that all personnel at the Pueblo Land Office be removed and that the Department of Justice institute criminal proceedings for fraud and perjury against all the individuals involved. On the basis of Robinson's report, the U.S. district attorney for Colorado called for a grand jury investigation, which indicted Moffat, Carr, and Cook for fraud.[45]

In his later history of Colorado, Frank Hall defended Elbert and asserted that his enemies engineered the whole scheme for the sole purpose of forcing his removal from office. When the U.S. District Court heard the case in 1878, it dismissed all charges for lack of evidence and ordered the land open again to pre-emption. While the court agreed that the previous claims were fraudulent because the parties who filed them did not exist, it could not prove that Moffat, Carr, or Cook were aware of the fraud.[46]

But the decision came too late. The damage had already been done, and many Coloradans assumed that members of the Denver Ring were just as corrupt as McCook. While the *Rocky News* insisted that fraud had not occurred, most newspapers in the territory, Democratic as well as Republican, criticized the entire scheme.[47] The *Greeley Tribune* expressed the general editorial attitude outside of Denver:

> For a long time Denver has been about the same thing as Colorado, and whatever was done there could injure scarcely anybody outside, because there was nobody outside. If they wanted land . . . they seized it, and nobody objected. . . . Now they have come into conflict with others who want a chance. It is quite likely that the people in the Arkansas valley wanted an opportunity to select choice land, . . . but the Denver ring, by the help of the Pueblo land office, was too sharp for them. This grabbing of land has been going on so long that it is likely that Denver people thought themselves perfectly in the right, and they had but a dim consciousness that they were committing perjury and fraud. . . . All this is far from being peculiar to Denver, only they have had a longer swing. The land laws are so imperfect that all new countries nurture a big corp [crop?] of perjured rascals.[48]

Suspicions about corruption in high circles were only strengthened when Elbert appointed Moffat as territorial treasurer, giving the impression that Moffat was being rewarded. At the same time members of the Denver Ring began petitioning President Grant to remove Moses Hallett as chief justice of the territorial supreme court. Inasmuch as Hallett was known to be politically independent but not sympathetic to the ring, the move appeared to many as an attack on the judicial system. With the Robinson report before him and with McCook undoubtedly keeping him abreast of every new rumor from the territory, Grant responded by reappointing Hallett to a second term but dismissing Elbert, Hall, and W. S. Lessig, surveyor general for Colorado.[49]

Stunned by their termination, both Hall and Elbert inquired about the reasons from friends in Washington, D.C. Schuyler Colfax informed Hall that his removal came merely to make the real reason less pointed: Grant was intent on getting rid of Elbert. The president was not dissatisfied with Hall's performance but felt that since the secretary had been in office since 1866, it was appropriate to remove him at this time. Mollified, Hall accepted the situation: "This removal has not made me a sorehead, nor will it drive me into hostility to my party." Elbert's response was less conciliatory. Ignoring a mass meeting in Denver held to protest the Las Animas land grab, Elbert insisted, "There has never been a period in the territory when the people are more satisfied with the Governor." Nor did he seem aware that Henry Teller, when called upon to speak at the meeting, was cheered upon saying, "the people of Colorado have been dissatisfied with [Elbert's] administration [because he] governs the territory for the benefit of the few." Elbert also thought it unfair that he should be removed for acts committed at the Pueblo Land Office because he did not appoint officials there and had no control over them. That Grant should disapprove of his appointment of Moffat perplexed Elbert. Not only was it made at Chaffee's request but there was no "well founded objection to the man himself" in the territorial Council, Elbert wrote, and the body could have easily rejected the nomination.[50]

Grant added insult to injury by nominating McCook to replace Elbert. He also nominated John Jenkins of Virginia and T. B. Searight of Pennsylvania to serve as territorial secretary and surveyor general respectively, and both men won easy confirmation. But the fight to approve McCook lasted five months. In Colorado reaction to McCook's appointment was mixed. Democratic newspapers and Republican journals opposed to the ring expressed approval. The *Colorado Chieftain* declared that only Elbert's "sonship in the Evans family makes him more available than McCook."[51] Even Henry Teller thought, "if McCook is confirmed we will have the Ring broken up completely." Elbert's supporters regarded McCook's nomination as a personal affront, and Chaffee was particularly disconcerted. Prior to the dismissal of Elbert, Chaffee and Grant had been close personal friends. According to tradition the two men fell out over a poker game, but the appointment struggle in Colorado probably played a major role in ending the friendship. At any rate, they were no longer speaking and the confirmation struggle became something of a personal feud. Chaffee even threatened to resign if McCook was confirmed but failed to follow through with the threat.[52]

In Washington, D.C., many senators expressed their surprise and opposition to Grant's appointment. Given the corruption of McCook's first administration, Senate approval seemed doubtful. But Grant became determined to win Senate confirmation even though Chaffee and a delegation of his supporters from Colorado fought to prevent it. During the months of testimony further accusations were leveled against McCook but still the Senate, by a one-vote majority, confirmed McCook as governor on June 19, 1874.[53]

Upon his return to Colorado, McCook sought revenge by persuading Grant to remove every political appointee that Chaffee had recommended. These included all Colorado land office officials and two justices of the territorial supreme court. Grant seemed only too willing to comply. He filled the vacancies with men who did not live in the territory, creating resentment and raising further cries from the locals that Colorado was being ruled by carpetbaggers. McCook was less successful when he tried to replace Elbert's appointees. They all refused to vacate their post, maintaining they had been appointed for fixed terms and could not be removed beforehand without cause. The U.S. attorney general upheld their argument and added that McCook's attempt to remove the men was illegal.

McCook's second administration lasted only eight months, and was a downhill slide all the way. The discontent caused by the new federal appointees and the bitter feuding among the Republicans renewed the desire for statehood and the opportunity for Coloradans to control their own destiny. The death of his wife, Mary, undoubtedly added to McCook's personal despondency, and, according to Frank Hall, "his drinking and moral conduct soon caused his supporters to desert him and it was not soon before he stood alone." Seeing the futility of retaining McCook, Grant secured his resignation and replaced him with John L. Routt. A plain-spoken Kentuckian with a reputation for honesty, Routt was made fully aware of the schism within the territorial Republican Party and was given the task of uniting the factions and preparing the territory for statehood.[54]

The negative impact of political infighting between 1872 and 1875 began to take effect almost immediately. Not only did the rift divide the Republican Party, but it also made rural Coloradans think that Denver was the root of all evil. Traveling through the mining districts and villages of the territory, a Denver newspaper reporter wrote, "We found an unfriendly feeling toward Denver. It comes from the general belief that people of Denver look down upon the rest of territory." SAJ, a resident of the Platte Cañon in Douglas County, blamed the territory's troubles on "that rotten Denver Ring" and urged the editor of the *Colorado Tribune* to "bury the entire pack of Ring scoundrels." Residents of southern Colorado blamed Denverites for giving visitors a negative impression of their region. "It has come to our attention," wrote the Colorado Springs *Gazette,* "that a number of hotels in Denver are telling people that there is nothing in this part of the territory worth traveling to. It is right that people will think their city the best," the editor continued, but those in Denver "step beyond this and besmirch the character of their neighbors." Several towns in northern Colorado leveled a similar charge, claiming, "the people [of Denver] are doing all in their power to persuade people to settle in the southern part of the territory."[55]

Political infighting among Republicans allowed the Democrats to elect a territorial delegate to Congress for the first time in the territory's history. The national Democratic Party began to regain some of its influence by taking control of the House of Representatives in 1874, and Colorado Territory was following the trend. Republicans came to their territorial convention in the fall of 1874 so split that reconciliation seemed impossible. One group called for resolutions condemning "land-grabbers," while another demanded the denunciation of President Grant and the carpetbaggers he had sent to rule the territory. Denver Republicans re-nominated Chaffee, who refused to run, and those outside the city gave the nod to H. P. H. Bromwell, a lawyer who had previously lived in Illinois and had been a member of Congress.[56]

Sensing victory, Democrats gathered in Colorado Springs and nominated Thomas M. Patterson, a newcomer who had come from Indiana in 1872 and practiced law in Denver. When the election results came in, Patterson won by a vote of 9,255 to 7,170. There were several reasons for Patterson's success: by electing a Democrat, Coloradans were repudiating Grant and his carpetbagger appointees; Patterson won because Republicans, disgusted about the infighting, did not vote; and Bromwell failed to secure backing from all Republicans because they thought he was McCook's choice. Contemporary newspapers placed the blame for the division within the Republican Party. "It is evident that the people are tired of war between the two republican [*sic*] factions for the spoils of office," wrote the *Fort Collins Standard.* "The fight . . . is a lasting disgrace to the territory and all those connected with either ring." The *Gazette* in Colorado Springs reached a similar conclusion: "Republicans have suffered a Democratic candidate, with little of qualification to recommend him, to win the race, and the Republican candidate . . . has been defeated because he rested under the suspicion of being favorable to the [McCook] regime."[57]

In the decade after the Civil War political infighting in Colorado reached such intensity that governors found it more and more difficult to govern. The territory had five governors during this period. Remarking on the rapid changeover, the Laramie (Wyoming) *Sentinel* stated: "We don't reckon there was ever a territory or state that required so many governors for home consumption as Colorado, and her future historians will likely go crazy in tracing out and recording them." According to Grace Greenwood, writing in 1873 during the height of the Elbert-McCook fight, the "general favorite [among the governors] in Colorado is Governor Hunt."[58] Several reasons accounted for this. Generally, people who lived in the territories regarded federal appointees from the outside as satraps, and territorial Coloradans expressed similar feelings. Hunt's long residence qualified him as a "native Coloradan," and few during his administration felt they were being governed by an outsider. Unlike the other governors of the period, Hunt dealt fairly with people, especially Native Americans, and there was no hint of personal dishonesty in his administration. But the end of his administration ushered in a period of political disruption that lasted for the remainder of the territorial period. It is interesting to ponder what turns Colorado's political history might have taken if President Grant had never appointed McCook and retained Hunt in office.

8 Statehood at Last

Colorado's final push for statehood began in 1872 and culminated four years later, in 1876. It came at a time when the nation appeared to be on the verge of economic and political unrest. A depression following the Panic of 1873 heightened a rising tide of discontent on both the agrarian and labor fronts. Businessmen engaged in cutthroat practices to eliminate their competition and, having achieved their goal, raised prices to recover any losses they had incurred. Partisan politics entered into public issues and sometimes determined their outcomes. Fearful of losing their control of the federal government because of scandal and corruption, Republicans utilized the same tactic they had used in 1864: admitting new states to influence the outcome of a presidential election. All these factors played a role in Colorado's last quest to enter the Union.[1]

Following the failure to achieve statehood in the post–Civil War years, Coloradans turned to more immediate concerns. Occasionally a newspaper editor or Denver politician raised the question of statehood but, on the whole, a general apathy about the issue prevailed. Nor was there any effort to raise the matter in Congress. In fact, Allen Bradford, Colorado's delegate between 1868 and 1871, opposed statehood and was only too willing to give the impression that Coloradans were not anxious for admission because the population was too small to assume the financial burdens of statehood. Moreover, Republicans in Congress saw little advantage in admitting the territory. They controlled both houses of Congress, the presidency, and most of the state governments and, for the moment, Colorado's political support was of little consequence.[2]

Governor McCook's political manipulations brought a change of attitude in the territory. The appointment of outsiders during his administration created resentment and raised complaints of carpetbag rule. "We have become tired, sick and disgusted of territorial pupilage and carpet-bag appointees and would rather 'paddle our own canoe,'" complained the *Colorado Chieftain.* A correspondent to the *New York Times* criticized federal appointees more directly. Territorial governors, he wrote, consider the territories as a place of exile and "the people look upon them and their associates as satraps, and themselves as very badly used in the matter of Federal appointments."[3]

A more concerted effort for statehood began when Jerome Chaffee replaced Bradford as delegate to Congress in 1871. A member of the Denver Ring, which had advocated statehood from the beginning, Chaffee took measures to strengthen the territory's chances for admission. To overcome the objection of a small population, Chaffee proposed annexing the southern portion of Wyoming Territory to Colorado. He saw two advantages in this scheme. First, it would increase Colorado's population; second, it would enhance the economic base because the Union Pacific Railroad ran through the proposed transfer. The idea had long been at the back of Chaffee's mind. As early as 1867 he wrote that he would do anything possible "to prevent any new territory being organized north of us because I covet a slice there." But the suggestion was not well received. While the *Rocky Mountain News* supported the plan as a means of giving "the people full control of their own Government and the choice of their officials," editors throughout the territory decried the idea as a scheme to "get our State admitted, even though we have to pillage the rights and property of our neighbors to accomplish it." Opposition was especially strong in the southern counties, where many believed that annexing part of Wyoming "would put Southern Colorado more outside the center of the state than it already is," and would "unite our interest with the Union Pacific. It ignored Colorado in building westward," wrote the *Colorado Chieftain,* "so why do we think it will benefit our interest now?" Made aware of the opposition at home and concerned about creating unfavorable impressions in Congress, Chaffee dropped the matter.[4]

Next, Chaffee introduced a resolution in the House of Representatives, requesting that one seat on the Committee on Territories be reserved for a territorial delegate. After the resolution was approved, Chaffee worked to secure the appointment for himself and used his position to work on Colorado's behalf. His ensuing move came in a measure to abolish all the territories. In their place he proposed combining the territories and then admitting them immediately or attaching them to existing states. The plan would have combined Colorado and Wyoming. Almost no one favored the idea and it was quickly shelved. Finally, Chaffee submitted a detailed report on Colorado's growth and future prospects to the Committee on Territories, which printed the information and distributed it to congressmen. Even though Chaffee failed to secure every proposal he introduced, his hard work and diligence gained him many friends both at home and in the nation's capital.[5]

While many Republicans in the House spurned Chaffee's early efforts, they became more receptive to the idea of statehood for Colorado during Grant's second term for numerous reasons. For one thing, the rupture between Liberal Republicans and conservative members of the party was becoming more pronounced and the loss of the Liberal's support was likely. For another, most of the scandals of Grant's presidency became public after 1872 and tainted leading party members, including the secretary of war and several members of Congress. Adding to Republican woes was the depression and the fact that all but three of the former Confederate states had fallen under the control of southern Democrats. Republican domination of national politics now appeared to be on the wane. The situation became more critical after 1874, when Democrats won control of the House of Representatives, a victory that implied that they could be victorious in the next presidential race. Indeed, Republican leaders began to regard three electoral votes from Republican-oriented Colorado as necessary if the party was to retain the White House in 1876.

Even the president advocated admission. Grant had a fondness for Colorado. He had visited the territory on the eve of his presidency in 1868 and again shortly after his second inauguration in 1873. He must have found the contrast between the two trips startling. On the first Grant had traveled by stagecoach over the Smoky Hill Route between Topeka, Kansas, and Denver, a trip that lasted a week with stops at ill-kept stage stations. In 1873 he rode in a private Pullman car described as "the most sumptuous and resplendent, not only in America but all over the world." In 1868 he passed through mostly uninhabited prairie; five years later hamlets and towns sat astride the railroad and townspeople came out to cheer and see the president. Colorado towns Grant had visited in 1868 were declining both in population and economically; now they were bustling with activity. It was estimated that Denver's population increased by 16,000 people since the 1870 census, while Central City's grew by 1,000. To display the territory's opulence, citizens wined and dined the president at every stop, and he walked over a silver brick sidewalk from his carriage to the Teller House in Central City. Chaffee accompanied the president and undoubtedly pointed out every improvement along the way.[6]

Impressed by what he saw, Grant recommended Colorado's admission when Congress convened in December 1873. The next day Chaffee introduced an Enabling Act, which passed the House by a partisan vote of 171 to 66. The delegate's hard work did not go unnoticed back home. "This favorable turn is largely attributable to the increasing zeal and energy of Hon. Mr. Chaffee," wrote the *Colorado Tribune.* "He has pressed our admission with scrupulous energy. Nothing has escaped his watchful attention and the attitude of the President demonstrates that he has not worked in vain." Success came easily in the House, which was still under Republican control and where Chaffee had made many friends, but the act faced strong resistance in the Senate.[7]

When the Senate took up the bill in December 1874, Democrats and some New England Republicans did all in their power to delay its passage. Democrats feared that the new state's electoral vote would go to the Republicans in 1876, and having gained control of the House in the November election, they sensed victory in the coming presidential election and were reluctant to diminish their party's chances. New Englanders had long opposed admitting states whose population did not entitle them to at least one representative. Many of them referred to Nevada (admitted in 1864) as a "rotten borough" and resented the increasing number of senators from the West whose presence in Senate lessened the impact of New England's influence.

Realizing they could not prevent passage, opponents attempted to amend the act, thereby delaying its passage or making its terms so unpalatable that Coloradans would refuse statehood rather than accept them. Chiefly they focused on the provisions regarding public land. Congress has always been generous in granting incoming states large portions of land so that they could use the proceeds to develop education, transportation, or other needs that arose. In the Enabling Act for Colorado, the House of Representatives gave the state two sections of land in every township to support common schools, plus 175 sections to provide for public buildings, expansion of the penitentiary, and a state university. Colorado was to receive, in addition, six sections of land surrounding twelve salt springs within its borders and 5 percent of the proceeds from all land that had been previously sold during the territorial period.[8]

Senator Aaron Sargent, a Democrat from California, began the process of delay by attempting to eliminate the 5 percent provision. He refused to withdraw his amendment even after colleagues pointed out that similar stipulations had been incorporated in every Enabling Act passed since 1816. Further, they argued, Sargent's amendment would leave Colorado without any financial resources to establish a government. The proposal was defeated because most senators regarded it as punitive. Next, George Edmunds, a Republican from Vermont, proposed that all public land in the territory previously granted to railroads be included in the total amount of land given to the new state. Midwestern senators came to Colorado's defense immediately, claiming that Edmunds's suggestion would leave the state with no public land of its own. Further, they pointed out, without land to sell, the new state would be bankrupt even before it was established. The amendment failed by a narrow margin, with only Democrats and New Englanders voting for it.

Stinging from his defeat, Edmunds motioned for adjournment again and again, hoping to delay consideration of the bill. Next, Democrat William Hamilton of Maryland interjected the issue of race. Knowing that any proposals dealing with racial issues always provoked extended debate, Hamilton moved to strike out a statement in the Enabling Act that forbade Coloradans from making any distinction in civil or political rights based on race. He argued that the provision was the same as the "reconstruction policy we have [forced] upon States South—a policy wrong always, and surely not required as to these people." Republicans were unwilling to get involved in a debate over their Reconstruction policy and quickly voted down Hamilton's amendment. Over the opposition of Democrats and New England Republicans, the Senate finally passed the Enabling Act by a decisive vote.[9]

By the time the Enabling Act arrived back in the House for approval of the Senate amendments, a number of political changes had occurred. Democrats had now taken control of the House, and many members adamantly opposed admitting Colorado. Some changed their minds only because Thomas Patterson, Colorado's new delegate, argued in favor of statehood. Offering his election as proof that the Democratic Party was becoming stronger in the territory, Patterson all but promised Colorado's electoral vote to the Democrats in the next presidential election. Along with Patterson, Chaffee, who had remained in the capital to work for admission, informed Republicans that Patterson's election was not an indication of changing political attitudes in the territory. Many Republicans had not voted in the recent election, he maintained, and those who voted for Patterson were casting a ballot against McCook's candidate, Bromwell. With statehood, Chaffee predicted, Coloradans would return to the Republican fold. Thus, while Chaffee was pledging Colorado's electoral vote to the Republicans, Patterson was promising it to the Democrats. With most of the objections seemingly overcome, leaders of both parties put pressure on their colleagues and the Enabling Act passed by a slim margin of five votes on March 3, 1875. The task had been difficult enough for Patterson to write, "Colorado is not a state yet, although by the time this reaches you, she may be. . . . Partisan character has crowded out all consideration of what is of the greatest moment to us in Colorado. . . . The danger is, that in their anxiety . . . that the next presidential election may be secure, . . . Republican[s] will forget the justice due to Colorado."[10]

National reaction to the Enabling Act followed sectional and political lines. Elements of the eastern press greeted the territory's potential entry with undisguised hostility. "There is something repulsive in the idea that a few handfulls [*sic*] of miners and reckless bushwhackers should have the same representation in the Senate as Pennsylvania, Ohio, and New York," wrote one editor. "There is not a single good reason for the admission of Colorado," another lamented, "Indeed, if it were not for the mines in that mountainous and forbidding region, there would be no population there at all." Coloradans were described as "an unsettled horde of adventurers who have no settled homes . . . and they are there solely because the state of semi-barbarism prevalent in that wild country suits their vagrant habits." The Democratic *Cincinnati Enquirer* concluded that Colorado's admission was championed by the "imperialist party" simply to hold the balance of power in the next presidential election. The editor calculated that Democrats controlled nineteen of the thirty-seven states in the Union and if the presidential election went to the House, they could quickly elect their candidate.[11] But the admission of Republican-oriented Colorado increased the number of states to thirty-eight and the vote would be evenly split, causing a long and drawn out contest.[12]

Other than referring to their critics as "salt water despots," Coloradans were not discouraged from moving forward. In the fall of 1875 they elected members to a constitutional convention, which met the following December in Denver. From the beginning everyone agreed that the constitution should be a nonpartisan effort and the document should not reflect the philosophy of any political party. Of the thirty-nine delegates, twenty-four were Republicans and fifteen Democrats. The majority had lived in New York or the Midwest, while two had been born in Germany and three in the British Isles. There were three Hispanic representatives: Casimiro Barela, J. M. Garcia, and Agapito Vigil. Lawyers comprised almost half of the professions represented, with bankers, merchants, ranchers, and farmers making up the remainder. Delegates referred to H. P. H. Bromwell, former congressmen from Illinois, as the "Blackstone of the convention" because he had more legal experience than the others and compromised a number of difficult issues. Missing from the delegation were well-known political figures from the territorial period. To give the convention a more nonpartisan tone, Teller, Evans, Elbert, and all of Colorado's former delegates to Congress did not participate. The *Colorado Tribune* noted their absence and dubbed the members of convention as the "new crowd" as opposed to the "old crowd."[13]

The more controversial issues at the convention involved religion. Should God be mentioned in the constitution? Should church property be taxed? Should parochial schools receive public funds? Some delegates even called for the prohibition of prayer and Bible reading in public schools, officially sanctioned religious holidays, and Sunday closings. Delegates dropped these more extreme demands after businessmen protested that incorporating such extreme restrictions into the constitution would give Colorado the appearance of being an anti-religious state and this would drive business and capital away. Debate on the religious issues became so heated that the *Colorado Tribune* suggested leaving them for future legislatures to deal with because they were "causing much agitation and may bring about the defeat of the document."[14]

The Civil War era was a religious age. Evangelical Protestantism had replaced the deistic thought of the Enlightenment, and references to the Divine Being in public documents became more frequent. Whereas state constitutions written before 1840 seldom mentioned God, those after often invoked His name in their preambles. The preamble to the Colorado document, as originally written, adopted the older practice and made no mention of God. Protest by both Protestant and Catholic clergy in Denver induced some delegates to add a clause specifically invoking the blessings of Jesus Christ, but it was removed after others pointed out that "this would be wrong because there are many citizens who do not believe he is a deity." In the end the preamble simply referred to "the Supreme Ruler of the Universe," thus, leaving the wording general enough for everyone to interpret it as he or she wished.[15]

Fear and disapproval of Roman Catholicism motivated attitudes regarding the taxation of church property and support for parochial schools. Many Protestants were suspicious of the Roman Catholic Church's dominance in southern Colorado and believed it would acquire and derive income from property that was not used for ecclesiastical purposes. Nor were their misgivings lessened by Bishop Joseph

Machebeuf's open declarations against taxing church property and demands for public monies to maintain parochial schools. Because he was a powerful figure in a growing Catholic population, Machefbeuf's attitude toward the final document could determine popular support, especially in the southern counties. Another complication to the school funding issue involved the considerable money that might become available for education. The Enabling Act had granted the new state 3,500,000 acres to establish a public education system, and it stipulated that the land could not be sold for less than $2.50 an acre, giving Colorado a potential windfall of almost $9,000,000. Few Protestant delegates, and especially those who opposed state support for any religious activity, were willing to share this money with religious-oriented schools.

The large number of petitions dealing with taxation of church property and school funding caused one editor to predict that the issues would "array . . . a large and influential element of our population against the constitution" and cause its rejection at the polls. After much debate and consideration, the convention excluded from taxation land and buildings that were used solely for worship or charitable purposes, schools, or cemeteries. Although parochial schools were not to be taxed, the constitution reserved the school fund for public institutions only.[16]

Arguments over the regulation of railroads indicated the increasing resentment against their growing influence. While railroads had done much to improve travel and the shipment of goods in Colorado, the major interstate lines were by the mid-1870s on their way to becoming monopolies, charging discriminatory rates, and engaging in other detrimental practices. Earlier, rural areas had favored more regulation but Denver business interests were able to quell any such moves in the legislature. And despite resolutions calling for stiffer railroad regulations in the convention, the delegates took a less aggressive approach. Railroad companies, some delegates believed, would refuse to build within the state if they were too restricted and those portions of Colorado needing faster transportation would suffer. Consequently, the constitution merely prohibited the legislature from granting irrevocable charters and stipulated that railroads were common carriers and could not charge unreasonable rates. Even these slight restrictions caused the Union Pacific to voice its opposition to the final document. Defending its action in a later "Address to the People," the delegates wrote: "We have endeavored to take a middle ground, believing it to be more safe, and in the end that it will give more general satisfaction."[17]

Almost as soon as the constitutional convention assembled, various groups begin agitating for woman suffrage. They organized a territorial

Woman Suffrage Society just as the convention opened, held mass meetings, and petitioned delegates to incorporate an equal suffrage provision in the constitution. In addition, suffragists enlisted strong backing from outside the territory. From Boston, the Massachusetts Woman Suffrage Association, at the urging of national suffragette Lucy Stone, memorialized the convention: "No part of the new Constitution of Colorado in this centennial Year, can be more appropriate . . . than the part which shall secure to women the right to a voice in making the laws they will have to obey." The executive committee of the Missouri Woman Suffrage Association voiced their support, hoping "woman may be remembered, and that here at last she may be endowed with the rights and privileges which we consider the birthright of every American citizen." When the committee on suffrage and elections rejected woman suffrage, H. P. H. Bromwell and Agapeta Vigil signed a minority report asking for the extension of the franchise. Urged by fellow delegates to abandon his effort, Vigil replied that "what the ladies asked was all right and he would vote for it."[18]

Unwilling to grant women full access to the polls, the delegates compromised by allowing them to vote in school elections and to hold school district offices. Hoping to remove the stigma for rejection from themselves, they also authorized the legislature to submit a woman suffrage proposition to the voters in the future. The lawmakers did submit one in October 1877, but voters rejected it by a two to one margin. Women in Colorado had to wait until 1893 before they gained full equality at the polls.[19]

Several considerations prompted the decision on woman suffrage. Pro-statehood advocates were pushing for Colorado to be admitted in 1876 so it would bear the motto "Centennial State," and they thought such a radical measure as woman suffrage would delay admission. Then, too, the Enabling Act required Colorado to meet all provisions for admission before the election of 1876, and the pro-state faction feared that Congress might deny admission if it failed to meet the deadline. Strong anti-suffragists argued that an equal suffrage provision was too extreme to be incorporated into the constitution without a separate vote on the issue. But most influential was the fear that if women were given the ballot, voters (all males) would reject the constitution when it was submitted for public approval. Even if voters approved it, other delegates worried that any controversial measure would cause the national government to question the document. As Ebenezer T. Wells, a delegate from Arapahoe County, said some years later: "Many of [the constitution's] provisions might have been framed in a wiser spirit, but for fear of its rejection."[20]

At the urging of Casimiro Barela, one of the last actions of the convention was to authorize the publication of the constitution in English, Spanish, and German. Then, going a step further, it stipulated that all laws, as well, should be published in the three languages until 1900. In doing so, the delegates recognized the importance of the non-English-speaking population. According to the Census of 1880, over one-fifth of Colorado's population was foreign-born (39,148 out of 194,327), and these individuals, added to the Mexican Americans, indicated a sizeable group of people whose native language was not English. Inasmuch as Colorado's laws allowed immigrants to vote once they had declared their intention to become U.S. citizens, it was important to encourage their participation by making it easier for them to be aware of the new constitution's contents.[21]

The convention adjourned on March 15, 1876, and called for a referendum on the constitution to be held on July 1. Public response to the constitution was unenthusiastic. In fact, by May the editor of the *Colorado Tribune* expressed concern about the apparent lack of interest and urged people and groups in favor of statehood to form clubs, publish letters, and send speakers throughout the territory. He worried that opponents would remain silent until just before the election and then present arguments against the document. This strategy would not give proponents enough time to respond and could defeat the constitution. The editorial sparked some reaction, for within the next month the *Colorado Chieftain* announced its neutrality with regard to statehood while the *Golden Transcript* and Colorado Springs *Gazette* declared their opposition.[22]

Arguments against statehood came from almost every element of society. Rural areas dreaded the increased taxes that statehood would bring and believed only the cities would benefit. Some areas opposed the railroad restrictions as not strong enough, others as too restrictive to encourage railroad expansion. The Union Pacific, which now also controlled the Kansas Pacific, was unhappy because the constitution labeled railroads as "common carriers" and prohibited their consolidation with competing lines. Among Mexican Americans a major anxiety was the increasing Anglo population and its political dominance in the new state. Referring back to the corruption during the McCook and Elbert administrations, the Colorado Springs *Gazette* insisted that the only people interested in statehood were those whose objective was "in the creation of offices they will fill." Led by Bishop Machebeuf, Catholics announced their opposition because the constitution taxed church property not used for ecclesiastical purposes and failed to provide public monies for parochial schools. Reviewing the various groups and the reasons for their opposition, one reporter calculated that the constitution was not a popular document.[23]

The referendum on the constitution reflected the general apathy. It was with a sense of relief that the *Miner's Register* announced "a majority . . . sufficient to place the charter beyond all danger of defeat." A total of 19,505 votes were cast in the election. While 15,443 voters approved the document and only 4,062 opposed it, the turnout was much lighter than anticipated. In southern Colorado, both Pueblo and El Paso counties rejected the document. To the north, Greeley also cast a negative vote but the other communities kept Weld County in the positive column. According to contemporary newspaper accounts, it was the overwhelmingly favorable vote cast in Arapahoe County, in which Denver was then located, that accounted for the large pro-state majority. Indeed, people in Denver were accused of voting early and often for statehood!

Some Coloradans blamed the low turnout on the time of year. July was a busy month for both farmers and miners and many were reluctant to leave their work. If that was the case, the number was considerable. According to Jerome Chaffee there were between 25,000 and 26,000 registered voters in Colorado. That number may be an exaggeration because it was included in the congressional report to support Colorado's admission to the Union. Still even with a slight exaggeration, it indicated that some 4,000 to 5,000 Coloradans did not care enough about statehood to came to the polls and cast their ballots on the constitution. Nevertheless, President Grant issued a proclamation setting August 1 as the official day of Colorado's admission to the Union.[24]

Colorado's admission received little notice throughout the nation. The news story of the summer of 1876 was the Battle of Little Big Horn, which occurred on June 25, and it relegated Colorado's constitutional election to the back pages, even within the new state. The nation was also celebrating the Centennial World's Fair in Philadelphia, and sports were becoming items of national interest. The establishment of the National League entrenched baseball into American culture, and 1876 saw the organization of the Intercollegiate Athletic Association and the Amateur Athletic Association. For those easterners disgruntled over Colorado's admission there was a more exciting event: William "Boss" Tweed, former mayor of New York City, was extradited from Spain to begin serving a prison term for political corruption on a scale larger than the nation had ever seen.[25]

Colorado's admission was grudgingly approved by some political elements. Not until January 1877 would Democrats finally accept the fact of Colorado's statehood. The difficulty arose from the presidential election of 1876, and the Colorado background to it lay in the constitutional convention.

The time between Colorado's admission and the presidential election was extremely tight. Congress stipulated in the Enabling Act that the referendum on the constitution could not be held before July 1, 1876. The constitutional convention had to provide enough time for the president to receive the election results and issue a proclamation admitting the state before any election for state officials could be held. Therefore, the convention set the election date for October 3, and for the convening of the first state legislature on November 1. The national presidential election was to be held on November 7.

Members of the convention realized that the legislature would have to organize before calling for a presidential election and, even at that, there would be less than a week to prepare. To overcome the problem, the judiciary committee recommended that the constitutional convention follow the example set by Nevada in 1864 and set the date for a presidential election. It appeared an acceptable solution until George H. Pease, representative from Park County, pointed out that the U.S. Constitution gives state legislatures the sole power to determine how presidential electors were appointed or chosen. Thus, only the state legislature could set the date of a presidential election. In 1864 no one objected to the decision of the Nevada convention because Lincoln's victory was not dependent upon Nevada's electoral vote. His majority was so overwhelming that Nevada's vote was superfluous. But everyone expected the upcoming presidential election to be much closer, and Colorado's electoral votes might be questioned if the convention, not the legislature, called for the presidential election. Persuaded by Pease's argument, the convention stipulated that the legislature would elect the presidential electors in 1876 only and then provide for a more popular method in subsequent years. Many state legislatures had chosen presidential electors until 1840 and South Carolina continued the practice until 1860. There could be no question about the legality of the procedure. As H. P. H. Bromwell told his fellow delegates, "this should be done with reluctance but there was no other practical solution."[26] The first state legislature was overwhelmingly Republican. It contained fifty-one Republicans and twenty-four Democrats. The lawmakers quickly organized and proceeded to elect U.S. senators and presidential electors. Jerome Chaffee and Henry Teller won the Senate seats. Regarding their election, the *New York Times* correspondent wrote, "It is generally conceded among the leaders of both parties that the election of

Mr. Chaffee is a fit recognition for his labors in behalf of admission and his important services to Colorado." The southern counties had hoped for the other Senate seat but accepted Teller as a compromise candidate. On November 7, 1876, the day of the national presidential election, the legislature, as expected, elected three Republicans, William L. Hadley, Otto Mears, and Herman Beckwerts, as presidential electors. Contrary to the hopes of national Democrats and Thomas Patterson's promises, Colorado remained a Republican stronghold in 1876.[27]

American presidential elections are determined by the electoral vote. Normally, the electoral vote reflects the popular will but occasionally, in 1876 and 2000, for example, problems arise. The number of votes in the electoral college, as it is called, is equal to the number of senators and representatives in Congress, and each state has the same number of electoral votes as it has U.S. senators and representatives. In 1876 there were 369 votes in the electoral college, and the winning candidate needed to secure 185 to be elected. When the vote was tallied Rutherford B. Hayes, the Republican candidate, had 165 votes, while Samuel J. Tilden, the Democratic opponent, had 184. Twenty votes were in dispute, and therefore not counted. One of them had been illegally cast but the situation was quickly corrected and the vote went to Hayes. The other nineteen came from South Carolina, Louisiana, and Florida. There southern Democrats were battling Republicans for control, and both parties had sent a separate set of electoral returns from each state—one for Hayes, the other for Tilden. Congress established an electoral commission to determine which candidate should be awarded these votes, and it, in turn, granted all the contested votes to Hayes. Thus, Hayes secured the minimum number of 185 votes and was declared the victor almost on the eve of his inauguration.

Tilden accepted his loss willingly but other Democrats began to look around for a scapegoat. They concluded that if Colorado had not been admitted, there would never have been a disputed election. Before the state's admission there were 366 votes in the electoral college. In order to win, the candidate needed 184 votes and Tilden received the requisite number when the ballots were first counted. Without Colorado's votes, Hayes's total could never have exceeded 182. For Democrats it was the admission of Colorado that caused their candidate's defeat. Had Colorado not been a state and had she not given her three electoral votes to Hayes, he could never have won the presidency, even with all twenty disputed votes. Some Democrats held a grudge against Patterson, and they regarded him with suspicion for his unfulfilled promise when he later served in Congress.[28]

When the House of Representatives convened in December, a group of Democrats, under the leadership of John Hurd of Ohio and William Springer of Illinois, went into action. They challenged the election of James Belford, who had been elected as representative from Colorado the previous October, for, they claimed, the state of Colorado did not exist. In their view, the Enabling Act was invalid because it authorized President Grant to issue a proclamation admitting Colorado after he had determined the state constitution met the requirements of the act. Admitting a state was a legislative function, they asserted, and Congress could not delegate this authority. Therefore, Colorado could not legally be admitted until Congress received and approved its constitution. Opponents resisted the argument on the grounds that Congress had given presidents similar authority in the past (indeed, Michigan, Missouri, Iowa, and Nevada had all been admitted by presidential proclamation) and that the Senate had already seated Chaffee and Teller. To get on with other business and avoid open confrontation, the matter was referred to the Judiciary Committee.[29]

The attack was overwhelmingly resented in Colorado. Even newspapers that had opposed statehood expressed strong disapproval. "The notions . . . are the last straw grasping at the attempt to secure Tilden's election," screamed the *Colorado Tribune.* The editors asked why Democrats did not notice this flaw in the Enabling Act earlier, since Congress was in session a full month after it was passed: "If leading Democrats doubted the . . . enabling act, they had time . . . to raise the question." The Colorado legislature petitioned Congress, calling the Democrats' argument an "injustice and a wrong," and requesting that Belford be seated immediately. Apparently the reaction in Colorado stunned some Democrats in Washington, D.C. At least, Springer demanded that Coloradans stop "portraying [the issue] as a party question." He threatened that "if they continue the Democratic members of this Congress and the next may just keep Colorado out of the Union."[30]

The Judiciary Committee reported back in January 1877. Six members wrote a majority report defending the Enabling Act, Grant's proclamation, and Colorado's constitution. It introduced a resolution declaring, "That Colorado is a State in this Union, and that James B. Belford, Representative-elect from said State, be sworn and admitted to his seat as such." Submitting a minority report, four members repeated the previous arguments and then presented their own resolution asserting that Colorado had met all the stipulations of the Enabling Act and "is hereby admitted into the Union." In order for the resolution to be effective it would have needed Senate approval but, at any rate, it would have admitted Colorado too late for its electoral vote to count. The ploy fooled few congressmen, and they overwhelmingly defeated the minority resolution. Colorado's electoral vote was counted in the presidential election of 1876.[31]

Statehood did not establish political harmony in Colorado. Within a year residents in the southern part of the state, irritated about the continued political dominance of the Denver region, began an unsuccessful movement to create the "Territory of San Juan." They contended that the disregard of Denver politicians for southern Colorado was as strong as that of federal appointees during territorial days. Besides, most of them had immigrated from the South, and they found it difficult to live with their "Yankee neighbors." In order to gain the support of the Mexican American population, they sought to incorporate part of New Mexico into the new territory. Denver politicians responded quickly to quash the movement. They began to listen more closely to the concern of southern Coloradans and even supported Frederick Pitkin from Ouray, in the San Juan region, for the governorship in 1879.[32]

Colorado prospered economically during the early years of statehood. Abundant rainfall from 1873 to 1885 provided sufficient grass for the range cattle industry and gave farmers substantial crop yields for their labor. Railroad profits increased and mining expanded greatly with the opening of the silver mines around Leadville. But prosperity also came at a cost. Legislative inaction allowed both industries to operate almost without restriction. Afraid that laws curtailing industry and business would hamper the state's economic growth, legislators did little to limit their abuses for the first decades of statehood. Railroads operated without any attempt to prevent rebates, pooling, and discriminatory rates. For a brief time after 1877 lawmakers prohibited the employment of children under fourteen in the mines but then repealed the law as an "unjust burden upon mine owners." And though the legislature provided for safety inspections in mines, it failed to enforce its own legislation.[33] Despite such drawbacks, Colorado continued to attract immigration and to grow into the economic and financial center of the Rocky Mountain region.

Epilogue

The quest for statehood had been long and trying. It began even before the territory was created with the "State of Jefferson" movement in 1859. The goal seemed achievable in 1864, but voters rejected a hastily drawn constitution. Even though the statehood issue was raised several times between 1865 and 1868, each consideration got bogged down in the struggle for power between President Johnson and the Senate. The pursuit of statehood finally ended in 1876, when President Grant issued a proclamation admitting the territory. But the years from 1859 to 1876 served Coloradans well and by the time they achieved statehood, the territory had reached a greater maturity and a more diversified economy. The mining frontier that existed in the founding days of the territory grew into agricultural and ranching frontiers as well. In 1859 Colorado's cities were small, untamed places. Most were regarded as rude hamlets where the law of the gun dominated until residents took matters into their own hands. The rudeness still remained in 1876 but visitors noted a growing refinement, especially in Denver and Colorado Springs. The beginning of the 1870s witnessed Colorado's closer ties to the rest of the nation as railroads provided faster transportation for both people and produce. Undoubtedly those Coloradans who lived in the territory from the beginning were aware of the many changes that had occurred and how they prepared the territory to take its place as a state in the Union.

The years following the admission of Colorado brought changes in the lives of many who had resided there during the territorial years.

William Hardin, Alexander Cummings, and Edward McCook left Colorado before 1876. Hardin moved to Cheyenne and, according to his descendants, may have spent his final years in Leadville. Cummings continued in public service and died while serving as U.S. consul in Ottawa, Canada. McCook returned to Chicago, where his wife's relatives lived.

Among the members of the Denver Ring, only Jerome Chaffee continued in politics but only for a brief time. He drew the short straw when he and Teller were sworn in as senators, and his term lasted only two years. After a tour of European cities, he, along with David Moffat, returned to their banking interests and to the First National Bank of Denver. John Evans became the chief financier of Colorado railroads and was influential in establishing the University of Denver. Samuel Elbert received an appointment to the Colorado Supreme Court and eventually became its chief justice. Two members of the ring devoted their efforts to preserving a record of Colorado's past. After he sold his interests in the *Rocky Mountain News,* William Byers became instrumental in founding the Colorado State Historical Society and served as its first president. Frank Hall turned his attention to writing and published the first multivolume history of Colorado in 1890.

Other individuals who had lived in Colorado during the territorial years became more active in both state and national politics. In addition to handling his business interests, John Routt served two terms as state governor in the ensuing years. Casimiro Barela represented Las Animas County in the state senate for twenty-five consecutive years. In addition to his mining and smelting endeavors, Nathaniel Hill served one term in the U.S. Senate. Thomas Patterson remained a lifelong Democrat and was elected to one term each in the U.S. House of Representatives and the Senate. Except for his three-year appointment from 1882 to 1885 as President Arthur's secretary of the interior, Henry Teller continued to serve in the U.S. Senate until 1909. The state's most renowned politician, he came to be called "Colorado's Grand Old Man."

Other individuals from the territorial era sought new ventures. Of the former governors, William Gilpin remained in Denver following his governorship and retained his interests in mining. A confirmed bachelor, he made an unfortunate marriage that caused him much regret in his later years. Alexander Hunt remained active in various business ventures but also dabbled in agricultural experimentation. William Palmer added coal mining to his railroad interests and continued to be one of the most influential individuals in the Colorado Springs area. Nathan

Meeker accepted an appointment as Indian agent to the White River Utes and was killed during an uprising in 1879. Robert Cameron served as superintendent of the Colorado State Prison during the 1880s.

Henry Wagoner, Sarah Hively, and Amelia Buss, among others, spent their remaining years quietly, but they along with the countless settlers who left no record of their activities all contributed to the building of the State of Colorado.

NOTES

Preface

1. Earl Pomeroy, "Toward a Reorientation of Western History," *Mississippi Valley Historical Review* 41 (Mar. 1955): 586; Clarence E. Carter, "The Territorial Papers of the United States: A Review and Commentary," *Mississippi Valley Historical Review* 42 (Dec. 1956): 521–22.

2. Howard Roberts Lamar, *Dakota Territory, 1861–1889: A Study of Frontier Politics* (New Haven, Conn., 1956); Lewis L. Gould, *Wyoming: A Political History, 1868–1896* (New Haven, Conn., 1968); Clark C. Spence, *Territorial Politics and Government in Montana, 1864–89* (Urbana, Ill., 1975); Jay J. Wagoner, *Arizona Territory, 1863–1912* (Tucson, Ariz., 1970); and Robert W. Larson, *New Mexico's Quest for Statehood, 1846–1912* (Albuquerque, N.M., 1968).

3. Howard Roberts Lamar, *The Far Southwest, 1846–1912: A Territorial History* (New Haven, Conn., 1966); Duane A. Smith, *The Birth of Colorado: A Civil War Perspective* (Norman, Okla., 1989).

Prologue

1. Henry Steele Commager, "The Northwest Ordinance," in *Documents of American History* (New York, 1963), 128–32.

2. Robert W. Johannsen, *Frontier Politics on the Eve of the Civil War* (Seattle, 1955), 52–53.

3. Gould, *Wyoming,* 17; Carl Abbott, Stephen J. Leonard, and David McComb, *Colorado: A History of the Centennial State* (Niwot, Colo., 1994), 66.

4. Colorado, Dakota, and Nevada in 1861; Idaho and Arizona in 1863; Montana in 1864: and Wyoming in 1868.

5. Earl Pomeroy, *The Territories and the United States, 1861–1890* (Seattle, 1969), 2; Gould, *Wyoming,* 17–19; Lamar, *Far Southwest,* 2–20; Lamar, *Dakota,* 11–27.

6. Lamar, Far Southwest, 212–17; Richard C. Willis, "Colorado Territory," in Ralph Y. McGinnis and Calvin N. Smith (eds.), *Abraham Lincoln and the Western Territories* (Chicago, 1994), 53–55; Thomas D. Isern, "Colorado Territory," in LeRoy H. Fisher (ed.), *The Western Territories in the Civil War* (Manhattan, Kans., 1977), 58–59.

Chapter 1: The New Territory

1. "Colorado Enabling Act, February 28, 1861," in *Statutes at Large, Dec. 5, 1859—Mar. 3, 1863,* part III, vol. XII (Boston, 1863), 172–77.

2. Lamar, *Far Southwest,* 217–21; Lamar, *Dakota,* 52–63; Willis, "Colorado," 56–57.

3. The official name of the river was the "Grand." Congress did not change it to the Colorado River until 1921 but, according to Frank Hall, local residents referred to it by the latter name before that time. Frank Hall, *History of the State of Colorado,* 4 vols. (Chicago, 1889–90), I, 258–65.

4. Isern, "Colorado," 59–60; Thomas L. Karnes, *William Gilpin: Western Nationalist* (Austin, Tex., 1970), 72–137. For Gilpin's writings on the West, see his *The Central Gold Region: The Grain, Pastoral and Gold Regions of North America With Some New Views of its Physical Geography and Observations on the Pacific Railroad* (Philadelphia, 1860) and *Address on the New Gold Mines, Delivered at Kansas City, by Col. Wm. Gilpin, accompanied by a map of the routes from Eastern Kansas to the mines* (Cincinnati, 1859).

5. (Denver) *Rocky Mountain News,* Dec. 21, 1861; Pomeroy, *Territories and U.S.,* 64; Sheldon S. Zweig, "The Civil Administration of Governor William Gilpin," *Colorado Magazine* 31 (July 1954): 179–93.

6. *Rocky Mountain News,* Aug. 26, 1861; Jason Howard Silverman, "Confederate Activities in Colorado Territory, 1861–1865" (M.A. thesis, Colorado State University, 1976), 98–101; Susan R. Ashley, "Colorado Territorial Days" (typescript, Colorado State Historical Society Library), n.p.

7. *Rocky Mountain News,* Dec. 26, 1861, Feb. 26, Mar. 6 and 28, 1862; Roy P. Basler (ed.), *The Collected Works of Abraham Lincoln, 9 vols.* (New Brunswick, N.J., 1956), V, 174; Smith, *Birth of Colorado,* 17, 25–28; Duane A. Smith, *Henry Teller: Colorado's Grand Old Man* (Boulder, Colo., 2002), 70–71; *History of the Arkansas Valley, Colorado* (Chicago, 1881), 550–70.

8. Harry E. Kelsey Jr., *Frontier Capitalist: The Life of John Evans* (Denver, 1969), 51–87.

9. Smith, *Birth of Colorado,* 153–54.

10. Rodman Wilson Paul, *Mining Frontiers of the Far West, 1848–1880* (New York, 1963), 116; James F. Rusling, *Across America; or, The Great West and the Pacific Coast* (New York, 1874), 68; Frank Fossett, *Colorado: Its Gold and Silver Mines, Farms and Stock Ranges, and Health and Pleasure Resorts. Tourist's Guide to the Rocky Mountains,* 2nd ed. (New York, 1880), 147.

11. *New York Times,* Mar. 11, 1866; (Black Hawk) *Daily Mining Journal,* Nov. 15, 1865; Charles W. Henderson, *Mining in Colorado: A History of Discovery, Development and Production* (U.S. Geological Survey, "Professional Paper" no. 138, Washington, D.C, 1926), 69; LeRoy Hafen (ed.), *Colorado and Its People: A Narrative and Topical History of the Centennial State,* 2 vols. (New York, 1948), II, 485–95; Paul, *Mining Frontiers,* 47–49; Rusling, *Across America,* 68.

12. Francis B. Heitman, *Historical Register and Dictionary of the United States Army, From its Organization, September 29, 1789 to Mar. 2, 1903,* 2 vols. (Washington, D.C., 1903), II, 285.

13. U.S. Department of War, *The War of the Rebellion: A Compilation of the Official Records of the Union and Confederate Armies,* ser. I, 70 vols. (Washington, D.C., 1880–1901), I, 42; Smith, *Birth of Colorado,* 253; Irving W. Stanton,

Sixty Years in Colorado: Reminiscences and Reflections of a Pioneer of 1860 (Denver, 1922), 9–10; Albert Castel, *William Clarke Quantrill: His Life and Times* (Norman. Okla., 1962), 178; Willis, "Colorado," 61.

14. Silverman, "Confederate Activities," 98; Eugene H. Berwanger, *The West and Reconstruction* (Urbana, Ill., 1981), 19–22.

15. Elma Dill Russell Spencer, *Green Russell and Gold* (Austin, Tex., 1966), 183; Silverman, "Confederate Activities," 98–100.

16. U.S. Bureau of the Census, *Eighth Census of the United States: 1860, Population* (Washington, D.C., 1864) 546; Paul, *Mining Frontiers*, 116.

17. No census was taken west of the Continental Divide in 1860. Colorado historian LeRoy Hafen calculated the figure for the South Platte Valley, and Kit Carson estimated the southern population in 1866. Fossett, *Colorado*, 147; *1860 Census, Population*, 549; U.S. Bureau of the Census, *Ninth Census of the United States: 1870, Population* (Washington, D.C., 1872), 16; U.S. Bureau of the Census, *Tenth Census of the United Sates: 1880, Population* (Washington, D.C., 1883), 5; LeRoy Hafen (ed.), *Colorado*, 2 vols. (New York, 1948), I, 82–85, 439; Rusling *Across America*, 94; Jerome C. Smiley, *Semi-Centennial History of the State of Colorado*, 2 vols. (Chicago, 1913), I, 440.

18. Pettis to Friend Hays, June 16, 1861, in Paul Giddens (ed.), "Letters of Newton S. Pettis, Associate Justice of the Colorado Supreme Court, Written in 1861," *Colorado Magazine* 15 (Jan. 1938): 7; Elliott West, *The Contested Plains: Indians, Goldseekers, & the Rush to Colorado* (Lawrence, Kans., 1998), 251–52; Frank Hall, *History of the State of Colorado*, 4 vols. (Chicago, 1889–90), I, 473; *1860 Census, Population*, 549; Hubert Howe Bancroft, *The Works of Hubert Howe Bancroft*, vol. XXV: *History of Nevada, Colorado and Wyoming, 1540–1888* (San Francisco, 1890), 536.

19. (Denver) *Rocky Mountain News*, May 16, June 16, 1865; *New York Times*, Feb. 18, 1866.

20. *Rocky Mountain News*, Oct. 9, 1865; *New York Times*, Jan. 28, 1866.

21. Dan E. Clarke, "The Movement to the Far West during the Decade of the Sixties," *Washington Historical Quarterly* 17 (Apr. 1926): 107; Samuel Bowles, *Across the Continent: A Summer's Journey to the Rocky Mountains, the Mormons, and the Pacific States* (Springfield, Mass., 1865), 179.

22. *New York Times*, Sept. 6, 1866; Percy Stanley Fritz, *Colorado: The Centennial State* (New York, 1942), 213; Berwanger, *West and Reconstruction*, 16.

23. Steele to Harper, Oct. 9, 1865, John Harper Papers (Western Americana Collection, University of Colorado, Boulder); Thomas J. Noel, Paul F. Mahoney, and Richard E. Stevens, *Historical Atlas of Colorado* (Norman, Okla., 1993), 25; Arrel Morgan Gibson, *The West in the Life of the Nation* (New York, 1976), 308. The Butterfield route originally ran through Texas and New Mexico, but during the Civil War it was moved north and followed the Republican and Smoky Hill rivers in Kansas.

24. Rusling, *Across America*, 75; Colin B. Goodykoontz, "Colorado as Seen by a Home Missionary, 1863–1865," *Colorado Magazine* 12 (Mar. 1935): 61–62; Kassler to Maria, Dec. 21, 1864, George Kassler Papers (Colorado State Historical Society Library); Hill to Alice, Mar. 9, 1865, N. P. Hill Papers (Colorado State Historical Society Library).

25. Louis L. Simonin, "Colorado in 1867 as Seen by a Frenchman," trans. Wilson O. Clough, *Colorado Magazine* 14 (Mar. 1937): 61.

26. Richard Hogan, *Class and Community in Frontier Colorado* (Lawrence, Kans., 1990), 21; Robert G. Athearn, *Westward the Briton* (New York, 1953), 38.

27. Goodykoontz, "Home Missionary," 62; Bancroft, *Colorado,* 550; Clarke to Irving W. Stanton, June 7, 1862, Irving W. Stanton Papers (Colorado State Historical Society Library); *Rocky Mountain News,* Apr. 27, 1865; Sherman to John Sherman, in Robert G. Athearn, *William Tecumseh Sherman and the Settlement of the West* (Norman, Okla., 1956), 20.

28. William Hepworth Dixon, *New America,* 2 vols. (London, 1867), I, 130; Bayard Taylor, *Colorado: A Summer Trip,* ed. William W. Savager Jr. and James H. Lazalier (Niwot, Colo., 1989), 37.

29. *1860 Census, Population,* 548; Rusling, *Across America,* 60–81; Raymond G. Colwell, Colorado City—Its Early Settlement" (typescript, Penrose Public Library, Colorado Springs), 2, 16–19.

30. James Meline, *Two Thousand Miles on Horseback, Santa Fé and Back. A Summer Tour Through Kansas, Nebraska, Colorado, and New Mexico in the Year 1866* (New York, 1867), 91–92; Joanne West Dodds, *They All Came to Pueblo: A Social History* (Virginia Beach, Va., 1994), 24–25; Minnie E. Stodddard, "Pueblo History" (typescript, Pueblo Public Library), 20–22.

31. Untitled essay in H. C. Waltz Papers (American Heritage Center Library, University of Wyoming), n.p.; Morris Taylor, *Trinidad, Colorado Territory* (Pueblo, Colo., 1966), 15–20.

32. *Rocky Mountain News,* Aug. 21, 1865; Dean F. Krakel, *South Platte Country: A History of Old Weld County, Colorado, 1739–1900* (Laramie, Wyo., 1954), 58–59; Fred H. Werner, *Historic Fort Sedgwick and Julesburg: A Study in Courage* (Greeley, Colo., 1987), 5–10; E. O. Davis, *The First Five Years of the Railroad Era in Colorado: June 16, 1867 to June 19, 1872, Julesburg to Pueblo in Five Years* (Denver, 1948) 6.

33. *Daily Mining Journal,* Apr. 5, 1864; Smith, *Birth of Colorado,* 196; see also 153–63 and 195–99.

34. Clark C. Spence, *British Investments and the American Mining Frontier, 1860–1901* (Ithaca, N.Y., 1958), 34; Taylor, *Summer Trip,* 61, 70; John H. Tice, *Over the Plains and on the Mountains, or Kansas and Colorado Agriculturally, Mineralogically, and Aesthetically* (Chicago, 1872), 225.

35. Goodykoontz, "Home Missionary," 64–65; Taylor, *Summer Trip,* 68–69; A. B. Legard, *Colorado* (London, 1872), 140–42; Nell Brown Propst, *Forgotten People: A History of the South Platte Trail* (Boulder, Colo., 1979), 39; Stoddard, "Pueblo History," 192–93; Ellen Coffin Pennock, "Incidents in My Life as a Pioneer," *Colorado Magazine* 30 (Apr. 1953): 130; Amelia Buss Diary, Sept. 16, 1866 (Western Americana Collection, University of Colorado); James Stratton Harlow Diary, n.d. (Fort Collins Public Library); *Chicago Tribune,* May 4, 1865.

36. *New York Times,* Feb. 18 and Sept. 6, 1866; Mrs. Daniel Witter, "Pioneer Life," *Colorado Magazine* 4 (Dec. 1927): 165–68.

37. Byers quoted in Stephen J. Leonard and Thomas J. Noel, *Denver: Mining Camp to Metropolis* (Niwot, Colo., 1990), 17; Krakel, *South Platte Country,* 86–92; *Official Records,* ser. I, vol. 34, part 1, 907 and part 4, 449; Statement of Mrs. Ewbanks, June 22, 1865, in U.S. Department of State, "Territorial Papers, Colorado Series," vol. I (microfilm); Raymond G. Carey, *A Collection of Documents Concerning the Battle of Sand Creek, November 29, 1864* (Denver, 1958),

176, 209–11; Propst, *Forgotten People,* 89; Smith, *Birth of Colorado,* 210; Lamar, *Far Southwest,* 246.

38. Charles Wentworth Dilke, *Greater Britain: A Record of Travel in English Speaking Countries During 1866 and 1867,* 2 vols. (London, 1868), I, 119; Cary, *Sand Creek Record,* 50; Michael Yates, *An Amusing Glance at Life and Leaders in Early Colorado* (Fort Collins, Colo., 1992), 84.

39. Evans quoted in Leonard and Noel, *Denver,* 21. See Kathleen Brosnan, *Uniting the Mountain and Plain: Cities, Law, and Environmental Change along the Front Range* (Albuquerque, 2002), 47–49, for a discussion of prejudice against Native Americans.

40. *Official Records,* ser. I, vol. 41, part 3, 242–43; *New York Times,* July 29, 1865; Alvin M. Josephy Jr., *Civil War in the American West* (New York, 1991), 315; Cary, *Sand Creek Record,* 208. The most balanced account of Sand Creek is Stan Hoig, *The Sand Creek Massacre* (Norman, Okla., 1961).

41. (Central City) *Daily Miners' Register,* Jan. 25, 1865; Gunther Barth, *Instant Cities: Urbanization and the Rise of San Francisco and Denver* (New York, 1975), 124.

42. *Rocky Mountain News,* Dec. 17, 1864, Feb. 4, Mar. 2 and 3, 1865; John H. Monnett, *The Battle of Beecher Island and the Indian War of 1867–1869* (Niwot, Colo., 1992), 31.

43. *Rocky Mountain News,* Mar. 2, July 11, 12, 18, Oct. 4, and 10, 1865; *Daily Mining Journal,* Oct. 10, 1865; Cary, *Sand Creek Record,* 198–219; *Official Records,* ser. I, vol. 48, 186; Hoig, *Sand Creek,* 171–72; Hall, *Colorado,* I, 350–52; Robert Black III, *Island in the Rockies: The History of Grand County, Colorado to 1930* (Boulder, Colo., 1969), 57.

44. Jerome Chaffee to Dear Judge [Bennet], Jan. 19, 1865, in Cary, *Sand Creek Record,* 62.

45. "Visiting the U.S. Mint in Denver: Its History and Coinage (pamphlet, Washington, D.C., 1995), 2 pp; Leonard and Noel, *Denver* 28–29; Abbot, Leonard, and McComb, *Colorado,* 65; Brosnan, *Mountain and Plain,* 18.

46. Thomas Jacob Noel, *Growing Through History with Colorado: The Colorado National Banks, the First 125 Years, 1862–1987* (Denver, 1987), xiii, xx, 1–4, and 16.

47. Samuel Bowles, *Our New West: Records of Travel Between the Mississippi River and the Pacific Ocean* (Hartford, Conn., 1869), 179–80.

Chapter 2: Subduing the Natives

1. Bent's statement implies a sense of regret. The son of William Bent and Owl Woman, a Southern Cheyenne, Bent spent his childhood at Bent's Fort, which his father and uncle operated in southeastern Colorado. In the late 1850s he was sent to St. Louis to be educated. There he joined the Confederate army following the bombardment of Fort Sumter. Wounded and captured during the Battle of Pea Ridge, he was released after taking an oath to never again bear arms against the United States. Union partisans in Colorado threatened to kill him upon his return home, so his father advised George to join his mother's people. From that time until his death Bent lived among the Southern Cheyenne. George E. Hyde, *The Life of George Bent: Written from his Letters,* ed. by Sovie Lottinville (Nor-

man, Okla., 1968), 25–50, 182; Moonlight to Grenville M. Dodge, n.d., in Smiley, *Colorado,* I, 428; Jean Afton, David Fridtjof Halaas, Andrew Masich, and Richard Ellis, *Cheyenne Dog Soldiers: A Ledgerbook History of Coups and Combat* (Denver, 1997), 294–96; A. R. Ross, "Indian Raids in Colorado, 1875," *Colorado Magazine* 24 (Nov. 1947): 262.

2. Ross, "Indian Raids," 261–63; Irving Howbert, *Memories of a Lifetime in the Pike's Peak Region* (Glorieta, New Mex., 1970, reprint), 188–93; Afton, *Dog Soldiers,* 294.

3. Hyde, *Bent,* 168–73; George Bird Grinnell, *The Fighting Cheyennes* (Norman, Okla., 1956), 181–82; *Official Records,* ser. I, vol. 48, part 1, 35; Werner, *Fort Sedgwick,* 19–20; Krakel, *South Platte Country,* 107–8.

4. Krakel, *South Platte Country,* 110–11; Afton, *Dog Soldiers,* 296–305.

5. Hyde, *Bent,* 188; Propst, *Forgotten People,* 96.

6. Report of Colonel Robert Livingston, in *Official Records,* ser. I, vol. 48, part 1, 89–92; Hall, *Colorado,* I, 359.

7. *Rocky Mountain News,* Jan. 19, 1865; Smiley, *Colorado,* I, 429.

8. *Official Records,* ser. I, vol. 48, part 1, 463; Hall, *Colorado,* I, 359–60; Smiley, *Colorado,* I, 427–29; Krakel, *South Platte Country,* 112–13.

9. Contrary to their belief, the Cheyennes originally lived along the Mississippi River in present-day Minnesota. They were pushed westward by migrating Sioux and first appeared in the Platte River region sometime between 1790 and 1800. For a full explanation see Donald J. Hughes, *American Indians in Colorado* (Boulder, Colo., 1977), 35–38; West, *Contested Plains,* 67.

10. Zachery Gussow, Leroy R. Hafen, and Arthur A. Ekrich Jr., *Arapaho-Cheyenne Indians* (New York, 1974), 22–23; Afton, *Dog Soldiers,* xviii; John H. Moore, *The Cheyenne Nation: A Social and Demographic History* (Lincoln, Neb., 1987), 198–200; John H. Monnett, *The Battle of Beecher Island and the Indian War of 1867–1869,* (Niwot, Colo., 1992), 198–200; Krakel, *South Platte Country,* 81.

11. Virginia Cole Trenholm, *Amanda Mary and the Dog Soldiers* (Lusk, Wyo., 1974), 21; Mari Sandoz, *Cheyenne Autumn* (New York, 1953), 113.

12. Hyde, *Bent,* 339.

13. Harry H. Anderson (ed.), "The Stand at the Arikaree," *Colorado Magazine* 41 (Fall 1964): 340; Stan Hoig, *The Peace Chiefs of the Cheyennes* (Norman, Okla., 1980), 85; Moore, *Cheyenne Nation,* 201; Afton, *Dog Soldiers,* xviii; Hyde, *Bent,* 113, 337–38; Sandoz, *Cheyenne Autumn,* xv.

14. Custer, Davis, and *Kansas Tribune* all quoted in Hoig, *Peace Chiefs,* 95–97; Trenholm, *Amanda Mary,* 8–9.

15. Bernitz quoted in Afton, *Dog Soldiers,* 310.

16. Rodenbough quoted in Hoig, *Peace Chief,* 97; Hyde, *Bent,* 216; Monnett, *Beecher Island,* 46.

17. Monnett, *Beecher Island,* 38.

18. Jess Augustin Castro, "Alexander Cameron Hunt: Colorado Territorial Governor, 1867–1869" (M.A. thesis, University of Denver, 1957), 57–56; Hoig, *Peace Chiefs,* 85–86; Monnett, *Beecher Island,* 31–39.

19. Sherman to John A. Rawlins, Sept. 12 and 30, 1866, in Athearn, *Sherman,* 76, 78; Sherman to Ellen, June 8, 1867, William Tecumseh Sherman Family Papers: Letters of William Tecumseh Sherman to Ellen Ewing Sherman (microfilm).

20. Hoig, *Peace Chiefs*, 251; Monnett, *Beecher Island*, 26–33; Sandoz, *Cheyenne Autumn*, 113; Gibson, *West in Nation*, 431.

21. Athearn, *Westward the Briton*, 133–34.

22. Hyde, *Bent*, 285; Castro, "Hunt," 70; Hall, *Colorado*, I, 361; Krakel, *South Platte Country*, 116; West, *Contested Plains*, 310.

23. Bernitz quoted in Grinnell, *Fighting Cheyennes*, 267–68; Robert G. Athearn, "Colorado and the Indian War of 1868," *Colorado Magazine* 33 (Jan. 1956): 3; Monnett, *Beecher Island*, 57–59.

24. (Pueblo) *Colorado Chieftain* quoted in Athearn, "Indian War," 46; Interview with B. F. Crowell, Sept. 18, 1886, in Hubert Howe Bancroft Collection (Western Americana Collection); Howbert, *Memoirs*, 183–84; Monnett, *Beecher Island*, 70–71.

25. Interview with George Aux, undated, Bancroft Collection; Sheridan to Hall, Aug. 28, 1868, in Territory of Colorado, *Biennial Report of the Adjutant-General of the Territory of Colorado for the two Years Ending, Dec. 31, 1869* (Central City, Colo., 1870); William S. Jenkins (ed.), "Records of the United States of America: A Microfilm Compilation. Colorado, 1861–1876" (Colorado State Archives) and *Colorado Council Journal, 1870* (Central City, Colo., 1870), both contain the complete correspondence between Hall and Sherman/Sheridan.

26. Monnett, *Beecher Island*. 124–41; Hoig, *Peace Chiefs*, 107.

27. Chauncey B. Whitney, "Diary of Chauncey B. Whitney," *Collections of the Kansas State Historical Society* 12 (1911–12): 296–302; George A. Forsyth, *Thrilling Days in Army Life* (Lincoln, Neb., 1994, reprint), 28–29; Hyde, *Bent*, 300; Grinnell, *Fighting Cheyennes*, 279–280.

28. Hurst quoted in Monnett, *Beecher Island*, 162.

29. Robert M. Utley, *Frontier Regulars: The United States Army and the Indian, 1866–1891* (New York, 1973), 148; Monnett, *Beecher Island*, 151–54; Grinnell, *Fighting Cheyennes*, 291.

30. Monnett, *Beecher Island*, 152–66.

31. H. C. Bankhead to Sheridan, Sept. 28, 1868, George Forsyth Papers (Colorado State Historical Society Library); Miles quoted in Monnett, *Beecher Island*, 1; *Rocky Mountain News*, Sept. 25, 1868.

32. Monnett, *Beecher Island*, 181; Grinnell, *Fighting Cheyennes*, 309.

33. Jack D. Filipiak, "The Battle of Summit Springs," *Colorado Magazine* 41 (Fall 1964): 346; Clarence Reckmeyer, "The Battle of Summit Springs," *Colorado Magazine* 6 (Nov. 1929): 211.

34. James T. King, *War Eagle: The Life of General Eugene A. Carr* (Lincoln, Neb., 1963), 84, 99–111; Moore, *Cheyenne Nation*, 162; Monnett, *Beecher Island*, 187–89; Hyde, *Bent*, 330; Filipiak, "Summit Springs," 347.

35. Controversy exists about who killed Tall Bull. Most historians agree that North killed the warrior, but "Buffalo Bill" Cody claimed credit in his road show, which ended with a reenactment of the battle. Don Russell, *The Lives and Legends of Buffalo Bill* (Norman, Okla., 1960), 132–37; Reckmeyer, "Summit Springs," 214–15; King, *Carr*, 116; West, *Contested Plains*, 378.

36. See West, *Contested Plains* for a detailed account of the battle. Emma Burke Conklin, comp., *A Brief History of Logan County, Colorado with Reminiscences by Pioneers* (Denver, 1928), 30.

37. King, *War Eagle,* 113; Hyde, *Bent,* 334; *Colorado House Journal, 1870* (Central City, Colo., 1870), Jan. 25, 1870; Afton, *Dog Soldiers,* 320; Hughes, *American Indians,* 61.

38. Samuel Elbert to John Pope, May 8, 1873, Samuel Elbert Letterbooks (Colorado State Archives); Frank Hall to John Pope, Mar. 13, 1874, in Jenkins, "Records"; F. H. to ed., Oct. 28, 1873 in (Denver) *Colorado Tribune,* Oct. 29, 1873.

39. *Rocky Mountain News,* May 18, 1865; Virginia McConnell Simmons, *The Ute Indians of Utah, Colorado, and New Mexico* (Boulder, Colo., 2000), 139–140; Robert Emmitt, *The Last War Trail: The Utes and the Settlement of Colorado* (Boulder, Colo., 2000), 22–23; Brosnan, *Mountain and Plain,* 48–49.

40. *Rocky Mountain News,* Aug. 7, 1865.

41. Simmons, *Ute Indians,* 121.

42. Ibid., 59–62.

43. Ibid, 116–18; *Official Records,* ser. I, vol. 22, part 2, 528; Castro, "Hunt," 71; Marshall Sprague, *Massacre: The Tragedy at White River* (Boston, 1957), 87–90; Emmitt, *Last War Trail,* xi.

44. Howard Roberts Lamar, *The Far Southwest,* 286; Frederic J. Athearn, *Land of Contrasts: A History of Southeast Colorado* (Denver, 1985), 80; Sprague, *White River,* 92–93; Castro, "Hunt," 72–79; Simmons, *Ute Indians* 132–33.

45. Ouray to Samuel Elbert, in Simmons, *Ute Indians,* 150.

46. Athearn, *Land of Contrasts,* 80; Simmons, *Ute Indians,* 148–49; Frances Leon Swadesh, *Los Prímeros Pobladores: Hispanic Americans of the Ute Frontier* (Notre Dame, Ind., 1974), 83; Hall, *Colorado,* II, 188–92.

Chapter 3: In Pursuit of Statehood

1. *Congressional Globe,* 39 Cong., 1 Sess., 210; Rex H. Moss, "Alexander Cummings, Governor of the Territory of Colorado, 1865–1867" (M.A. thesis, University of Denver, 1965), 42–43; Smiley, *Colorado,* I, 436.

2. Robert E. Smith, "Thomas M. Patterson, Colorado Statehood, and the Presidential Election of 1876," *Colorado Magazine* 53 (Spring 1976): 154.

3. *Rocky Mountain News,* Dec. 4, 1867; Leonard and Noel, *Denver,* 35; Abbott, Leonard, and McComb, *Colorado,* 82.

4. Harry E. Kelsey Jr., *Frontier Capitalist: The Life of John Evans* (Denver, 1969), 164; Robert W. Larson, *New Mexico's Quest for Statehood, 1846–1912* (Albuquerque, N.M., 1968), 30–42; Hall, *Colorado,* I, 367.

5. *Congressional Globe,* 39 Cong., 1 Sess., 1351; Moss, "Cummings," 41; *Rocky Mountain News,* Sept. 19, 1865; Eugene H. Berwanger, "Reconstruction on the Frontier: The Equal Rights Struggle in Colorado, 1865–1867," *Pacific Historical Review* 44 (Aug. 1975): 315.

6. Berwanger, "Reconstruction on the Frontier," 315–16; *Rocky Mountain News,* Aug. 4, 1865.

7. The U.S. government and most states did not recognize blacks as citizens until the adoption of the Fourteenth Amendment in 1868.

8. *1860 Census, Population,* 548; *1870 Census, Population,* 16; Berwanger, *West and Reconstruction,* 143–50.

9. Berwanger, *West and Reconstruction,* 143–50; *Rocky Mountain News,* Aug. 1, 1865.

10. William Hanchett, "'His Turbulent Excellency,' Alexander Cummings, Governor of Colorado Territory, 1865–1867," *Colorado Magazine* 34 (Apr. 1957): 83–85; Hall, *Colorado,* I, 374.

11. Hall, *Colorado,* I, 369; *Rocky Mountain News,* Oct. 19 and Nov. 16, 1865; *Daily Mining Journal,* Jan. 8, 1866.

12. *New York Times,* Feb. 18, 1866; Henry Teller to David H. Nichols, Dec. 29, 1865, David H. Nichols Papers (Western Americana Collection, University of Colorado).

13. Cummings's proclamation of December 23, 1865, in Territory of Colorado, "Governors of Colorado: Record of Executive Proceedings, Colorado Territory. Executive Papers, 1861–1870," Book A (microfilm, Colorado State Archives); Moss, "Cummings," 20; Hanchett, "Turbulent Excellency," 85–86.

14. Matthew Simpson to John Evans, Aug. 4, 1865, John Evans Papers (Colorado State Historical Society Library).

15. Cummings to William H. Seward, Jan. 7, 1866, U.S. Department of State, "Territorial Papers, Colorado Series, Vol. I: 1859–1874" (microfilm); Cummings to Seward, Jan. 9, 1866, Samuel Elbert Papers (Colorado State Historical Society Library).

16. Cummings to Seward, Feb. 19, 1866, Elbert Papers; Hanchett, "Turbulent Excellency," 87–89.

17. Cummings to Elbert, Jan. 9, 1866; Elbert to David Chever (executive secretary in Elbert's office), Jan. 10, 1866; Chever to Elbert, Jan. 11, 1866; and Elbert to Cummings, Jan. 11, 1866, all in *Daily Mining Journal,* Jan. 18, 1866. Manuscript copies of these letters are found in the Elbert Papers.

18. *Daily Mining Journal,* Jan. 30, Feb. 9, and Mar. 2, 1866; Hall, *Colorado,* I, 377.

19. Hall, *Colorado,* I, 377; Brosnan, *Mountain and Plain,* 52–53.

20. Cummings to Lafayette Foster (president of the U.S. Senate), Dec. 23, 1865, U.S. Senate, "Territorial Papers of the United States Senate: Colorado, Apr. 3, 1860-Feb. 20, 1868" (microfilm); Cummings's special message on black suffrage, Jan. 23, 1866, State Department Territorial Papers; *Rocky Mountain News,* Jan. 15, 1866.

21. *Daily Mining Journal,* Jan. 27, 30, Feb. 8, 9, and Mar. 2, 1866; *Rocky Mountain News,* Jan. 15, 1866.

22. *Daily Mining Journal,* Jan 27, 1866; Territory of Colorado, *Council Journal of the Legislative Session of the Territory of Colorado, Sixth Session, 1866–1867* (Central City, Colo., 1867), 17–18.

23. Alexander Cummings, *Speech of Alexander Cummings Delivered at Williamsport, Pa., September, 1856, on the Question, "Did the Constitution Establish Slavery,* (n. p., n. d., pamphlet), 31 pp.; *Official Records,* ser. I, vol. xxiv, part ii, 404; ser. III, vol. iv, 121, 124.

24. *Congressional Globe,* 39 Cong., 1 Sess., 1329–31, 1352, 1365.

25. *Rocky Mountain News,* May 4, and July 28, 1866; *Congressional Globe,* 39 Cong., 1 Sess., 2148, 2210, 2600–2603, 3476.

26. *Congressional Globe,* 39 Cong., 2 Sess., 362; Hanchett, "Turbulent Excellency," 86–90.

27. *Congressional Globe,* 39 Cong., 2 Sess, 364–65, 382, 398–99, 840; Berwanger, *West and Reconstruction,* 150–53.

28. (Central City) *Daily Miner's Register,* Mar. 24, 1867; (Golden) *Colorado Transcript,* Jan. 17, 1867; *Rocky Mountain News,* Apr. 1 and 3, 1867; Hall to his Mother, Apr. 14, 1867, Frank Hall Papers (Colorado State Historical Society Library).

29. Hall to his Father, Nov. 7 and 17, 1866, Hall Papers; "Statement on Hunt-Chilcott election," undated, Alexander Cameron Hunt Papers (Colorado State Historical Society Library); Hall, *Colorado,* I, 386–89; *Congressional Globe,* 40 Cong., 1 Sess., 225–33.

30. Rusling, *Across America,* 61; *Daily Mining Journal,* Sept. 14, 1866; Hall, *Colorado,* I, 388–89.

31. *Rocky Mountain News,* Dec. 18 and 19, 1866; Moss, "Cummings," 77; Hanchett, "Turbulent Excellency," 96–100.

32. Undated petition to Andrew Johnson, State Department Territorial Papers.

33. Bradford to Johnson, Feb. 7, 1867, ibid.

34. Cummings to Seward, Mar. 5, 1867, State Department Territorial Papers; House of Representatives, *House Miscellaneous Documents,* 39 Cong., 2 Sess. 9–15. Although wheeled vehicles were not able to go over Berthoud Pass, the *Rocky Mountain News* gave the opposite impression as early as 1865. See Black, *Island in the Rockies,* 52–53; *Rocky Mountain News,* Sept. 25 and 28, 1865.

35. Cummings to Seward, March 5, 1867, State Department Territorial Papers; *House Miscellaneous Documents,* 9–15.

36. Report of E. Pershine Smith, Examiner of Claims, Mar. 7, 1867, State Department Territorial Papers.

37. *Rocky Mountain News,* Apr. 24, 1867; Moss, "Cummings," 101; Hall, *Colorado,* I, 391–92.

38. *Daily Miner's Register,* Apr. 25, 1867; Moss, "Cummings," 101; Hancett, "Turbulent Excellency," 81.

39. Samuel Elbert, "Public Men and Measures" (typewritten), Bancroft Collection; "Petition of Colored Citizens," Feb. 10, 1868, Senate Territorial Papers; Frank Hall to Thaddeus Stevens, Apr. 13, 1868, Hall Papers; *Rocky Mountain News,* Mar. 14, 1868; Elmer Ellis, "Colorado's First Fight for Statehood, 1865–1868," *Colorado Magazine* 8 (Jan. 1931): 29–30; Kelsey, *Frontier Capitalist,* 163–65; Smiley, *Colorado,* I, 375.

40. Hall, *Colorado,* I, 363–64, 453, 464–68; Marshall Sprague, *Newport of the Rockies: The Life and Good Times of Colorado Springs* (Denver, 1961), 27.

Chapter 4: A Rebounding Economy

1. Hafen, *Colorado,* II, 636–37.

2. Hall, *Colorado,* I, 492.

3. Peter Day to Dodge, n.d., quoted in Black, *Island in the Rockies,* 41; Robert Ormes, *Railroads and the Rockies: A Record of Lines in and near Colorado* (Denver, 1963), 21–22, 384; Robert G. Athearn, *High Country Empire: The High Plains and the Rockies* (New York, 1960), 160. Dodge contradicted himself regarding who actually made the decision to avoid the Colorado Rockies. In an essay entitled "How We Built the Union Pacific Railway," he contended that he

traveled the "country from the Laramie Cañon on the north to the Arkansas River on the South" but failed to find a satisfactory crossing. In another essay entitled "Civil Engineering," he wrote that a party led by P. T. Brown spent the summer of 1866 attempting to locate a possible rail route through the Colorado mountains. See Grenville M. Dodge, *How We Built the Union Pacific Railway* (reprint, Denver, 1965), 21; and, Dodge, "The Civil Engineering in an Early Day and in the Civil War-Address Delivered Before the Western Society of Civil Engineers," in *How We Built the Union Pacific Railway,* 110.

4. Hall, *Colorado,* I, 425.

5. S. D. Mock, "The Financing of Early Colorado Railroads," *Colorado Magazine* 18 (Nov. 1941): 202; Krakel, *South Platte Country,* 69–70; Wilbur Fisk Stone (ed.), *History of Colorado,* 5 vols. (Chicago, 1918), I, 332–36; Hafen, *Colorado,* II, 323, 637–39; Hall, *Colorado,* I, 493.

6. Ormes, *Railroads and the Rockies,* 226–30.

7. Leonard and Noel, *Denver,* 351; Barth, *Instant Cities,* 214; Davis, *Railroad Era,* 14; Stone, *Colorado,* I, 336.

8. Stone, *Colorado,* I, 338–40; Kelsey, *Frontier Capitalist,* 174.

9. The four men were Bela Hughes and John Evans, both of whom have been mentioned; John Pierce, an early miner who turned to railroad investing; and Robert Carr, an executive for the Union Pacific Railroad. Billy L. Boyles, *The St. Vrain Valley: Its Early History* (Longmont, Colo. 1967), 58; Fossett, *Colorado,* 134.

10. Hafen, *Colorado,* II, 642; Kelsey, *Frontier Capitalist,* 175–77.

11. Ormes, *Railroads and the Rockies,* 277.

12. The Mississippi had been bridged earlier, in 1857.

13. *1860 Census, Population,* 548; *1870 Census, Population,* 95; Fossett, *Colorado,* 327; Stone, *Colorado,* I, 341–42.

14. Hall, *Colorado,* I, 494.

15. Hall to Mother, Sept. 9. 1867, Hall Papers; Fossett, *Colorado,* 218; Hall, *Colorado* I, 352–53; II, 214–15.

16. Duane A. Smith, *Rocky Mountain Mining Camps: The Urban Frontier* (Bloomington, Ind., 1967), 129–30; Hall, *Colorado,* II. 209.

17. Hall, *Colorado,* I, 493.

18. Ormes, *Railroads and the Rockies,* 128–30; Hafen, *Colorado,* II, 644–50; Davis, *Railroad Era,* 153.

19. Hall, *Colorado,* II, 92–95; Ormes, *Railroads and the Rockies,* 274–76.

20. James E. Fell Jr., *Ores to Metals: The Rocky Mountain Smelting Industry* (Lincoln, Neb., 1979), 53–55; Hall, *Colorado,* I, 95–98.

21. Athearn, *High Country Empire,* 162–63; (Denver) *Colorado Tribune,* May 4, 1876.

22. Palmer quoted in Raymond Colwell, "The Railroad Age, 1871–1890," *The Pikes Peak Region: A Sesquicentennial History,* ed. Harvey I. Carter (Colorado Springs, 1956), 15; Hafen, *Colorado,* II, 647–49.

23. Hafen, *Colorado,* II, 647–49; Hall, *Colorado,* II, 102–3, 363.

24. Athearn, *High Country Empire,* 163; Hafen, *Colorado,* I, 326; Stanton, *Sixty Years,* 177; *Colorado Tribune,* May 4, 1876.

25. Hall, *Colorado,* II, 102–3; Noel, *Historical Atlas of Colorado,* 28.

26. Athearn, *High Country Empire,* 159; Barth, *Instant Cities,* 216; Leonard and Noel, *Denver,* 39.

27. Quotation in Tice, *Over the Plains,* 225; Henderson, *Mining in Colorado,* 29; Paul, *Mining Frontiers,* 121.

28. Frank Fossett, *Colorado: Historical, Descriptive and Statistical Work on the Rocky Mountains, Gold and Silver Mining Region* (Denver, 1876), 93.

29. Liston E. Leyendecker, "Colorado and the Paris Universal Exposition, 1867," *Colorado Magazine* 46 (Winter 1969): 1–15; *1870 Census, Population,* 347; Paul, *Mining Frontiers,* 122.

30. Paul, *Mining Frontiers,* 122.

31. Hill to Alice Hill, Oct. 16, 1864, in Fell, *Ores to Metals,* 18; Paul, *Mining Frontiers,* 43.

32. Fell, *Ores to Metals,* 22–35; Spence, *British Investments,* 101–2.

33. Fossett, *Historical Colorado,* 163, 203; Fell, *Ores to Metals,* 24.

34. Paul, *Mining Frontiers,* 43; Lamar, *Far Southwest,* 265.

35. Fell, *Ores to Metals,* 52–55.

36. Liston E. Leyendecker, *Georgetown: Colorado's Silver Queen, 1859–1876* (Fort Collins, Colo., 1977), 20–35; Walter T. K. Nugent, *Money and American Society, 1865–1880* (New York, 1968), 104; Fossett, *Historical Colorado,* 101–2, 162–63, 464; Hafen, *Colorado,* I, 336.

37. Hafen, *Colorado,* I, 337–38; Stone, *Colorado,* I, 266–71.

38. George W. Pine, *Beyond the West: An Account of Two Years Travel in the other Half of Our Great Continent* (Utica, N.Y., 1871), 113; Gilbert C. Fite, *Farmers' Last Frontier, 1865–1900* (New York, 1966), 181.

39. *1880 Census, Population,* 382; Fite, *Farmers' Last Frontier,* 183–84; Maurice Frink, W. Turrentine Jackson, and Agnew Wright Spring, *When Cattle was King: Contributions to the Western Range Cattle Industry* (Boulder, Colo., 1956), 45.

40. Hall, *Colorado,* I, 509–10; Fossett, *Colorado,* 172, 190.

41. Robert G. Dunbar, "History of Agriculture," in LeRoy Hafen (ed.), *Colorado,* II, 121–22.

42. Bancroft, *Colorado,* 539; Hafen, *Colorado,* I, 122; Dunbar, "Agriculture," 122–24; James Earl Sherow, *Watering the Valley: Development Along the High Plains Arkansas River, 1870–1950* (Lawrence, Kans., 1990), 11–15.

43. Dunbar, "Agriculture," 127.

44. Hall, *Colorado,* II, 177.

45. Hall, *Colorado,* I, 449; Smiley, *Colorado,* I, 458; Harlow Diary, n.d., 36; Evans to Dear Wife, Aug. 9, 1876, Evans Papers.

46. Statement in Amelia Block Papers, n. d. (Western Americana Collection); Hall to Bolling Hall, July 22, 1874, in John D. W. Guice, "Alabama Planters in the Rockies," *Colorado Magazine* 52 (Winter 1976): 22.

47. Harlow Diary, n.d., 36; Donald Danker (ed.), *Mollie: The Journal of Mollie Dorsey Sanford in Nebraska and Colorado Territories, 1857–1866* (Lincoln, Neb. 1959), 192.

48. Cozens to W. Z. Cozens, Feb. 26, 1874, William Z. Cozens Papers (Colorado State Historical Society Library).

49. *Colorado Tribune,* Aug. 8, Nov. 20 and 22, 1873; Jan. 5 and June 14, 1874; Jan. 18, 1875; Jan. 23 and 25, 1876; Abbott, Leonard, and McComb, *Colorado,* 127.

50. *New York Times,* Aug. 12, 1874; Hall, *Colorado,* II, 207.

51. Bancroft, *Colorado*, 543; Stone, *Colorado*, I, 503; Dilke, *Greater Britain*, 90.

52. Edward Everett Dale, *The Range Cattle Industry: Ranching on the Great Plains from 1865 to 1925* (Norman, Okla., 1960), 71–72; Ernest Staples Osgood, *The Day of the Cattleman* (Minneapolis, 1929), 37–40; Stone, *Colorado*, I, 519; Clifford P. Westeremeier, "Legal Status of Colorado Cattlemen, 1867–1887," *Colorado Magazine* 25 (May 1948): 111.

53. Fossett, *Colorado*, 180; Tarbox quoted in *Colorado Chieftain*, Sept. 5, 1873.

54. Frink, *When Cattle Was King*, 369; West, *Contested Plains*, 248–49.

55. West, *Contested Plains*, 147–48, 248–49.

56. "John Wesley Prowers," in P. G. Scott Collection (Colorado State Historical Society Library), n.p.; Propst, *Forgotten People*, 74; Krakel, *South Platte Country*, 192.

57. Frink, *When Cattle Was King*, 337–38, 349, 369; Propst, *Forgotten People*, 108; Krakel, *South Platte Country*, 191–92; Athearn, *High Country Empire*, 137–38; Dale, *Range Cattle Industry*; John M. Kuykendall, "The First Cattle North of the Union Pacific Railroad," *Colorado Magazine* 6 (Mar. 1936): 70; *Cheyenne* [Wyoming] *Leader*, Feb. 13, 1878.

58. "Prowers," Scott Collection; West, *Contested Plains*, 247–50; Athearn, *Land of Contrast*, 85–87; *Colorado Chieftain*, May 29, 1872 and Feb. 21, 1873.

59. West, *Contested Plains*, 249; Brosnan, *Mountain and Plain*, 67; Krakel, *South Platte Country*, 172; Frink, *When Cattle Was King*, 247; Osgood, *Day of the Cattleman*, 118–19; Eugene H. Berwanger, "The Absurd and the Spectacular: The Historiography of the Plains-Mountains States-Colorado, Montana, Wyoming," *Pacific Historical Review* 50 (Nov. 1981): 462–63; *Colorado Tribune*, Oct. 19, 1872.

Chapter 5: Settling the Plains

1. R. B. Townshend, *A Tenderfoot in Colorado* (Norman, Okla., 1968), 3, 109; Werner, *Fort Sedgwick*, 5; Conklin, *Logan County*, 57–58.

2. Werner, *Fort Sedgwick*, 31; Stephen Ambrose, *Nothing Like it in the World: The Men Who Built the Transcontinental Railroad, 1863–1869* (New York, 2000), 219–20.

3. Townshend, *Tenderfoot in Colorado*, 3; Davis, *Railroad Era*, 11–12.

4. James Willard, *The Union Colony at Greeley, Colorado, 1869–1870* (Boulder, Colo., 1918), x–xi; *Colorado Tribune*, May 22, 1869; Krakel, *South Platte Country*, 205; Boyles, *St. Vrain Valley*, 58; Fritz, *Colorado*, 229–33; Brosnan, *Mountain and Plain*, 73–74.

5. Stone, *Colorado*, I, 158–59.

6. Robert Hine, *Community on the American Frontier: Separate but Not Alone* (Norman, Okla., 1980), 221–22; Katherine Harris, *Long Vistas: Women and Families on Colorado Homesteads* (Niwot, Colo., 1993), 80–81; Fite, *Farmers' Last Frontier*, 181; Krakel, *South Platte Country*, 206; Willard, *Union Colony*, xviii.

7. Willard, *Union Colony*, xiv–xv.

8. Ibid., xviii–xix; Fritz, *Colorado*, 229; Krakel, *South Platte Country*, 206.

9. James Willard and Colin B. Goodykoontz, *Experiments in Colorado Colonization: Selected Contemporary Records relating to the German Colonization Company and the Chicago-Colorado, St. Louis-Western and Southwestern Colonies* (Boulder, Colo., 1926), xvi–xxiii: *Colorado Tribune,* May 25, 26, and June 14, 1870.

10. *Colorado Tribune,* June 14, 1870; Willard and Goodykoontz, *Experiments in Colorado Colonization,* xxiii; Boyles, *St. Vrain Valley,* 59–60; Legard, *Colorado,* 69.

11. *Colorado Chieftain,* Feb. 24, Mar. 10 and 17, 1870; Willard and Goodykoontz, *Experiments in Colorado Colonization,* xxi, 66–70.

12. *Rocky Mountain News,* Apr. 25, 1870; *Colorado Tribune,* Apr. 27, 1870; *Daily Miner's Register,* Mar. 20, 1870.

13. *Colorado Chieftain,* Apr. 28, 1870; *Colorado Tribune,* Apr. 30, 1870; *Rocky Mountain News,* May 2, 1870; Willard and Goodykoontz, *Experiments in Colorado Colonization,* 104–7.

14. Willard and Goodykoontz, *Experiments in Colorado Colonization,* xx–xxiv; interview with Mrs. Warren R. Fowler, n.d., Bancroft Collection; *Greeley* (Colorado) *Tribune,* Apr. 10, 1871.

15. David Boyd, *A History: Greeley and the Union Colony of Colorado* (Greeley, Colo., 1890), 39; Krakel, *South Platte Country,* 209–17; Propst, *Forgotten People,* 127.

16. *Rocky Mountain News,* June 1, 1870; *Colorado Tribune,* May 26, 1870; unidentified and undated newspaper clipping in Nathan Meeker Papers (Colorado State Historical Society Library); Hafen, *Colorado,* I, 331; Smiley, *Colorado,* I, 450; Willard, *Union Colony,* 268–69; Krakel, *South Platte Country,* 216.

17. See especially Lewis Eslick to Meeker, n.d.; Alfred Chapman to Meeker, Feb. 29, 1872; James N. Bowden to Meeker, Oct. 28, 1872; Frank B. McClellan to Meeker, Nov. 4, 1872; Arthur A. Parrish to Meeker, Nov. 6, 1872; and Iday Hiser to Meeker, Nov. 13, 1872, all in Meeker Papers.

18. Propst, *Forgotten People,* 134.

19. Interview with Thomas Bell, Aug. 5, 1880, Bancroft Collection; James M. Clark, *Colonial Days* (Greeley, Colo., 1902), 11; Luella Shaw, *True History of Some of the Pioneers of Colorado* (Hotchkiss, Colo., 1909), 237; William Edgar Pabor, *Colorado As an Agricultural State: It's Farms, Fields, and Garden Lands* (New York, 1883), 32–33; Hafen, *Colorado,* I, 328–29; *Rocky Mountain News,* June 27, 1870.

20. Krakel, *South Platte Country,* 36–43; Boyd, *Greeley and the Union Colony,* 175.

21. *Greeley Tribune,* Dec. 7, 1870 and Feb. 1, 1871.

22. *Colorado Tribune,* May 26, 1870; Willard and Goodykoontz, *Experiments in Colorado Colonization,* xxxi.

23. John Erastus Lester, *The Atlantic to the Pacific: What to See and How to See It* (London, 1873), 221.

24. *Greeley Tribune,* Mar. 1, 1871; *Colorado Tribune,* Aug. 1, 1871; Willard and Goodykoontz, *Experiments in Colorado Colonization,* xxxiii–xxxvi; Krakel, *South Platte Country,* 219–20; Willard, *Union Colony,* xviii; Robert G. Athearn, *The Coloradans* (Albuquerque, N.M., 1976), 119.

25. "Annals of the *Longmont Times*" in Longmont pamphlet file, Western Americana Collection; Willard and Goodykoontz, *Experiments in Colorado Colonization,* xxiv, 139.

26. Byers to C. N. Pratt, Jan. 26, 1871, in Willard and Goodykoontz, *Experiments in Colorado Colonization,* 224; Tice, *Over the Plains,* 149; Mabel Downer Durning, *The Chicago-Colorado Colony: Founding of Longmont* (Longmont, Colo., 1975), 7; Boyle, *St. Vrain Valley;* Krakel, *South Platte Country,* 216.

27. *Colorado Tribune,* Apr. 10, 1871, and Sept. 22, 1873; *Boulder* (Colorado) *County News,* Apr. 15, 1871; Willard and Goodykoontz, *Experiments in Colorado Colonization,* xxvii.

28. *Boulder County News,* July 14, 1876; Boyles, *St. Vrain Valley;* St. Vrain Historical Society, *They Came to Stay: Longmont, Colorado, 1858–1920* (Longmont, Colo., 1971), 176; Charles Bullard and Sally Vecchio Martin, *Longmont's History in Architecture Today* (Boulder, Colo., 1986), 7.

29. Boyles, *St. Vrain Valley,* 61–62; Hafen, *Colorado,* I, 331–32; Bullard, *Longmont's History,* 8.

30. *Colorado Tribune,* Apr. 12 and May 26, 1870.

31. *Rocky Mountain News,* Apr. 30, 1871; Clark, *Colonial Days,* 49–50; Sprague, *Newport of the Rockies,* 30–31; Ansel Watrous, *History of Larimer County, Colorado* (Fort Collins, Colo., 1972 reprint), 270.

32. *Greeley Tribune,* Apr. 28, 1876; Krakel, *South Platte Country,* 62; Conklin, *Logan County,* 75–78, 92, 323.

33. Conklin, *Logan County,* 74–78; Kathryn Young, "Pioneer Days in Sterling," *Colorado Magazine* 4 (Mar. 1927): 62; Propst, *Forgotten People,* 133; Harris, *Long Vistas,* 27.

34. Watrous, *Larimer County,* 231–40; Stone, *Colorado,* 166; interview with James B. Arthur, Sept. 26, 1885, Bancroft Collection; *1880 Census, Population,* 113.

35. Athearn, *Land of Contrasts,* 93–99; *Colorado Tribune,* Nov. 7, 1873; Hafen, *Colorado,* I, 422–26.

36. *Colorado Tribune,* Sept. 25, 1872.

37. *Rocky Mountain News,* Apr. 14, 1870; *Colorado Chieftain,* Apr. 14, 1870; *Colorado Tribune,* Apr. 17, 1871; Willard and Goodykoontz, *Experiments in Colorado Colonization;* Marshall to Smiley, undated, in Jerome C. Smiley, *History of Denver: with Outlines of the Earlier History of the Rocky Mountain Country* (Denver, 1901), 453.

38. Frink, *When Cattle Was King,* 55; Colorado Springs (Colorado) *Gazette,* Jan. 4, 1873.

39. Palmer to his wife, undated, in Amanda Ellis, *The Colorado Springs Story* (Colorado Springs, Colo., 1954), 9; Smiley, *Colorado,* I, 455.

40. Ellis, *Colorado Springs Story,* 7–9; Colwell, "Colorado City," 16.

41. Sprague, *Newport of the Rockies,* 23–39; Kenneth E. Englert, "History of Colorado Springs" (typescript, Penrose Library), n.p.

42. *Colorado Tribune,* July 1, 1872; Sprague, *Newport of the Rockies,* 70; Colwell, "Railroad Age," in Carter, *Pike's Peak Region,* 17; *1880 Census, Population,* 113.

43. Athearn, *Coloradans,* 96; Englert, "Colorado Springs," n.p.

44. Townshend, *Tenderfoot in Colorado,* 187; Englert, "Colorado Springs," n.p.; Sprague, *Newport of the Rockies,* 87; *Greeley Tribune,* Sept. 24, 1873.

45. Fossett, *Historical Colorado*, 442, 452; Muirhead, *Land of Contrasts*, 212; *Colorado Tribune*, Jan 11. 1875; Sprague, *Newport of the Rockies*, 70.

46. Hogan, *Class and Community*, 159, 195.

47. *1870 Census, Population*, 16, 95; *1880 Census, Population*, 51–52; Isabella Bird, *Isabella Lucy Bird's "A Lady's Life in the Rocky Mountains,"* ed. Ernest S. Bernard (Norman, Okla., 1999), 5, 12, 55, 89, 116, 207.

48. Black, *Island in the Rockies*, 78–85; *1880 Census, Population*, 96; Duane Vandenbushe and Duane A. Smith, *A Land Alone: Colorado's Western Slope* (Boulder, Colo., 1981), 30–31, 41–47; Fred Espinosa, "Del Norte-Past and Present," *Colorado Magazine* 5 (June 1928): 98; Hall, *Colorado*, II, 192–93; Stone, *Colorado*, I, 156.

49. Hall, *Colorado*, I, 518; Abbott, Leonard, and McComb, *Colorado*, 78; Brosnan, *Mountain and Plain*, 77; West, *Contested Plains*, 251; Territory of Colorado, Territorial Board of Immigration, *Resources and Advantages of Colorado, Prepared and Published by Authority of the Territorial Board of Immigration* (Pamphlet, Denver, 1872), 47 pp.

50. Gould, *Wyoming*, 9–15; Spence, *Montana*, 119–28; Lamar, *Dakota Territory*, 149–50 Lamar, *Far Southwest*, 174–76, 393, 437–38; *1870 Census, Population*, 8–9, and 16; *1880 Census, Population*, 2–3 and 51–52; U.S. Department of the Interior, Census Bureau, *Report of the Population of the United States at the Eleventh Census, 1890*, part l (Washington, D.C., 1895), 75–80 and 236.

51. Alvin Steinel, *History of Agriculture in Colorado* (Fort Collins, Colo., 1926), 50–51; *1870 Census, Population*, 16; *1880 Census, Population*, 51–51.

Chapter 6: Town and Country Society

1. Greeley quoted in Carl Ubbelohde, Maxine Benson, and Duane Smith, *A Colorado History*, 8th ed. (Boulder, Colo., 2001), 93; Hall, *Colorado*, I, 233–34.

2. Stephen J. Leonard, *Lynching in Colorado, 1859–1919* (Boulder, Colo., 2002), 163–73; John W. Cook (comp.), *Hands Up; or, Thirty-five Years of Detective Life in the Mountains and on the Plains. Reminiscences of General D. J. Cook, Chief of the Rocky Mountain Detective Association* (Denver, 1897), 26, 92–125.

3. Cook, *Hands Up*, 41.

4. Ibid., 57–91; Colorado State Archives, "Prisoner's Index, 1871–1973" (http://www.archives.state.co.us/pen/index/html).

5. *Rocky Mountain News*, Feb. 23, 1870; Boyles, *St. Vrain Valley*, 46–51; James H. Pickering, *"This Blue Hollow," Estes Park, the Early Years, 1859–1915* (Niwot, Colo., 1999), 70–75; Watrous, *Larimer County*, 78.

6. Routt to Sherman, July 20, 1875, John Routt Letterbook (Colorado State Archives); John Ophus, "The Lake County War, 1874–1875," *Colorado Magazine* 47 (Spring 1970): 119–28.

7. Leonard, *Lynching in Colorado*, 32; Meline, *Two Thousand Miles*, 56; Athearn, *Westward the Briton*, 37–38, 40–41, 142; no author, *The Dome of the Continent: Colorado in 1872; including trips to Central City, Georgetown, Idaho Springs, Grays Peaks, Denver, with Geological, Mineralogical, and Biological Notes*, (Olympic Valley, Calif., 1977), 4; Maurice O'Conner Morris, *Ram-*

bles in the Rocky Mountains; with a Visit to the Gold Fields of Colorado (London, 1864), 78.

8. Rusling, *Across America,* 59–62.

9. Athearn, *Westward the Briton,* 38; Melvin H. Schoberlin, *From Candles to Footlights: A Biography of Pike's Peak Theatre, 1859–1876* (Denver 1941), 193; Smith, *Birth of Colorado,* 171; Lamar, *Far Southwest,* 284; Liston E. Leyendecker, *Georgetown: Colorado's Silver Queen, 1859–1876* (Fort Collins, Colo., 1977), 27; Taylor, *Trinidad,* 25.

10. Hall, *Colorado,* I, 207; Dixon, *New America,* I, 136.

11. *1870 Census, Population,* 624; *1880 Census, Population,* 560.

12. Mary Blake, *On the Wing: Rambling Notes of a Trip to the Pacific* (Boston, 1883), 46; Stanton, *Sixty Years,* 169–70.

13. *Rocky Mountain News,* June 14, 1865; Randall quoted in Athearn, *Westward the Briton,* 65; Dixon, *New America,* I, 136.

14. Pennock, "Incidents in Life," 126; Propst to Cousin, June 13, 1874, quoted in Conklin, *Logan County,* 153.

15. Journal of Mrs. Andrew Paul (Sarah) Hively, August 15, 1863 (Western History Department, Denver Public Library); Propst to Cousin, June 23, 1874, quoted in Conklin, *Logan County,* 152; Danker, *Mollie Sanford Journal,* 191; Pennock, "Incidents in Life," 129.

16. Buss Diary, Sept. 17, 1866; Hively Journal, June 19, 1864.

17. Interview with H. Slate, Sept. 4, 1885, Bancroft Collection; Dorothy Large, *Old Burlington: First Town on the St. Vrain, 1860–1871,* (Longmont, Colo., 1984), 33.

18. Danker, *Mollie Sanford Journal,* 128; Whitter, "Pioneer," 166; Riethmann statement, n.d., in Amelia Block Papers (Western Americana Collection); Clark Secrest, *Hell's Belles: Prostitution, Vice, and Crime in Early Denver,* rev. ed. (Boulder, Colo., 2002), 74–75.

19. Statement of Mrs. Mote, n.d., in Frances Boyle Papers (Western History Department, Denver Public Library); Young, "Pioneer Days," 62; St. Vrain Historical Society, *They Came to Stay,* 195.

20. Buss Diary, Sept. 17, 1866, Sept. 21, Oct. 9, and Oct. 24, 1867.

21. Pennock, "Incidents in Life," 127; Hively Journal, May 22, 1863; Mrs. J. A. Davis, "Interesting Account of Pioneer Life," in Pamphlet File (Western Americana Collection); Buss Diary, Sept. 21, 1867; see especially Oct. 1866, and Feb. and Mar. 1867, for statements on loneliness.

22. Pennock, "Incidents in Life," 126–27; Harris, *Long Vistas,* 21; Propst, *Forgotten People,* 47.

23. Barth, *Instant Cities,* 172–73.

24. West, *Contested Plains,* 184–87; Barth, *Instant Cities,* 126; Leonard and Noel, *Denver,* 34.

25. *Rocky Mountain News,* May 24 and Sept. 30, 1865; Alice Polk Hill, *Colorado Pioneers in Picture and Story* (Denver, Colo., 1915), 224; Grace Greenwood, *New Life in New Lands: Notes of Travel* (New York, 1873), 43; *Colorado Tribune,* Oct. 18 and 25, 1872.

26. Hall to Mother, Jan. 20, 29, 1867 and June 28, 1868, Frank Hall Papers (Colorado State Historical Society Library); *Colorado Tribune,* July 12, 1873, May 11, 1876.

27. Frink, *When Cattle Was King,* 60.

28. Virginia McConnell, "A Gauge of Popular Taste in Early Colorado," *Colorado Magazine* 46 (Fall 1969): 338–50; Athearn, *Coloradans*, 157–58.

29. McConnell, "Popular Taste," 347; Thomas J. Noel, *The City and the Saloon: Denver, 1858–1916* (Niwot, Colo., 1996), 18.

30. *Colorado Tribune*, July 23, 1872; *Greeley Tribune*, n.d., quoted in Schoberlin, *From Candles to Footlights*, 208.

31. Fritz, *Colorado*, 225; Stone, *Colorado*, I, 661–69.

32. Stone, *Colorado*, I, 681–87; Hafen, *Colorado*, I, 642; II, 203; Hall, *Colorado*, I, 207; H. C. Waltz to G. I. Reed, Jan. 1, 1875, Waltz Papers.

33. *1870 Census, Population*, 16, 95; *1880 Census, Population*, 381–82.

34. U.S. Bureau of the Census, "Population Schedules of the Ninth Census of the United States, 1870: Colorado" (microfilm), NARG 29; Berwanger, *West and Reconstruction*, 25.

35. Noel, *City and the Saloon*, 26–27; Morris, *Rambles in the Rocky Mountains*, 77.

36. Quintard Taylor, *In Search of the Racial Frontier: African-Americans in the American West, 1528–1990* (New York, 1998), 203.

37. *Rocky Mountain News*, Apr. 12, 1871; *Colorado Tribune*, July 15, 1872.

38. Walter Lumley Shelly, "The Colorado Republican Party: The Formative Years, 1861–1876" (M.A. thesis, University of Colorado, 1963), 67–71; *Denver Times*, n.d., in Elmer Ellis, *Henry Moore Teller: Defender of the West* (Caldwell, Idaho, 1941), 88; *Rocky Mountain News*, Sept.14, 1875; *Colorado Tribune*, Mar. 24 and Sept. 14, 1875; see the *Colorado Chieftain* and the *Colorado Tribune*, Mar. to Aug., 1876, for articles on crimes committed by blacks.

39. Bowles, *Our New West*, 190; *Rocky Mountain News*, Jan. 2, 1868.

40. John Lawrence Dairy (Western Americana Collection), n.p.; Rusling, *Across America*, 92; Bowles, *Across the Continent*, 21; Howbert, *Memories*, 167.

41. M. Sheldon interview, n.d., Bancroft Collection; Legard, *Colorado*, 101–2.

42. U. B. Holloway to David Nichols, July 9, 1866, David H. Nichols Papers (Western Americana Collection); Swadesh, *Los Prímeros Pobladores*, 91–92; *New York Times*, Oct. 25, 1873.

43. *Colorado Chieftain*, May 2, 1872.

44. *Colorado Chieftain*, July 10, 17, Aug. 3, 29, 1873; Taylor, *Summer Trip*, 51.

45. *Rocky Mountain News*, Jan. 3, 6, 13, and 27, 1868; Taylor, *Trinidad*, 60–75.

46. Hall to Gen. A. J. Smith, Mar. 2, 1868, in William S. Jenkins (ed), "Records of the United States of America: A Microfilm Compilation. Colorado 1861–1876" (Colorado State Archives); Taylor, *Trinidad*, 73–75.

47. Noel, *City and the Saloon*, 28; *1880 Census, Population*, 382; Hall, *Colorado*, I, 496; *Colorado Tribune*, July 14, 1873.

48. *Colorado Tribune*, Oct. 10, 1872, July 14, 1873, Jan. 26 and June 8, 1876.

Chapter 7: Reform and Corruption

1. John G. Sproat, *"The Best Men": Liberal Reformers in the Gilded Age* (New York, 1968), 66–85.

2. Elliott West, "Of Lager Beer and Sonorous Songs," *Colorado Magazine* 48 (Spring 1971): 113–17; U.S. Congress, House of Representatives, 43 Cong., 1

Sess., "Admission of Colorado as a State" (Committee on Territories Report, No. 619), 4; Bird quoted in Noel, *City and the Saloon,* 115.

3. Dodds, *Pueblo,* 22.

4. West, "Of Lager Beer," 109; Athearn, *Westward the Briton,* 75; Noel, *City and the Saloon,* 17.

5. Noel, *City and the Saloon,* 23–29; *Colorado Tribune,* Nov. 16, 1872; *Rocky Mountain News,* June, 15, 1865.

6. Noel, *City and the Saloon,* 23–29, 134.

7. *Greeley Tribune,* Nov. 16, 1870, Oct. 11, 1871, and Jan. 24, 1872; *Rocky Mountain News,* Oct, 25, 1870; *Colorado Tribune,* Aug. 8, 1872; Howbert, *Memoirs,* 234–36.

8. *Colorado Chieftain,* July 15, 1874; Howbert, *Memoirs,* 234–36; Sprague, *Newport of the Rockies,* 66.

9. Colorado Springs *Gazette,* Nov. 21, 1874 and Apr. 10, 1875; Sprague, *Newport of the Rockies,* 65; Durning, *Chicago-Colorado Colony,* 14; *Colorado Tribune,* June 3, 1871, and May 3, 1875.

10. Fred Anderson, "Prohibition in Fort Collins, Colorado, Prior to the Passage of the Volstead Act" (typescript in possession of author), 1–4; Evadene Burris Swanson, *Fort Collins Yesterdays* (Fort Collins, Colo., 1975), 22–24.

11. Thomas P. Lowry, *The Story the Soldiers Wouldn't Tell: Sex in the Civil War* (Mechanicsburg, Pa. 1994), 11–88; James C. Mohr, *Radical Republicans in the North: State Politics During Reconstruction* (Baltimore, 1976), 8, 106.

12. Swanson, *Fort Collins Yesterdays,* 25; *Colorado Tribune,* July 14, 1873; Secrest, *Hell's Belles,* 89.

13. Joanne West Dodds, *What's a Nice Girl Like You Doing in a Place Like This?: Prostitution in Southern Colorado, 1860–1911* (Pueblo, Colo., 1996), 3–5; Anne M. Butler, *Daughters of Joy, Sisters of Mercy: Prostitutes in the American West, 1865–1890* (Urbana, Ill., 1985), xvi–xvii; *Colorado Tribune,* July 14, 1873.

14. *Rocky Mountain News,* Nov. 30, 1872; Oct. 26, 27, 1873; Mar. 6, 7, 19, Aug. 30, Sept. 2, 3, 1874; and Apr. 20, 1875.

15. *Rocky Mountain News,* Sept. 23, 1874 and Apr. 20, 1875; Secrest, *Hell's Belles,* 104; Butler, *Daughters of Joy,* 63–64.

16. *Rocky Mountain News,* Aug. 12, 1874; Butler, *Daughters of Joy,* 63–64; Secrest, *Hell's Belles,* 91.

17. Secrest, *Hell's Belles,* 91–102; Butler, *Daughters of Joy,* 65–69.

18. *Colorado Tribune,* Feb. 10, 1867; the most complete account of the Kansas referendum is found in Ellen Carol DuBois, *Feminism and Suffrage: The Emergence of an Independent Women's Movement in America, 1848–1869* (Ithaca, N.Y., 1978). Despite the dates in the title the bulk of her book focuses on the post–Civil War period.

19. Stone, *Colorado,* I, 668

20. *Council Journal, 1870,* 19, 131–38; *Colorado Tribune,* Feb. 10, 1870; Kassler to Mae, June 28, 1871, George Kassler Papers (Colorado State Historical Society Library).

21. *Colorado Tribune,* Jan. 13, 21, 17, Feb. 1, 9, 10, 13, Mar. 19, and Apr. 14, 1870.

22. Efay Nelson Grigg, "Social Legislation and the Welfare Program," in Hafen, *Colorado,* II, 333–34; Thomas J. Noel, Stephen J. Leonard, and Kevin E. Rucker, *Colorado Givers: A History of Philanthropic Heroes* (Niwot, Colo., 1998), 2–10.

23. *Denver Weekly Times,* July 15, 1875; *Colorado Tribune,* May 6, 1876; John E. Ray, D. C. Dudley, and G. W. Veditz, *A Brief Historical Sketch and Handbook of the Colorado School for the Deaf and Blind from its Inception to Mar., 1st, 1893* (Colorado Springs, Colo., 1893), 3–12; Colwell, "Railroad Age," 16; Stone, *Colorado,* I, 821.

24. Samuel Hoyt to Orville Browning, Mar. 7, 1869 and Feb. 5,1870, in U.S. Department of Interior, "Territorial Papers, Colorado 1861–1888: Letters Received Relating to the Penitentiary at Cañon City, Jan. 18, 1868-Dec. 27, 1875, and Miscellaneous Subjects, Oct. 26-May 31, 1876" (Mss, National Archives Microfilm Publication #431); quotation from *Colorado Chieftain,* June 29, 1873; "Proclamation of Governor McCook re territorial penitentiary, June 6, 1871, in Territory of Colorado, Governors of Colorado, "Record of Executive Proceedings, Colorado Territory. Executive Papers, 1861–1870, Book A" (Mss, Colorado State Archives); Virgil V. Peterson, "Penal, Correctional and Eleemosynary Institutions in Colorado," in Hafen, *Colorado,* II, 609–11.

25. *1860 Census, Population,* 546; Inez Johnson Lewis, "Progress of Education in Colorado," in Hafen, *Colorado,* II, 159–61; Smiley, *Colorado,* I, 441; Fritz, *Colorado,* 222–23.

26. "Reports of the Superintendent of Public Instruction," for 1871, 1872, 1874, and 1875, all in Jenkins, "Records"; Mohr, *Radical Republicans in the North,* 17, 68, 106; Lewis, "Education in Colorado," 162–63; Berwanger, "Reconstruction on the Frontier," 326–27.

27. Michael McGiffert, *The Higher Learning in Colorado: An Historical Study, 1860–1940* (Denver, 1964), 6, 24; George Willard Frasier and William Hartman, "History of Higher Education in Colorado," in Hafen, *Colorado,* II, 477; Stone, *Colorado,* I, 611–13.

28. Frasier, "Higher Education," 479; Stone, *Colorado,* I, 603–4, Athearn, *Coloradans,* 155.

29. *Boulder County News,* Nov. 3, 1871; McGiffert, *Higher Learning,* 7.

30. *Greeley Tribune,* May 27, 1876; McGiffert, *Higher Learning,* 6–7.

31. Noel, *Colorado Givers,* 57; Frasier, "Higher Education," 480.

32. Colorado Springs *Gazette,* n.d., quoted in McGiffert, *Higher Learning* 26; Frasier, "Higher Education," 477; Fritz, *Colorado,* 225.

33. Noel, *Growing Through History,* 23; Abbott, Leonard, and McComb, *Colorado,* 67.

34. Stanton, *Sixty Years,* 181, 209–10; unsigned and undated statement in Bancroft private notes, Bancroft Collection.

35. Hall, *Colorado,* I, 448–49; *New York Times,* Mar. 5, 1875.

36. Hall, *Colorado* I, 467.

37. *Colorado Tribune,* May 26, 1869.

38. *Council Journal, 1870,* 19; *Colorado Tribune,* Jan. 5, 1870; Hall, *Colorado* I, 528.

39. Lamar, *Far Southwest,* 287; Simmons, *Ute Indians,* 134.

40. Elliott West, "Jerome B. Chaffee and the McCook-Elbert Fight," *Colorado Magazine* 46 (Spring 1969): 154–55; Lamar, *Far Southwest,* 286–87; Hall, *Colorado,* II, 167–70.

41. Hall, *Colorado,* II, 169; West, "McCook-Elbert Fight," 153–54.

42. *Rocky Mountain News,* Dec. 12, 1872; Thompson to McCook, Dec. 12 and 20, 1872; Feb. 5 and 18, 1873, James B. Thompson Papers (Western History Department, Denver Public Library).

43. *Colorado Tribune,* Apr. 27 and May 5, 1874.

44. Hall, *Colorado,* II, 164–67; *Congressional Globe,* 43 Cong., 1 Sess., part I, vol. II, 103–603; *Colorado Tribune,* Jan. 14, 1874; *Colorado Chieftain,* Dec. 20, 1873; West, "McCook-Elbert Fight," 149.

45. Robinson's report was published in full in the *Colorado Chieftain,* Feb. 1, 1874; *Colorado Tribune,* Jan. 30 and Feb. 2, 1874; *Rocky Mountain News,* July 15, 1874.

46. Hall, *Colorado,* II, 167.

47. The *News*'s defense was in part motivated by Byers's friendship with Moffat and Carr. Perhaps he sympathized with them because he was, at the same time, involved in a lawsuit over land he had obtained by questionable means. In 1854 Congress had issued script to mixed-blood Indians in Minnesota authorizing them to claim up to 480 acres of surveyed public land. Ten years later, Byers's brother-in-law received permission from Susan Boshman, a half-caste French-Canadian Sioux, to take up land on her behalf. He claimed 160 acres around Hot Sulphur Springs and immediately sold it to Byers. Simultaneously two other brothers-in-law each laid claim to 160 acres adjacent to Byers's land and then transferred title to the editor. In 1875 Boshman's relatives sued to regain her portion of the land but finally settled for monetary compensation after several years. See Black, *Island in the Rockies,* 63–73.

48. *Greeley Tribune,* Feb. 4, 1874.

49. *Colorado Tribune,* Feb. 2 and 15, 1874; Hall, *Colorado,* II, 157.

50. Colfax to Hall, Feb. 20, 1874, Hall Papers (Colorado State Historical Society Library); Hall to Harper Orahood, Dec. 25, 1874, Harper Orahood Papers (Western Americana Collection); Elbert to Jerome Chaffee, Feb. 1, 1874, Elbert Papers; (Georgetown) *Colorado Miner,* Feb 5, 1874; *Rocky Mountain News,* Jan. 28, 1874.

51. Elbert was the son-in-law of John Evans.

52. *Colorado Tribune,* Jan. 30, 1874; *Colorado Chieftain,* Dec. 29, 1872, and Jan. 30, 1874; *Boulder County News,* Jan 30, 1874; Teller to Harper Orahood, Jan. 25, 1874, Orahood Papers; Charles S. Thomas, "The Pioneer Bar of Colorado," *Colorado Magazine* 1 (1924): 201.

53. West, "McCook-Elbert Fight," 146–56; Smiley, *Colorado,* I, 377; Hall, *Colorado,* II, 157–58, 170: *Colorado Tribune,* Feb. 4, Mar. 24, Apr. 8, 17, and June 19, 1874.

54. Hall, *Colorado,* II, 173; *Colorado Tribune,* May 16, 1874; Lamar, *Far Southwest,* 289; Fossett, *Historical Colorado,* 128.

55. Colorado Springs *Gazette,* Mar. 29, 1873, and June 26, 1875; (Longmont) *Colorado Press,* July 3, 1873; *Colorado Tribune,* Oct. 2, 1873, and Feb. 5, 1874.

56. *New York Times,* Aug. 12, 1874; Hall, *Colorado,* II, 212–13; Lamar, *Far Southwest,* 288–89.

57. *Fort Collins Standard,* Aug. 29, 1874; Colorado Springs *Gazette,* Sept. 12, 1874; West, "McCook-Elbert Fight," 164–65; Robert E. Smith, "Patterson," 157.

58. *Laramie* (Wyoming) *Sentinel,* n.d., quoted in Ubbelohde, Benson, and Smith, *A Colorado History,* 147; Greenwood, *New Life in New Lands,* 127.

Chapter 8: Statehood at Last

1. Lamar, *Far Southwest,* 271–72.

2. *Colorado Tribune,* Jan. 1, 1871; *Colorado Chieftain,* Jan. 26, 1873.

3. *Colorado Chieftain,* Dec. 18, 1872; *New York Times,* Aug. 4, 1874.

4. Chaffee to Irving Stanton, Dec. 20, 1871, Irving W. Stanton Papers (Western History Department, Denver Public Library); Chaffee to Evans, Nov. 20 1867, Evans Papers; *New York Times,* Jan. 3, 1872; *Colorado Chieftain,* Dec. 24, 1872.

5. *Colorado Tribune,* May 4, 1876; Hall, *Colorado,* II, 122–25; U.S. Congress, House of Representatives, 43 Cong., 1 Sess., "Admission of Colorado as a State," *House Report* #619, 6 pp.

6. "Admission of Colorado," 4; Hall, *Colorado,* I, 453; II, 155; Ambrose, *Nothing Like It in the World,* 185; Lamar, *Far Southwest,* 289–90.

7. *Colorado Tribune,* Dec. 29, 1873; Smiley, *Colorado,* I, 484; Hall, *Colorado,* I, 268.

8. "Colorado Enabling Act," *Statutes at Large of the United States from December, 1873 to Mar., 1875,* vol. XVIII, part 3 (Washington, D.C., 1875), 474–76.

9. *Cong. Record,* 43 Cong., 2 Sess., 1671–90.

10. Patterson to Kate, Feb. 21, 1875, Thomas M. Patterson Family Papers (Western Americana Collection); Smith, "Patterson," 158; Hall, *Colorado,* II, 268–72.

11. When a presidential election goes to the House of Representatives, each state is entitled to one vote and the candidate must receive a majority of the votes cast.

12. *New York Times,* June 28, 1875; Smith, "Patterson," 160; Theo. F. Van-Wagenen, "Views on the Admission of Colorado in 1876," *Colorado Magazine* 3 (Aug. 1926): 86–88; Hall, *Colorado,* II, 270–72.

13. *Proceedings of the Constitutional Convention Held in Denver, December 20, 1875 to Frame a Constitution for the State of Colorado Together with the Enabling Act, the Address to the People, and The Constitution as Adopted and the President's Proclamation* (Denver, 1907), 15–17; *Colorado Tribune,* Feb. 14, 1876; Lamar, *Far Southwest.* 290–91; Henry J. Hersey, "The Colorado Constitution," *Colorado Magazine* 3 (Aug. 1921): 69–70.

14. *Colorado Tribune,* Jan. 23, 1876.

15. *Proceedings,* 42, 102, 108, 149, 623, 663; Colin G. Goodykoontz, "Some Controversial Questions Before the Colorado Constitutional Convention of 1876," *Colorado Magazine* 17 (Jan. 1940): 4; *Colorado Tribune,* Jan. 23, 1876.

16. *Proceedings,* 146, 152, 158, 163, 165, 183, 228, 235–36, 261, 277–78, 296, 309, 320, 329; *Colorado Tribune,* Jan. 23, 1876; Goodykoontz, "Controversial Questions," 6–8.

17. "Address to the People," in *Proceedings,* 728; see also *Proceedings,* 55, 59, 72, 116, 119, 334, 697–700; Hafen, *Colorado,* I, 349; Goodykoontz, "Controversial Questions," 10.

18. *Proceedings,* 109, 112, 165, 261, 266–71, 314–15; Susan B. Anthony claimed opposition on the part of the Hispano population delayed the granting of woman suffrage in Colorado. For a refutation of the idea see William B. Faherty, "Regional Minorities and the Woman Suffrage Struggle," *Colorado Magazine* 33 (July 1956): 215.

19. *Proceedings,* 683; *Colorado Tribune,* Feb. 19, 1876; Fatherty, "Regional Minorities," 216; Hafen, *Colorado,* I, 249–50.

20. Wells quoted in *Legislative, Historical and Biographical Compendium of Colorado, Embracing Information . . . of its Territorial and State Governments, Together with . . . Biographical Sketches of the Governor, State Officers, Senators, and Representatives of the Sixth Biennial Legislature* (Denver, Colo., 1887), 168; *Colorado Tribune,* Jan. 25, 1876; Faherty, "Regional Minorities," 215.

21. *Proceedings,* 100, 282, 702; José Emilio Fernández, *The Biography of Casimiro Barela,* trans. A. Gabriel Melédez (Albuquerque, N.M., 2003), 39; *1870 Census, Population,* 305; *1880 Census, Population,* 560–61; Hafen, *Colorado,* I, 347.

22. *Colorado Tribune,* May 19, June 7, and June 21, 1876; Colorado Springs *Gazette,* Feb. 20, 1875, and June 17, 1876.

23. Colorado Springs *Gazette,* Jan. 17, 1874; *Colorado Tribune,* June 9, 15, 16, 21, and 22, 1876; *New York Times,* Mar. 24, 1876.

24. *Daily Miner's Register,* July 3, 1876; *Colorado Chieftain,* July 2, 1876; *Rocky Mountain News,* July 6, 1876; "Admission of Colorado," 5; Fernández, *Barela,* 42; Hall, *Colorado,* II, 328; Hafen, *Colorado,* I, 355–56.

25. *The Encyclopedia of American Facts and Dates,* 7th ed. (New York, 1979), 208–312.

26. *Proceedings,* 11, 655–60, 671–72, 706–7; *Colorado Tribune,* Mar. 11 and 15, 1876; *Legislative Compendium,* 165.

27. *New York Times,* Oct. 26, 1876; State of Colorado, "House Journal, 1st Sess, 1876–1877 (Ms, Colorado State Archives—the proceedings of the first session of the legislature were never published).

28. Smith, "Patterson," 162.

29. *Cong. Record,* 44 Cong., 2 Sess., 3–11.

30. *Colorado Tribune,* Jan. 4, 1877; Colorado Springs *Gazette,* Dec. 17, 1876; *Rocky Mountain News,* Dec. 19, 1876, and Jan. 27, 1877; *Boulder County News,* Dec. 15, 1876; *Cong. Record,* 44 Cong., 2 Sess., 92, 1060; Springer to editor, Dec. 23, 1876, in *Colorado Chieftain,* Jan. 7, 1877.

31. *Cong. Record,* 44 Cong., 2 Sess., 1140–54; *New York Times,* Jan. 4, 1877.

32. Dudley Taylor Cornish, "The First Five Years of Statehood," *Colorado Magazine* 25 (July 1948): 220–32; Hall, *Colorado,* 484–87.

33. Abbott, Leonard, and McComb, *Colorado,* 127–28; Hall, *Colorado,* I, 548; II, 480.

BIBLIOGRAPHY

Papers, Diaries, and Journals

H. William Axford Papers, American Heritage Center, University of Wyoming, Laramie.

Rose Bell Diary, Colorado State Historical Society Library, Denver.

Amelia Block Papers, Western Americana Collection, University of Colorado, Boulder.

Alanzo Boardman Papers, Western History Department, Denver Public Library.

Frances Boyle Papers, Western History Department, Denver Public Library.

Amelia Buss Diary, Western Americana Collection, University of Colorado.

William Z. Cozens Papers, Colorado State Historical Society Library.

F. W. Cragen Papers, Western Americana Collection, University of Colorado.

Leonard Eicholtz Papers, American Heritage Center, University of Wyoming

Samuel Elbert Letterbook, Colorado State Archives, Denver.

Samuel Elbert Papers, Colorado State Historical Society Library.

John Elsner Papers, Western History Department, Denver Public Library.

John Evans Papers, Colorado State Historical Society Library.

George Forsyth Papers, Colorado State Historical Society Library.

Frank Hall Papers, Colorado State Historical Society Library.

Frank Hall Papers, Western Americana Collection, University of Colorado.

James Stratton Harlow Diary, Fort Collins Public Library.

John Harper Papers, Western Americana Collection, University of Colorado.

Jacob O. Hays Papers, American Heritage Center, University of Wyoming.

N.P. Hill Papers, Colorado State Historical Society Library.

Sarah (Mrs. Andrew Paul) Hively Journal, Western History Department, Denver Public Library.

Ann Honselman Papers, Western Americana Collection, University of Colorado.

Alexander Cameron Hunt Papers, Colorado State Historical Society Library.

George Kassler Papers, Colorado State Historical Society Library.

John Lawrence Diary, Western Americana Collection, University of Colorado.

Edward McCook Papers, Colorado State Historical Society Library.

Samuel Mallary Papers, Western Americana Collection, University of Colorado.

Nathan Meeker Papers, Colorado State Historical Society Library.

David H. Nichols Papers, Western Americana Collection, University of Colorado.

Airlio Ogilvy Papers, Western Americana Collection, University of Colorado.

Harper Orahood Papers, Western Americana Collection, University of Colorado.

William Jackson Palmer Papers, Colorado State Historical Society Library.

Thomas M. Patterson Family Papers, Western Americana Collection, University of Colorado.
Morton E. Post Papers, American Heritage Center, University of Wyoming.
John Routt Letterbooks, Colorado State Archives.
John Routt Papers, Colorado State Historical Society Library.
Hal Sayre Papers, Western Americana Collection, University of Colorado.
P. G. Scott Papers, Colorado State Historical Society Library.
William Tecumseh Sherman Family Papers: Letters of William Tecumseh Sherman to Ellen Ewing Sherman (microfilm).
Silas Soule Papers, Western History Department, Denver Public Library.
Irving W. Stanton Papers, Colorado State Historical Society Library.
Irving W. Stanton Papers, Western History Department, Denver Public Library.
Samuel F. Tappan Papers, Colorado State Historical Society Library.
Henry M. Teller Papers, Western Americana Collection, University of Colorado.
James B. Thompson Papers, Western History Department, Denver Public Library.
H. C. Waltz Papers, American Heritage Center, University of Wyoming.
Daniel Witter Papers, Colorado State Historical Society Library.

Statements and Memoirs

Ashley, Susan R., "Colorado Territorial Days," Colorado State Historical Society Library.
Bancroft, Hubert Howe Collection, Western Americana Collection, University of Colorado.
Bennet Family Memoirs, Western Americana Collection, University of Colorado.
Canon, Benton, "History of the Georgia Colony," Colorado State Historical Society Library.
Davis, Mrs. J. A., "Interesting Account of Pioneer Life," Western Americana Collection, University of Colorado.
Ellinwood, L. E. "Memoirs of Old Colorado City," Penrose Public Library, Colorado Springs.
Scott, P. G. Collection, Colorado State Historical Society Library.

Official Manuscripts

Colorado, State of. "House Journal, 1st Session, 1876–1877," Colorado State Archives.
Colorado, Territory of. "Governors of Colorado: Record of Executive Proceedings, Colorado Territory. Executive Papers, 1861–1870: Book A," Colorado State Archives (microfilm).
Jenkins, William S. (ed.), "Records of the United States of America: A Microfilm Compilation. Colorado 1861–1876," Colorado State Archives.
U.S. Bureau of the Census. "Population Schedules of the Ninth Census of the United States: 1870." National Archives, Record Group 29 (microfilm).

U.S. Department of the Interior. "Territorial Papers, Colorado, 1861–1888. Letters Received Relating to the Penitentiary at Cañon City, January 18, 1868–December 27, 1875, and Miscellaneous Subjects, October 26, 1861–Mar. 31, 1875" (microfilm).

U.S. Department of State. "Territorial Papers: Colorado Series, Vol. I: Incoming Letters and their Enclosures, Proclamations, Petitions, and Memorials, December 26, 1859–Apr. 22, 1874" (microfilm).

U.S. Senate. "Territorial Papers of the United States Senate, 1789–1873: Colorado, Apr. 3, 1860–February 20, 1868" (microfilm).

Internet Sources

Colorado State Archives. "John Evans" (http://www.state.co.us./archives/govs/html)

Colorado State Archives. "Prisoner's Index, 1871–1973" (http://www.state.co.us/pen/index/html)

Colorado State Archives. "William Gilpin" (http://www.state.co.us/archives/govs/html)

Newspapers

Note: Colorado newspaper titles often changed; to avoid confusion I cite the most frequently used title.

Black Hawk *Daily Mining Journal.*

Boulder County News.

Central City *Daily Miners' Register.*

Cheyenne (Wyoming) *Leader.*

Chicago Tribune.

Central City *Daily Miners' Register.*

Colorado Springs *Gazette.*

Denver *Colorado Tribune.*

Denver *Rocky Mountain News.*

Denver Weekly Times.

Fort Collins Standard.

Georgetown *The Colorado Miner.*

Golden *Colorado Transcript.*

Greeley Tribune.

Longmont *Colorado Press.*

Longmont Times.

New York Times.

Pueblo *Colorado Chieftain.*

Published Sources and Documents

Ashley, Susan R. "Reminiscences of Colorado in the Early Sixties," *Colorado Magazine* 13 (Nov. 1936): 219–30.

Basler, Roy P. (ed.). *The Collected Works of Abraham Lincoln.* 9 vols. New Brunswick, N.J., 1956.

Biographical Directory of the American Congresses, 1774–1949. Washington, D.C., 1949.

Carey, Raymond G. *A Collection of Documents Concerning the Battle of Sand Creek, November 29, 1864.* Denver, 1958.

Carroll, John M. *The Sand Creek Massacre: A Documentary History.* New York, 1973.

Colorado Business Directory, 1876. Denver, 1876.

Colorado, Territory of. *Biennial Report of the Adjutant-General of the Territory of Colorado for the two years ending, December 31, 1869.* Central City, 1870.

———. *Council of the Legislative Session of the Territory of Colorado,* 1866, 1867, 1870, 1872, 1874, 1876. Title and imprint vary.

———. *House Journal of the Legislative Session of the Territory of Colorado, Eighth Session, 1870.* Central City, 1870.

———. Territorial Board of Immigration. *Resources and Advantages of Colorado, Prepared and Published by Authority of the Territorial Board of Immigration.* Pamphlet. Denver, 1873.

Commager, Henry Steele. *Documents of American History.* New York, 1963.

Cummings, Alexander. *Speech of Alexander Cummings Delivered at Williamsport, Pa., September 1856, on the Question, "Did the Constitution Establish Slavery."* Pamphlet, n.p., n.d.

Danker, Donald (ed.). *Mollie: The Journal of Mollie Dorsey Sanford in Nebraska and Colorado Territories, 1857–1866.* Lincoln, Neb., 1959.

Giddens, Paul (ed.). "The Letters of Newton S. Pettis, Associate Justice of the Colorado Supreme Court, Written in 1861," *Colorado Magazine* 15 (Jan. 1938): 3–14.

McDonough, Marian McIntyre. "Diary of a Tenderfoot on the Denver and Rio Grande Survey in 1871," *The Denver Westerners Brand Book* 28 (1972): 113–36.

Mattes, Merrill J. (ed.). "The Beecher Island Battlefield Diary of Sigmund Schlesinger," *Colorado Magazine* 29 (July 1952): 160–69.

Proceedings of the Constitutional Convention Held in Denver, December 20, 1875, to form a Constitution for the State of Colorado together with the Enabling Act, the Address to the People, The Constitution as Adopted and, the President's Proclamation. Denver, 1907.

Sanford, Mollie E. Dorsey. "The Diary of a Pioneer Woman," *The Denver Westerners Brand Book* 10 (1954): 295–329.

Spring, Agnes Wright (ed.). "The Diary of Mary Ellen Jackson Barley Bailey," *The Denver Westerners Brand Book* 18 (1962): 109–34.

Statutes at Large of the United States from December, 1859, to Mar., 1863. Vol. XII. Boston, 1863.

Statutes at Large of the United States from December, 1873, to Mar., 1875. Vol. XVIII, part 3. Washington, D.C., 1875.

Statutes at Large of the United States from December, 1875, to Mar., 1877. Vol. XIX, part 1. Washington, D.C., 1877.

Thorndike, Rachel Sherman. *The Sherman Letters: Correspondence Between General Sherman and Senator Sherman from 1837 to 1891.* New York, 1967.

U.S. Bureau of the Census. *Eighth Census of the United States: 1860, Population.* Washington, D.C., 1864.

———. *Ninth Census of the United States: 1870, Population.* Washington, D.C., 1872.

———. *Tenth Census of the United States: 1880, Population.* Washington, D.C., 1883.

———. *Eleventh Census of the United States: 1890, Population.* Washington, D.C., 1895.

U.S. Bureau of the Mint. "Visiting the U.S. Mint in Denver: its History and Coinage." Pamphlet. Washington, D.C., 1995.

U.S. Congress. *Congressional Globe,* 39, 40, 41, 42 Congresses, 1865–73.

———. *Congressional Record,* 43, 44, 45 Congresses, 1874–77.

———. House of Representatives. *House Miscellaneous Documents:* "Superintendent of Indian Affairs for Colorado," 39 Congress, 2 Sess., No. 81.

———. House of Representatives. *House Miscellaneous Documents:* "Admission of Colorado as a State," 43 Congress, 1 Sess., No. 619.

U.S. Department of War. *The War of the Rebellion: A Compilation of the Official Records of the Union and Confederate Armies.* Series I. 70 vols. Washington, D.C., 1880–1901.

Whitney, Chauncey B. "Diary of Chauncey B. Whitney," *Collections of the Kansas State Historical Society* 12 (1911–12): 296–302.

Books and Articles

Abbott, Carl, Stephen J. Leonard, and David McComb. *Colorado: A History of the Centennial State.* Niwot, Colo., 1994.

Afton, Jean, David Fridtjof Halaas, Andrew Masich, and Richard Ellis. *Cheyenne Dog Soldiers: A Ledgerbook History of Coups and Combat.* Denver, 1997.

Allen, Alonzo H. "Early Days in Longmont," *Colorado Magazine* 14 (Sept. 1937): 191–98.

Ambrose, Stephen E. *Nothing Like it in the World: The Men Who Built the Transcontinental Railroad, 1863–1865.* New York, 2000.

American Encyclopedia of Facts and Dates. 7th ed. New York, 1979.

Anderson, Fred. "Prohibition in Fort Collins, Colorado, Prior to Passage of the Volstead Act," typescript in possession of author.

Anderson, Harry H. (ed.). "Stand at the Arkiaree," *Colorado Magazine* 41 (Fall 1964): 337–42.

Ashby, George. *Major Grenville M. Dodge (1836–1916): Maker of History in the Great West.* New York, 1947.

Athearn, Frederic J. *Land of Contrasts: A History of Southeast Colorado.* Denver, 1985.

Athearn, Robert G. "Colorado and the Indian War of 1868," *Colorado Magazine* 33 (Jan. 1956): 42–51.

———. *High Country Empire: The High Plains and the Rockies.* New York, 1960.

———. *Rebel of the Rockies: A History of the Denver & Rio Grande Western Railroad.* New Haven, Conn., 1962.

———. *The Coloradans.* Albuquerque, N.M., 1976.

———. "The Denver and Rio Grande and the Panic of 1873," *Colorado Magazine* 35 (Apr. 1958): 121–38.

———. *Westward the Briton.* New York, 1953.

———. *William Tecumseh Sherman and the Settlement of the West.* Norman, Okla., 1956.

Axford, H. William. *Gilpin County Gold: Peter McFarlane, 1848–1929, Mining Entrepreneur in Central City, Colorado.* Chicago, 1976.

Baker, James, ed. *History of Colorado,* 5 vols. Denver, 1927.

Bancroft, Caroline. *Six Racy Madams of Colorado.* Boulder, Colo., 1965.

Bancroft, Hubert Howe. *History of Nevada, Colorado, and Wyoming, 1540–1888.* Vol. XXV, *The Works of Hubert Howe Bancroft.* San Francisco, 1890.

Barth, Gunther. *Instant Cities: Urbanization and the Rise of San Francisco and Denver.* New York, 1975.

Beaman, James. "Concise History of Pueblo," typescript, Pueblo Public Library.

Beck, Warren A., and Ynez D. Hasse. *Historical Atlas of New Mexico.* Norman, Okla., 1969.

Beecher Island Annual: Sixty-Second Anniversary of the Battle of Beecher Island, Sept. 17, 18, 1868. Wray, Colo., 1930.

Bender, Norman J. "Crusade of the Blue Banner of Colorado," *Colorado Magazine* 47 (Spring 1970): 91–118.

Bernard, Ernest S. *Isabella Lucy Bird's "A Lady's Life in the Rocky Mountains."* Norman, Okla., 1999.

Berwanger, Eugene H. "Reconstruction on the Frontier: The Equal Rights Struggle in Colorado, 1865–1867," *Pacific Historical Review* 44 (Aug. 1975): 313–29.

———. "William J. Hardin: Colorado Spokesman for Racial Justice, 1863–1873," *Colorado Magazine* 52 (Winter 1975): 52–65.

———. "The Absurd and the Spectacular: The Historiography of the Plains-Mountain States: Colorado, Montana, Wyoming," *Pacific Historical Review* 50 (Nov. 1981): 445–75.

———. *The West and Reconstruction.* Urbana, Ill., 1981.

Beshoar, Michael. *All About Trinidad and Las Animas County, Colorado: Their History, Industries, Resources, Etc.* Denver, 1882.

Billington, Ray Allen. *Westward Expansion: A History of the American Frontier.* 2nd ed. New York, 1963.

Black, Robert C., III. *Island in the Rockies: The History of Grand County, Colorado to 1930.* Boulder, Colo., 1969.

Blake, Mary. *On The Wing: Rambling Notes of a Trip to the Pacific.* Boston, 1883.

Bluemel, Elinor. *One Hundred Years of Colorado Women.* Denver, 1973.

Bowles, Samuel. *Across the Continent: A Summer's Journey to the Rocky Mountains, the Mormons, and the Pacific States.* Springfield, Mass., 1865.

———. *Our New West: Records of Travel Between the Mississippi River and the Pacific Ocean.* Hartford, Conn., 1869.

Boyd, David. *A History: Greeley and the Union Colony of Colorado.* Greeley, Colo., 1890.

Boyles, Billy L. *The St. Vrain Valley: Its Early History.* Longmont, Colo., 1967.

Brayer, Herbert O. "History of Colorado Railroads," in LeRoy R. Hafen (ed.), *Colorado and Its People: A Narrative and Topical History of the Centennial State.* 2 vols. New York, 1948, II, 635–90.

Brosnan, Kathleen. *Uniting Mountain and Plain: Cities, Law, and Environmental Change along the Front Range.* Albuquerque, N.M., 2002.

Bullard, Charles, and Salley Vecchio-Martin. *Longmont's History in Agriculture Today.* Boulder, Colo., 1986.

Burkey, Elmer R. "The Site of the Murder of the Hungate Family By Indians in 1864," *Colorado Magazine* 13 (July 1935): 139–42.

Butler, Anne M. *Daughters of Joy, Sisters of Mercy: Prostitutes in the American West, 1865–90.* Urbana, Ill., 1985.

Byers, William N. "The Centennial State," typescript, Bancroft Collection, Western Americana Collection, University of Colorado.

Carey, Raymond. "The Puzzle of Sand Creek," *Colorado Magazine* 41 (Oct. 1946): 278–98.

Carter, Clarence E. "The Territorial Papers of the United States: A Review and a Commentary," *Mississippi Valley Historical Review* 42 (1956): 510–24.

Carter, Harvey I. (ed.). *The Pike's Peak Region: A Sesquicentennial History.* Colorado Springs, Colo., 1956.

Castel, Albert. *Civil War Kansas: Reaping the Whirlwind.* Lawrence, Kans., 1997.

———. *William Clark Quantrill: His Life and Times.* Norman, Okla., 1999.

Castro, Jess Augustin. "Alexander Cameron Hunt: Colorado Territorial Governor, 1867–1869." M.A. thesis, University of Denver, 1967.

Clark, C. M. *A Trip to Pike's Peak & Notes By the Way.* Ed. Robert Greenwood. San Jose, Calif., 1958.

Clark, James M. *Colonial Days.* Greeley, Colo., 1902.

Clarke, Dan E. "The Movement to the Far West During the Decade of the Sixties," *Washington Historical Quarterly* 17 (Apr. 1926): 105–13.

Collins, George W. "Colorado's, Territorial Secretaries" *Colorado Magazine* 43 (Summer 1966): 185–208.

Colton, Ray C. *The Civil War in the Western Territories.* Norman, Okla., 1959.

Colwell, Raymond G. "Colorado City—Its Early Settlement," typescript, Penrose Public Library, Colorado Springs.

———. "The Railroad Age: 1871–1890," in Harvey I. Carter (ed.), *The Pike's Peak Region: A Sesquicentennial History* (Colorado Springs, 1956), 15–22.

Conklin, Emma Burke. *A Brief History of Logan County, Colorado, with Reminiscences By Pioneers.* Denver, 1928.

Cook, John W. (comp). *Hands Up; or, Thirty-five Years of Detective Life in the Mountains and on the Plains: Reminiscences by General D. J. Cook, Chief of the Rocky Mountain Detective Association.* Denver, 1897.

Cornish, Dudley Taylor. "The First Five Years of Statehood," *Colorado Magazine* 25 (July 1948): 220–32.

Cox, C. Jefferson. "Summit Springs," *The Denver Westerners Brand Book* 25 (1969): 297–308.

Craig, Reginald S. *The Fighting Parson: The Biography of Colonel John M. Chivington.* Los Angeles, 1959.

Cruden, Robert. *The War That Never Ended: The American Civil War.* New York, 1973.

Dale, Edward Everett. *The Range Cattle Industry: Ranching on the Great Plains from 1865 to 1925*. Norman, Okla., 1960.

Davis, E. O. *The First Five Years of the Railroad Era in Colorado: June 16, 1867 to June 19, 1872, Julesburg to Pueblo in Five Years*. Denver, 1948.

Dawson, Thomas F. "Major Thompson, Chief Ouray, and the Utes," *Colorado Magazine* 7 (May 1930): 113–22.

DeVoto, Bernard. "Geopolitics with Dew," *Harper's* 188 (Mar. 1944): 313–23.

Dilke, Charles Wentworth. *Greater Britain: A Record of Travel in English Speaking Countries During 1866 and 1867*. London, 1868.

Dixon, William Hepworth. *New America*. 2 vols. London, 1867.

Dodds, Joanne West. *They All Came to Pueblo: A Social History*. Virginia Beach, Va., 1994.

———. *What's a Nice Girl Like You Doing in a Place Like This?: Prostitution in Southern Colorado, 1860–1911*. Pueblo, Colo., 1996.

Dodge, Grenville M. *How We Built the Union Pacific Railway*. Reprint. Denver, 1965.

———. "The Civil Engineer in an Early Day and in the Civil War: Address Delivered Before the Western Society of Civil Engineers," in *How We Built the Union Pacific Railway*. Reprint. Denver, 1965, 97–125.

Dome of the Continent: Colorado in 1872, including Trips to Central City, Georgetown, Idaho Springs, Gray's Peak, and Denver, with Geological, Mineralogical and Biological Notes. Olympic Valley, Calif., 1977.

Dorset, Phillis Flanders. *The New Eldorado: The Story of Colorado's Gold and Silver*. New York, 1970.

Downing, Sybil, and Robert E. Smith. *Tom Patterson: Colorado Crusader for Change*. Boulder, Colo., 1995.

DuBois, Ellen Carol. *Feminism and Suffrage: The Emergence of an Independent Women's Movement in America, 1848–1869*. Ithaca, N.Y., 1978.

Dunbar, Robert G. "History of Agriculture," in LeRoy R. Hafen (ed.). *Colorado and Its People: A Narrative and Topical History of the Centennial State*. 2 vols. New York, 1948, II, 121–57.

Durning, Mabel Downer. *The Chicago—Colorado Colony: Founding of Longmont*. Longmont, Colo., 1975.

Ellis, Amanda. *The Colorado Springs Story*. Colorado Springs, Colo., 1954.

Ellis, Elmer. "Colorado's First Fight for Statehood, 1865–1868," *Colorado Magazine* 13 (Jan. 1931): 23–30.

———. *Henry Moore Teller: Defender of the West*. Caldwell, Idaho, 1941.

Ellis, Erl H. *Colorado Mapology*. Frederick, Colo., 1983.

Emmit, Robert. *The Last War Trail: The Utes and the Settlement of Colorado*. Boulder, Colo., 2000.

Englert, Kenneth E. "History of Colorado Springs," typescript, Penrose Public Library.

Espinosa, Fred. "Del Norte—Its Past and Present," *Colorado Magazine* 5 (June 1928): 95–102.

Faherty, William B. "Regional Minorities and the Woman Suffrage Struggle," *Colorado Magazine* 33 (July 1956): 212–17.

Fell, James E., Jr. *Ores to Metals: The Rocky Mountain Smelting Industry*. Lincoln, Neb., 1979.

Fernández, José Emilio. *The Biography of Casimiro Barela.* Trans. A Gabriel Meléndez. Albuquerque, N.M., 2003.
Fetter, Richard. *Frontier Boulder.* Boulder, Colo., 1983.
Filipiak, Jack D. "The Battle of Summit Springs," *Colorado Magazine* 41 (Fall 1964): 343–54.
Fite, Gilbert C. *The Farmers' Last Frontier, 1865–1900.* New York, 1966.
Folwell, William Watts. *A History of Minnesota.* 4 vols. St. Paul, Minn., 1956.
Forsyth, George A. *Thrilling Days in Army Life.* Reprint. Lincoln, Neb., 1994.
Fossett, Frank. *Colorado: Historical, Descriptive and Statistical Work on the Rocky Mountain Gold and Silver Mining Region.* Denver, 1876.
———. *Colorado: Its Gold and Silver Mines, Farms and Stock Ranges, and Health and Pleasure Resorts. Tourist's Guide to the Rocky Mountains.* 2nd ed. New York, 1880.
Frasier, George Willard, and William Hartman, "History of Higher Education in Colorado," in LeRoy R. Hafen (ed.), *Colorado and Its People: A Narrative and Topical History of the Centennial State.* 2 vols. New York, 1948, II, 475–84.
Freeman, Winfield, "The Battle of the Arickaree," *Collection of the Kansas State Historical Society* 6 (1897–1900): 346–57.
Frink, Maurice, W. Turrentine Jackson, and Agnes Wright Spring. *When Cattle was King: Contributions to the Western Range Cattle Industry.* Boulder, Colo., 1956.
Fritz, Percy Stanley. *Colorado: The Centennial State.* New York, 1941.
Gaines, A. P. "The Battle of Beecher's Island," *The Denver Westerners Brand Book* 25 (1969): 109–24.
Gibson, Arrell Morgan. *The West in the Life of the Nation.* New York, 1976.
Goodykoontz, Colin B. "Colorado As Seen by a Home Missionary, 1863–1868," *Colorado Magazine* 12 (Mar. 1935): 60–68.
———. "Some Controversial Questions Before the Colorado Constitutional Convention of 1876," *Colorado Magazine* 17 (Jan. 1940): 1–17.
Gould, Lewis L. *Wyoming: A Political History, 1868–1896.* New Haven, Conn., 1968.
Gower, Calvin W. "Gold Fever in Kansas Territory: Migration to the Pikes's Peak Gold Fields, 1858–60," *Kansas Historical Quarterly* 9 (1973): 58–74.
Greenwood, Grace. *New Life in New Lands: Notes of Travel.* New York, 1873.
Gregg, Efay Nelson. "Social Legislation and the Welfare Program," in LeRoy R. Hafen (ed.), *Colorado and Its People: A Narrative and Topical History of the Centennial State.* 2 vols. New York, 1948, II, 333–68.
Grinnell, George Bird. *By Cheyenne Campfires.* New Haven, Conn., 1962.
———. *The Fighting Cheyennes.* Norman, Okla., 1956.
Guice, John D. W. "Alabama Planters in the Rockies," *Colorado Magazine* 52 (Winter 1976): 1–47.
———. "Colorado's Territorial Courts," *Colorado Magazine* 45 (Summer 1968): 204–24.
Gussow, Zachary, LeRoy R. Hafen, and Arthur K. Ekrich Jr. *Arapaho-Cheyenne Indians.* New York, 1974.
Hafen, Anne W. and LeRoy R. Hafen. "The Beginning of Denver University," *Colorado Magazine* 24 (Mar. 1947): 58–66.
Hafen, LeRoy R. (ed.). *Colorado and Its People: A Narrative and Topical History of the Centennial State.* 2 vols. New York, 1948.

———. *Colorado: The Story of a Western Commonwealth.* Denver, 1933.

———. "Colorado's First Legislative Assembly," *Colorado Magazine* 20 (Apr. 1943): 44–49.

———. "Steps to Statehood in Colorado," *Colorado Magazine* 3 (Aug. 1926): 97–110.

Hagie, C. E. "Gunnison in Early Days," *Colorado Magazine* 8 (July 1931): 121–29.

Halaas, David Fridtjof, and Andrew E. Masich. *Halfbreed: The Remarkable True Story of George Bent.* New York, 2003.

Hale, Jesse D. "The First Successful Smelter in Colorado," *Colorado Magazine* 13 (Sept. 1936): 161–67.

Hall, Frank. *History of the State of Colorado.* 4 vols. Chicago, 1889–90.

Hanchett, William. "'His Turbulent Excellency,' Alexander Cummings, Governor of Colorado Territory, 1865–1867," *Colorado Magazine* 34 (Apr. 1957): 81–104.

Hansen, James E., II. *Democracy's College in the Centennial State: A History of Colorado State University.* Fort Collins, Colo., 1977.

Harris, Katherine. *Long Vistas: Women and Families on Colorado Homesteads.* Niwot, Colo., 1993.

Harvey, James R. "Negroes in Colorado," *Colorado Magazine* 26 (July 1949): 145–76.

Heitman, Francis B. *Historical Register and Dictionary of the United States Army, From its Organization, September 29, 1789 to Mar. 2, 1903.* 2 vols. Washington, D.C., 1903.

Helzler, Rosemary, and John Helzler. *Colorado Springs and Pike's Peak Country: A Pictorial History.* Norfolk, Va., 1989.

Henderson, Charles W. *Mining in Colorado: A History of Discovery, Development and Production.* Professional Paper # 138, U.S. Geological Survey. Washington, D.C., 1926.

Hensel, Donald W. "Statehood Aspirations and Constitutions of Early Colorado," *Denver Westerners Brand Book* 14 (1958): 97–116.

Hersey, Henry J. "The Colorado Constitution," *Colorado Magazine* 3 (Aug. 1926): 65–76.

Hill, Alice Polk. *Colorado Pioneers in Picture and Story.* Denver, 1915.

Hine, Robert. *Community on the American Frontier: Separate but Not Alone.* Norman, Okla. 1980.

Hirshson, Stanley P. *Grenville M. Dodge: Soldier, Politician, Railroad Pioneer.* Bloomington, Ind., 1967.

History of the Arkansas Valley. Chicago, 1881.

Hogan, Richard. *Class and Community in Frontier Colorado.* Lawrence, Kans., 1990.

Hoig, Stan. *The Peace Chiefs of the Cheyennes.* Norman, Okla., 1980.

———. *The Sand Creek Massacre.* Norman, Okla., 1961.

Hollister, Ovando. *The Mines of Colorado.* Springfield, Mass., 1967.

Hoover, Ethel. "Consumer Price Index, 1850–1880," in Ralph Andreano (ed.). *Economic Impact of the American Civil War.* Cambridge, Mass., 1967, 222–35.

Horner, John Willard. *Silver Town.* Caldwell, Idaho, 1950.

Howbert, Irving. *Memories of a Lifetime in the Pike's Peak Region.* Reprint. Glorieta, N.M., 1970.

Hughes, J. Donald. *American Indians in Colorado.* Boulder, Colo., 1977.

Hutchins, Mark E. "The Julesburg Indian Attacks, January 7 and February 2, 1865," *The Denver Westerners Brand Book* 32 (1995): 207–18.

Hyde, George E. *The Life of George Bent, Written from His Letters.* Ed. Sovie Lottinville. Norman, Okla, 1968.

Isern, Thomas D. "Colorado Territory," in LeRoy H. Fischer (ed.), *The Western Territories in the Civil War.* Manhattan, Kans., 1977, 57–71.

Jeffrey, Julie Roy. *Frontier Women: The Trans-Mississippi West, 1840–1880.* New York, 1979.

Johannsen. Robert W. *Frontier Politics on the Eve of the Civil War.* Seattle, 1955.

Johnson, Harrison. *Johnson's History of Nebraska.* Omaha, 1880.

Josephy, Alvin M., Jr. *Civil War in the American West.* New York, 1991.

Karnes, Thomas L. *William Gilpin: Western Nationalist.* Austin, Tex., 1970.

Kelsey, Harry E., Jr. *Frontier Capitalist: The Life of John Evans.* Denver, 1969.

King, James T. *War Eagle: The Life of General Eugene A. Carr.* Lincoln, Neb., 1963.

Krakel, Dean F. *South Platte Country: A History of Old Weld County, Colorado, 1739–1900.* Laramie, Wyo., 1954.

Kuykendall, John M. "The First Cattle North of the Union Pacific Railroad," *Colorado Magazine* 6 (Mar. 1930): 69–74.

Lamar, Howard Roberts. *Dakota Territory, 1861–1889: A Story in Frontier Politics.* New Haven, Conn., 1956.

———. *The Far Southwest, 1856–1912: A Territorial History.* New York, 1970.

Large, Dorothy. *Old Burlington: First Town on the St. Vrain.* Longmont, Colo., 1984.

Larson, Robert W. *New Mexico's Quest for Statehood, 1846–1912.* Albuquerque, N.M., 1968.

Lecompte, Janet. "Sand Creek," *Colorado Magazine* 41 (Oct. 1964): 314–35.

Legard, A. B. *Colorado.* London, 1872.

Legislative, Historical & Biographical Compendium of Colorado. Denver, 1887.

Leonard, Stephen J. *Lynching in Colorado, 1859–1919.* Boulder, Colo., 2002.

Leonard, Stephen, and Thomas J. Noel. *Denver: Mining Camp to Metropolis.* Niwot, Colo., 1990.

Lester, John Erastus. *The Atlantic to the Pacific: What to See and How to See it.* London, 1873.

Lewis, Inez Johnson. "Progress of Education in Colorado," in LeRoy R. Hafen (ed.), *Colorado and Its People: A Narrative and Topical History of the Centennial State.* 2 vols. New York, 1948, II, 159–97.

Leyendecker, Liston E. "Colorado and the Paris Universal Exposition, 1867," *Colorado Magazine* 46 (Winter 1969): 1–15.

———. *Georgetown: Colorado's Silver Queen, 1859–1876.* Fort Collins, Colo., 1977.

Lowry, Thomas P. *The Story the Soldiers Wouldn't Tell: Sex in the Civil War.* Mechanicsburg, Pa., 1994.

MacKell, Jan. *Brothels, Bordellos, and Bad Girls: Prostitution in Colorado, 1860–1930.* Albuquerque, N.M., 2004.

McConnell, Virginia. "A Gauge of Popular Taste in Early Colorado," *Colorado Magazine* 46 (Fall 1969): 338–50.

McGiffert, Michael. *The Higher Learning in Colorado: An Historical Study, 1860–1940*. Denver, 1964.

McKay, R. H. *Little Pills: An Army Story*. Pittsburg, Kans., 1918.

McMechan, Edgar C. "John Hittson, Cattle King," *Colorado Magazine* 11 (Sept. 1934): 164–70.

———. *The Life of Governor Evans: Second Territorial Governor of Colorado*. Denver, 1924.

Meline, James. *Two Thousand Miles on Horseback, Santa Fé and Back. A Summer Tour Through Kansas, Nebraska, Colorado, and New Mexico in the Year 1866*. New York, 1867.

Milligan, Edward W. "John Wesley Iliff," *The Denver Westerners Brand Book* 6 (1950): 43–60.

Mock, S. D. "The Financing of Early Colorado Railroads, *Colorado Magazine* 18 (Nov. 1941): 200–208.

Mohr, James C. *Radical Republicans in the North: State Politics During Reconstruction*. Baltimore, 1976.

Monnett, John H. *The Battle of Beecher Island and the Indian War of 1867*. Niwot, Colo., 1992.

Moore, John H. *The Cheyenne Nation: A Social and Demographic History*. Lincoln, Neb., 1987.

Morgan, Nicholas. "Mormon Colonization in the San Luis Valley," *Colorado Magazine* 27 (Oct. 1950): 269–93.

Morris, Maurice O'Conner. *Rambles in the Rocky Mountains: with a Visit to the Gold Fields of Colorado*. London, 1864.

Moss, Rex H. "Alexander Cummings, Governor of the Territory of Colorado, 1865–1867." M.A. thesis, University of Denver, 1965.

Mothershead, Harmon. "Negro Rights in the Colorado Territory," *Colorado Magazine* 40 (July 1963): 212–23.

Muirhead, James Fullarton. *The Land of Contrasts: A Briton's View of his American Kin*. Boston, 1898.

Murray, Robert B. "The Supreme Court of Colorado Territory," *Colorado Magazine* 44 (Winter 1967): 20–34.

"Nathaniel S. Seith and Two of his Early Colorado Letters," *Colorado Magazine* 17 (Mar. 1940): 65–72.

Noel, Thomas J. *Growing Through History with Colorado: The Colorado National Banks, The First 125 Years, 1862–1987*. Denver, 1987.

———. *The City and the Saloon: Denver, 1858–1916*. Niwot, Colo., 1996.

———. "The Multifunctional Frontier Saloon: Denver, 1858–1876," *Colorado Magazine* 52 (Spring, 1975): 114–36.

———, Paul F. Mahoney, and Richard E. Stevens. *Historical Atlas of Colorado*. Norman, Okla., 1993.

———, Stephen J. Leonard, and Kevin R. Rucker. *Colorado Givers: A History of Philanthropic Heroes*. Niwot, Colo., 1998.

Nostrand, Richard L. *The Hispano Homeland*. Norman, Okla., 1992.

Nugent, Walter T. K. *Money and American Society, 1865–1880*. New York, 1968.

O'Conner, Thomas. "Bishop Machebeuf," *Colorado Magazine* 13 (July 1935): 130–39.

Ophus, John. "The Lake County War, 1874–75," *Colorado Magazine* 47 (Spring 1970): 119–35.

Ormes, Robert M. *Railroads and the Rockies: A Record of Lines in and near Colorado.* Denver, 1963.

Osborn, James. "Theater in Denver, 1859–1991," *The Denver Westerners Golden Anniversary Brand Book* 32 (1995): 167–76.

Osgood, Ernest Staples. *The Day of the Cattleman.* Minneapolis, 1929.

Pabor, William Edgar. *Colorado As an Agricultural State, Its Farms, Fields, and Garden Lands.* New York, 1883.

Paul, Rodman Wilson. "Colorado as a Pioneer of Science in the Mining West," *Mississippi Valley Historical Review* 47 (June 1960): 34–50.

———. *Mining Frontiers of the Far West, 1848–1880.* New York, 1963.

Peake, Ora Brooks. *The Colorado Range Cattle Industry.* Glendale, Calif., 1937.

Pennock, Ellen Coffin. "Incidents in My Life as a Pioneer," *Colorado Magazine* 30 (Apr. 1953): 124–33.

Peterson, Virgil V. "Penal, Correctional and Eleemosynary Institutions in Colorado," in LeRoy R Hafen (ed.), *Colorado and its People: A Narrative and Topical History of the Centennial State.* 2 vols. New York, 1948, II, 609–39.

Pickering, James H. *"This Blue Hollow": Estes Park, the Early Years, 1859–1915.* Niwot, Colo., 1999.

Pine, George W. *Beyond the West: An Account of Two Years Travel in the Other Half of the Great Continent.* Utica, N.Y., 1871.

Polakoff, Keith Ian. *The Politics of Inertia: The Election of 1876 and the End of Reconstruction.* Baton Rouge, La., 1973.

Pomeroy, Earl S. *The Territories and the United States, 1961–1890.* Seattle, 1969.

———. "Toward a Reorientation of Western History," *Mississippi Valley Historical Review* 41 (Mar. 1955): 579–600.

Prentice, C. A. "Captain Silas S. Soule, a Pioneer Martyr," *Colorado Magazine* 12 (Nov. 1935): 224–28.

Propst, Nell Brown. *Forgotten People: A History of the South Platte Trail.* Boulder, Colo., 1979.

Randall, James G., and David Donald. *The Civil War and Reconstruction.* 2nd ed. Lexington, Mass., 1969.

Ray, John E., D. D. Dudley, and G. W. Veditz. *A Brief Historical Sketch and Handbook of the Colorado School for the Deaf and Blind from its Inception to Mar., 1st, 1893.* Colorado Springs, Colo., 1893.

Reckmeyer, Clarence, "The Battle of Summit Springs," *Colorado Magazine* 6 (Nov. 1929): 211–20.

Rist, Martin, "History of Religion in Colorado," in LeRoy R. Hafen (ed.), *Colorado and Its People: A Narrative and Topical History of the Centennial State.* 2 vols. New York, 1948, II, 199–224.

Rockafellow, B. F. "History of Fremont County," in *History of the Arkansas Valley, Colorado.* Chicago, 1881, 543–687.

Ross, A. R. "Indian Raids in Colorado, 1875," *Colorado Magazine* 24 (Nov. 1947): 258–63.

Rusling, James F. *Across America: or, The Great West and the Pacific Coast.* New York, 1874.

Russell, Don. *The Lives and Legends of Buffalo Bill.* Norman, Okla., 1960.

St. Vrain Historical Society. *They Came to Stay: Longmont, Colorado, 1858–1920.* Longmont, Colo., 1971.

Sandoz, Mari. *Cheyenne Autumn.* New York, 1953.

Sanford, Albert B. "John L. Routt: First State Governor of Colorado," *Colorado Magazine* 3 (Aug. 1926): 81–86.

Schoberlin, Melvin H. *From Candles to Footlights: A Biography of Pike's Peak Theatre, 1859–1876.* Denver, 1941.

Secrest, Clark. *Hell's Belles: Prostitution, Vice, and Crime in Early Denver.* Rev. ed. Boulder, Colo., 2002.

Shaw, Luella. *True History of Some of the Pioneers of Colorado.* Hotchkiss, Colo., 1909.

Shelly, Walter Lumley. "The Colorado Republican Party: The Formative Years, 1861–1876." M.A. thesis, University of Colorado, 1963.

Sherow, James Earl. *Watering the Valley: Development along the High Plains Arkansas River, 1870–1950.* Lawrence, Kans. 1990.

Silverman, Jason Howard, "Confederate Activities in Colorado Territory, 1861–1865." M.A. thesis, Colorado State University, 1976.

Simmons, Virginia McConnell. *The Ute Indians of Utah, Colorado, and New Mexico.* Boulder, Colo., 2000.

Simonin, Louis L. "Colorado in 1867 as Seen by a Frenchman," *Colorado Magazine* 14 (Mar. 1937): 56 63.

———. *The Rocky Mountain West in 1867.* Trans. Wilson O. Clough. Lincoln, Neb., 1966.

Smiley, Jerome C. *The History of Denver: with Outlines of the Earlier History of the Rocky Mountain Country.* Denver, 1901.

———. *Semi-Centennial History of the State of Colorado.* 2 vols. Chicago, 1913.

Smith, Barbara. *The First Hundred Years of Greeley, Colorado, 1870–1970.* Greeley, Colo., 1970.

Smith, Duane A. *Henry Teller: Colorado's Grand Old Man.* Boulder, Colo., 2002.

———. *Rocky Mountain Mining Camps: The Urban Frontier.* Bloomington, Ind., 1967.

———. *The Birth of Colorado: A Civil War Perspective.* Norman, Okla., 1989.

Smith, Henry Nash. *Virgin Land: The American West as Symbol and Myth.* Cambridge, Mass., 1950.

Smith, Robert E. "Thomas M. Patterson, Colorado Statehood, and the Presidential Election of 1876," *Colorado Magazine* 53 (Spring 1976): 153–62.

Socolofsky, Homer E., and Huber Self. *Historical Atlas of Kansas.* 2nd ed. Norman, Okla., 1972.

Spence, Clark C. *British Investments and the American Mining Frontier, 1860–1901.* Ithaca, N.Y., 1958.

———. *Territorial Politics and Government in Montana, 1864–89.* Urbana, Ill., 1975.

Spencer, Elma Dill Russell. *Green Russell and Gold.* Austin, Tex., 1966.

Sprague, Marshall. *Colorado: A Bicentennial History.* New York, 1976.

———. *Massacre: The Tragedy at White River.* Boston, 1957.

———. *Newport of the Rockies: The Life and Good Times of Colorado Springs.* Denver, 1961.
Sproat, John G. *"The Best Men": Liberal Reformers in the Gilded Age.* New York, 1968.
Stanton, Irving W. *Sixty Years in Colorado: Reminiscences and Reflections of a Pioneer of 1860.* Denver, 1922.
"Statehood Celebration of 1876," *Colorado Magazine* 3 (Aug. 1926): 94–97.
Steinel, Alvin T., *History of Agriculture in Colorado.* Fort Collins, Colo., 1926.
Stephen, Barbara Carpenter. *Dearest Grandchildren: A Grandmother's Account of the Beginning and Growth of Horace Greeley's Union Colony.* Greeley, Colo., 1986.
Stoddard, Minnie E. "Pueblo History," typescript, Pueblo Public Library.
Stone, Wilbur Fisk (ed.). *History of Colorado.* 5 vols. Chicago, 1918–19.
Swadesh, Frances Leon. *Los Prímeros Pobladores: Hispanic Americans of the Ute Frontier.* Notre Dame, Ind., 1974.
Swanson, Evadene Burris. *Fort Collins Yesterdays.* Fort Collins, Colo., 1975.
Taylor, Bayard. *Colorado: A Summer Trip.* Ed. William W. Savager Jr. and James H. Lazalier. Niwot, Colo., 1989.
Taylor, Morris. *Trinidad, Colorado Territory.* Pueblo, Colo., 1966.
Taylor, Ouintard. *In Search of the Racial Frontier: African-Americans in the American West, 1528–1990.* New York, 1998.
Thomas, Charles S. "The Pioneer Bar of Colorado," *Colorado Magazine* 1 (Jan. 1924): 193–204.
Tice, John H. *Over the Plains and on the Mountains, or Kansas and Colorado Agriculturally, Mineralogically, and Aesthetically.* Chicago, 1871.
Townshend, Richard B. *A Tenderfoot in Colorado.* Norman, Okla., 1968.
Trenholm, Virginia Cole. *Amanda Mary and the Dog Soldiers.* Lusk, Wyo., 1974.
Ubbelohde, Carl, Maxine Benson, and Duane Smith. *A Colorado History.* 8th ed. Boulder, Colo., 2001.
Utley, Robert M. *Frontier Regulars: The United States Army and the Indian, 1866–1891.* New York, 1973.
Vandenbusche, Duane and Duane A. Smith. *A Land Alone: Colorado's Western Slope.* Boulder, Colo., 1981.
Van Wagenen, Theo. F. "Views of the Admission of Colorado in 1876," *Colorado Magazine* 3 (Aug. 1926): 86–88.
Walters, R. J. (Mrs.). "Colorado's Statehood Celebration, 1876," *Colorado Magazine* 11 (Sept. 1934): 161–64.
Ware, Eugene F. *The Indian War of 1864: Being a Fragment of the Early History of Kansas, Nebraska, Colorado, and Wyoming.* Topeka, Kans., 1911.
Watrous, Ansel. *History of Larimer County Colorado.* Reprint. Fort Collins, Colo., 1972.
Werner, Fred H. *Heroic Fort Sedgwick and Julesburg: A Study in Courage.* Greeley, Colo., 1987.
———. *The Beecher Island Battle, September 17, 1868.* Greeley, Colo., 1989.
West, Elliott. "Jerome B. Chaffee and the McCook-Elbert Fight," *Colorado Magazine* 46 (Spring 1969): 145–65.
———. "Of Lager Beer and Sonorous Songs," *Colorado Magazine* 48 (Spring 1971): 108–28.

———. *The Contested Plains: Indians, Goldseekers and the Rush to Colorado.* Lawrence, Kans., 1998.

———. *The Saloon on the Rocky Mountain Mining Frontier.* Lincoln, Neb., 1979.

Westermeier, Clifford P. "The Legal Status of Colorado Cattlemen, 1867–1887," *Colorado Magazine* 25 (May 1948): 109–18, and (July 1948): 157–66.

Wharton, Junius E. *History of the City of Denver from Its Earliest Settlement to the Present Time.* Denver, 1909.

Wilder, Daniel W. *The Annals of Kansas.* Topeka, 1875.

Willard, James. *The Union Colony at Greeley, Colorado, 1869–1871.* Boulder, Colo., 1918.

Willard, James, and Colin B. Goodykoontz. *Experiments in Colorado Colonization: Selected Contemporary Records Relating to the German Colonization Company and the Chicago-Colorado, St. Louis-Western, and Southwestern Colonies.* Boulder, Colo., 1926.

Willis, Richard C. "Colorado Territory," in Ralph Y. McGinnis and Calvin Smith, *Abraham Lincoln and the Western Territories,* Chicago, 1994, 53–71.

Winther, Oscar Osburn. *The Transportation Frontier: The Trans-Mississippi West, 1869–1890.* New York, 1964.

Witter, Daniel (Mrs.). "Pioneer Life," *Colorado Magazine* 4 (Dec. 1927): 165–74.

Yates, Michael. *An Amusing Glance at Life and Leaders in Early Colorado.* Fort Collins, Colo., 1992.

Young, Kathryn. "Pioneer Days in Sterling," *Colorado Magazine* 4 (Mar. 1927): 58–63.

Zweig, Sheldon S. "The Civil Administration of Governor William Gilpin," *Colorado Magazine* 31 (July 1954): 179–93.

INDEX

EUGENE H. BERWANGER lives in Fort Collins, Colorado.

The University of Illinois Press
is a founding member of the
Association of American University Presses.

University of Illinois Press
1325 South Oak Street
Champaign, IL 61820-6903
www.press.uillinois.edu